Honey, I Want to Start My Own Business

Honey, I Want to Start My Own Business

A Planning Guide for Couples

Azriela Jaffe

Foreword by John Gray, Ph.D.

HarperBusiness
A Division of HarperCollins*Publishers*

HarperCollins books may be purchased for educational, business, or sales promotional use. For information please write: Special Markets Department, HarperCollins Publishers, Inc., 10 East 53rd Street, New York, NY 10022.

FIRST EDITION

Designed by Nancy Singer

ISBN 0-88730-795-7

96 97 98 99 00 ❖/RRD 10 9 8 7 6 5 4 3 2 1

This book is dedicated to my husband and beshert,
Stephen Jaffe

Contents

Foreword

T he traditional male and female roles of provider and nurturer are changing. A man used to derive his sense of self from being the sole provider for the family. He could depend on his wife to provide him with emotional support when he came home from a long day at the office. Now, the modern male may be working with his wife as a full business partner, and the clear distinction between male and female roles has disappeared. It's hard for him to expect emotional support from his wife after a hard day at the office when she spent the day at his side, and she's exhausted, too! Husbands and wives who build a company together need a new job description for how to be successful business and marriage partners at the same time.

Even the modern woman who occupies the traditional role of supportive spouse to her entrepreneurial husband needs help. Often she is working a job to help support the family, and yet she still has primary responsibility for child rearing and managing the household. She is overworked, overstressed, and feels unsupported. Her husband used to think he could make her happier by being a better provider. Now she is complaining about the long hours he's working, the riskiness of his venture, and the travel that's required. He is confused about how to respond. Traditionally, if problems arose at home, his approach to solving them was to become more successful at work. But now the problems are *originating* from his work, so what does he do?

The entrepreneur of the nineties needs a new job description, one that defines the requirements and skills that will keep his or her spouse happy while growing a successful business.

Whether you are just thinking about quitting your job, or you have already launched your business; whether you are working with your spouse to grow a business or depending on your spouse to support your efforts to be self-employed, *Honey, I Want to Start My Own Business* is *the* manual you need to manage the challenges of business ownership. No other book captures so succinctly a practical commonsense approach to reducing the stress of business ownership on your marriage.

The voices of other entrepreneurial couples will reassure you that you are not alone in your struggle, and though their stories portray a sometimes frightening but realistic picture of the challenges of self-employment, the overall message of this book is an optimistic one. *Honey, I Want to Start My Own Business* shows you that it *is* possible to have a joyful fulfilling marriage and a thriving business at the same time. Place this book next to your bed or on your desk, and refer to it often throughout your journey together as an entrepreneurial couple.

> *John Gray, Ph.D.*
> Author of the bestselling books *Men Are from Mars, Women Are from Venus* and *Mars and Venus in the Bedroom*

Preface

I remember the acrid smell of ammonia emanating from the blueprint machine in our basement when I was a young girl. My dad housed his start-up electronics company in a spare bedroom upstairs. After school I looked forward to getting a peek into the room jammed full with mysterious gadgets and electronic equipment. When my mother became pregnant with my brother Joel, Dad lost his home office to the family's need for the spare bedroom. He moved his fledging business to a facility outside our home. I was sad to see him go.

I knew very little about the family business. I knew that my father was an electrical engineer (whatever that meant). Money was extremely tight because we were living off my mother's meager teaching salary while my dad started his own company. I knew nothing about risk, nor did I fully understand the demands of a small business start-up. The adventure was exciting in the beginning, until it translated over a period of years into my dad's regular absence from home because of work demands. My mom raised three kids, worked full-time, and managed the household budget on less than we needed. I remember she always seemed tired.

After a decade, my dad sold the company. He and Mom took another entrepreneurial plunge, this time as full partners in a computer skills training center. Mom quit her teaching career to join Dad in the business world. They converted a den in the house to their home office and eventually rented space outside the home as their company grew. Their desire to spend all day and evening together amazed me. I wondered if I would ever share a marriage that intimate.

Mom and Dad retired recently. They still enjoy spending virtually every hour of the day together. They were my earliest role models for how a couple can successfully combine entrepreneurship and marriage. My mom was undyingly faithful to my dad's earliest entrepreneurial dreams. Her contribution to the household was essential to his business success. I'm sure they had their challenges as a couple working together in their second business, but their respect for each other and devotion to a common dream kept their marriage on track. My parents showed me that two things are possible: prosperity from business ownership and a marriage strong enough to withstand the pressures of entrepreneurial life.

In my late twenties I pursued my own entrepreneurial dreams. I was single at the time and had only my own life to consider when I quit a high-paying, but tedious job as a human resource executive to become an H.R. consultant. I wanted the freedom to work my own hours and the flexibility to pursue my dreams of becoming a published writer.

I supplemented my first human resource clients with a multi-level marketing (MLM) business selling Matol Botanical products. I prospered in the MLM business when I had sold to everyone in my network who was easy for me to influence. When it became necessary to cold-call prospects, my thriving MLM business started to wane.

In 1989 I gratefully accepted a job offer from my biggest client to become their human resources director. I reentered the entrepreneurial world when I married my husband Stephen in 1993. Following in my mother's footsteps, I agreed to support my husband's entrepreneurial dreams. I gave up my condo and the single life and moved in with Stephen and his teenage sons. Two weeks before our honeymoon Stephen quit his job to start his own consulting business, and we embarked on our first of several entrepreneurial journeys together.

If our first years of marriage had been all roses and romance I wouldn't have written this book. The optimism and fantasy that accompanies romantic love strongly influenced our decision making. We were naive about the hardships that would follow our decision for Stephen to quit his job.

We underestimated the psychological impact on our relationship of my supporting the family with my salary. We were unprepared for the challenges that arose when Stephen worked out of our home. We planned only for Stephen's business success, and didn't predict how difficult it would be for Stephen to land clients or collect accounts receivables. During our first year of marriage we suffered a miscarriage, brought our daughter Sarah into the world, and created a new stepfamily. Financial worries, lack of sleep, and limited intimate time together made it difficult to keep the initial romance of our courtship alive.

I conceived the idea for this book during my first pregnancy. I worked full-time in my human resource job, and then worked late into the night interviewing entrepreneurial couples and transcribing my notes into the computer. While Stephen struggled to become successful with his own business, he now also became the supportive spouse for my new entrepreneurial dream: to publish a book to help couples meet the kinds of entrepreneurial challenges we were coping with. Despite Stephen's fatigue and business worries, he made time for collaborating with me, editing my manuscript, and giving me emotional support to manage the hardships of pregnancy, stepparenting, and my insane schedule.

My daughter Sarah was born in October 1994. After a maternity leave I returned to my job as a human resource director on a part-time basis. Shortly after I returned to work, HarperCollins awarded me a contract to write this book. Stephen and I knew that I couldn't continue to work full-time, take care of a family, and write the book nights and weekends. My health and our relationship would deteriorate to a dangerous level. I was also now pregnant with our second child. The ordeal of prospecting clients discouraged Stephen and he considered closing his business down. In the spring of 1995 we made another major life change.

We sold our home in Massachusetts and moved our family to Lancaster, Pennsylvania, to a new community conducive to raising children and finding employment. Stephen and I switched roles and I became the entrepreneur in the family. With three children to support, and a fourth on the way, Stephen went back to work in a corporate job so that we could rely on some steady income. He was fortunate to find a challenging position in an entrepreneurial company. Stephen's transition back to corporate life was difficult for both of us in some ways. As we struggled with Stephen's being gone from the home for long hours, we missed the freedom and flexibility of Stephen's former self-employment. We knew that it was the right decision for our family, however, and we were grateful that Stephen was able to find a job he enjoys.

Our second daughter, Elana, was born in February 1996, a few months before the release of this book. We are adjusting to our new home and community, our new livelihoods, and our expanded family. Living with a teenaged stepson, an active toddler, and a newborn is a daily challenge. Though my husband and I have just celebrated our second wedding anniversary, it feels like much longer. We have endured many hardships and celebrated many blessings in our brief time together. Our commitment to each other remains rock solid. We continue to learn, grow, and deepen our love and respect for each other.

This book will share with you our entrepreneurial journey in great detail. I share this overview with you so that you will understand as you go forward that I know from personal experience the matters about which I write. I have experienced the challenges and rewards of being self-employed, being married to an entrepreneur, raising a family, and keeping a marriage healthy and strong. As any author, I am also writing a book on the subject I need to know the most about. I don't have all the answers; I am learning as I go along just like you. I expect that you and your partner will find your own answers. This book will help you discover the questions to ask and will give you the benefit of the wisdom of those entrepreneurial couples who came before you.

Acknowledgments

Hundreds of people helped to make this book a reality. Though I may have given this work its vision and shape, I was never working alone. I gratefully acknowledge all those who participated with me in the process. The following people deserve special mention.

My husband, Stephen, my biggest fan and supporter, who graciously allowed our private story to become public. He is my *beshert* and lifetime partner.

My parents, Phil and Maude Ackerman, who gave me a role model for growing a successful business and sustaining a thriving marriage at the same time.

My agent, Denise Stinson, who shared my vision and believed in my ability to pull it off.

My editor, Kirsten Sandberg, who patiently helped shape the manuscript into a finished piece.

My friend and mentor, Susan Page, who inspired me to go for my dream of being published and helped me to get there.

The following people who took the time to give me valuable feedback on my draft manuscript in process: Susan Page, Margaret Lichtenburg, Jane Hilburt Davis, Mary Korman, David and Platt Arnold, Stan Fried, Scott Stanley, Pat Zorn, Sharon Kleinberg, Chris Mogil, Anne Slepian, Olivia Mellan, Victoria Collins, Cliff Smith, Tom Bickford, Greg Godek, Eva Friederichs, Pat Boyd, Ty Boyd, Dayne Lamb, Gardner Stratton, Liz Curtis Higgs, Linda

Weltner, Beverly Williams, Sara Linquist, and Robert Fishbone.

The entrepreneurial couples who spent their time and shared their hearts and souls with me so that we could all learn from their experience. Their individual names are found in the directory of couples who participated in the research for this book (p. xviii).

The spirit guides and guardian angels who linked me to the critical people involved in this project and channeled the wisdom that flowed through my writing.

Research Participants

*H*oney, *I Want to Start My Own Business* draws from the experience of more than 125 entrepreneurial couples across the country, as well as experts in the fields of marriage counseling, business consulting, franchising, multilevel marketing, and financial planning. It was important to the author from the outset that this book be research based, rather than simply a memoir of her own entrepreneurial journey.

Care was taken to assure that the research sample was representative across the following criteria:

- All models of combining entrepreneurship and marriage, including working partners, dual entrepreneurs, and supportive spouses.
- Thriving couples, struggling couples, divorced or close-to-divorced couples.
- Geographic location—all regions of the country.
- Age—ranging from age twenty-four to age seventy-two.
- Family makeup, including no children, up to seven children, grown children, stepfamily.
- Nature of relationship, including living together, first through fourth marriage.
- Ethnicity and sexual preference—interviews include minority and gay and lesbian couples.
- Type of business, including service, retail, manufacturing, sole

proprietorship, agriculture, multilevel marketing, and franchising.
- Company size, ranging from $15,000 to $40 million a year in gross sales.
- Length of time in business, ranging from a few months to three decades.
- When business started, ranging from years before intimate relationship formed to years after intimate relationship formed.

All couples were assured confidentiality. Therefore, their identities are disguised in the stories shared in the book. In some cases, to ensure complete privacy, stories are composites of more than one couple.

Couples were located through networking and magazine and newspaper articles in national publications. Phone and in-person interviews took place over a period of one year.

Listed below are the couples who granted up to two hours of time for in-depth interviews with the author. Research included interviews with some couples who are not listed here, as they asked not to be identified in any manner. Total interviews with couples and experts in the field numbered more than 150.

DIRECTORY OF PARTICIPATING COUPLES

Laura Berman-Fortgang, business and personal coach, New York
Mark Berman-Fortgang, television producer, New York

Deborah Bloom, human resource consultant, Massachusetts
Walter Dardano, retired entrepreneur, Massachusetts

Constance and Stan Freid, partners, Multinational Services
    Group, Inc., New York

Cindy Hyken, full-time mother, Missouri
Shep Hyken, professional speaker and consultant, Missouri

Madeline Homan, business and personal coach, New York
John Hickok, actor/director, New York

Lianne and Stuart Hunt, partners, Great Harvest Bread Co.,
    Massachusetts

Carla LaFave, dog breeder, Massachusetts
Mike LaFave, human resource consultant, Massachusetts

Carol Reiko, psychotherapist, Massachusetts
Richard, owner of mattress franchise, Massachusetts*

Jan Rybeck, full-time mother, Rhode Island
Chick Rybeck, chiropractor, Rhode Island*

Millie Cushing, full-time mother and volunteer, New Jersey
Tom Cushing, president of International Metal Trading Company,
    New Jersey

Mikki Williams, professional speaker, Connecticut
Dutch De Groot, operations manager, Connecticut

Anne and Ron Burke, owners, MailBox Etc., Massachusetts

Eileen Silva and Taylor Hegan, partners, First Fitness multilevel
    marketing organization, Texas

Marge Segal, manager, retail store and professional speaking
    business, Massachusetts
Rick Segal, owner, retail store, and professional speaker,
    Massachusetts

Angie and Steve Sirico, partners, D'Valda and Sirico Dance
    Center, Connecticut

---

*Represented by spouse at interview.

Celia Wakefield, professional organizer, New York
Victor Wakefield, business consultant, New York

Maude Ackerman, vice president, and Phil Ackerman, president,
    Entech computer training center, New York

Lois Malech, full-time mother, New York
Bob Malech, retired entrepreneur, New York

Elizabeth Jeffries, professional speaker and author, Kentucky
Stephen Tweed, health care strategist, speaker, and author,
    Kentucky

Mary Landry, jewelry maker, Massachusetts
Leo Landry, bookstore manager, Massachusetts

Marjorie Brady, professional speaker, Pennsylvania
Dr. Alan Frieman, dentist, Pennsylvania

Judy and Ed Blair, partners, desktop publishing business, New York

Vickie Kilmer, librarian, Pennsylvania
Jim Kilmer, president, Remlick Foods, Pennsylvania

Kirsten Gamble and Charles Flood, partners, Flood, Gamble
    Associates investment firm, New York

Beverly Gorden, foster parent, Tennessee
Dave Gorden, professional speaker and consultant, Tennessee

Lauve Metcalfe, principal, Organizational Health Consultants,
    Arizona
J. R. Dubler, sales manager for sports apparrel company, Arizona*

Kitty Granquist, Shaklee sales leader, Massachusetts
Bob Granquist, owner, picture framing shop, Massachusetts*

---

*Represented by spouse at interview.

Audrey and Al Fontaine, master franchisors, Miracle Method of
    NE, Massachusetts

Ellen and Tom Zimmerman, partners, Synergy counseling and
    consulting, Texas

Gail Vankleeck, president of interior design firm and independent
    distributor, I.D.N., Massachusetts
Parker Babbidge, independent distributor, I.D.N., Massachusetts

Nancy Miller and Mike Round, partners, Rounds, Miller and
    Associates, California

Deborah Penta, president, marketing and P.R. firm,
    Massachusetts
Dave Kurlan, president, sales management consulting firm,
    Massachusetts

Melanie Ullman, school librarian, Massachusetts
Rabbi Alan Ullman, founder, School for Jewish Studies,
    Massachusetts

Anonymous, flower shop owner, Massachusetts
Anonymous, health care administrator, Massachusetts

Pat and Ty Boyd, partners, professional speaking business, North
    Carolina

Nancy Gianchiglia, full-time mother, Massachusetts
Bob Gianchiglia, financial adviser, Massachusetts

Dee Jolly, vice president, and William Jolly, president,
    InspirTainment, Plus, Washington, D.C.

Tracey Godek, physical therapist and feldencriast practitioner,
    Massachusetts
Greg Godek, author and publisher, Massachusetts

Jan and Tom Bickford, owners, Spiritcraft Drums, Massachusetts

Susan Smith, midwife, Massachusetts
Bob Smith, retired cabinetmaker, Massachusetts*

Roberta Taylor, retired advertising agency owner, Massachusetts
David Taylor, stockbroker, Massachusetts*

Lucy Elliot, secretary, Massachusetts
Dick Elliot, president, outplacement consulting firm,
    Massachusetts

Ruth and Wallace Becker, owners, Congresional Insurance
    agency, Maryland

Liz Beard, software systems consultant, Massachusetts
Dave Ploss, president, environmental and safety consulting firm,
    Massachusetts

Ella Walsh, contract health agent, Massachusetts
Howard Walsh, owner, Academy of Learning franchise,
    Massachusetts

Samantha Koumanelis, founder, Street Smarts, Massachusetts
Philip Picco, retired firefighter and golf store owner,
    Massachusetts

Barbara Buckland, program manager, social services, New
    Hampshire
Jim Buckland, owner of transportation company, New Hampshire

Naomi and Jim Rhode, owners, SmartPractice, health care
    training, Arizona

Susan Wood, president, and Lee Easter, vice president, Spec:
    Edit, technical communication firm, Massachusetts

---

*Represented by spouse at interview.

Nancy Wainer Cohen, author and midwife, Massachusetts
Dr. Paul Cohen, dentist, Massachusetts*

Claudine Wilder, consultant and author, Massachusetts
Tad Jankowski, lawyer, Massachusetts*

Marcia Stone, president and CEO, HybriVet Systems,
    Massachusetts
Travis Stone, software engineer, Massachusetts

Pat Higgins, secretary, Massachusetts
Joe Higgins, owner, Eastern Auto and Truck Service,
    Massachusetts

Platt Arnold, title researcher, Connecticut
David Arnold, psychotherapist, Connecticut

Cynthia Sprock, executive assistant, California
Vance Sprock, owner, Cupertino bicycle shop, California

Prue Berry and Doug Wilson, codirectors, Rowe Camp and
    Conference Center, Massachusetts

Nancy Martini, partner, Shearson Publishing Co., Massachusetts
Paul Martini, president, A.J. Martini Inc., Massachusetts

Irene Applebaum, principal, AppleGraphic design company,
    Massachusetts
Stephen Fish, principal, Springfield Associates, Massachusetts

Iris Hatfield, president, HuVista Int., handwriting analysis
    company, Kentucky
Wayne Hatfield, quality assurance S.P.C., Kentucky

---

*Represented by spouse at interview.

Deborah Hoffman, professional speaker and consultant,
    New Hampshire
David Hoffman, president, Hoffman Sales, specialty advertising,
    New Hampshire

Claudia Liebesny, principal, Human Resource Research Inc.,
    Massachusetts
John Liebesny, president, SmartRoute Systems, Massachusetts

Linda Moore, president, Harvest Ventures Group, Inc.,
    Massachusetts
Bill Moore, president, Franchise Spectrum Inc., Massachusetts

Ellen Yenawine, associate, and Gardner Yenawine, principal,
    Gardner Yenawine and Associates, Massachusetts

Penny Patterson and Bob Mendes, Shaklee sales leaders,
    Massachusetts

Priscilla and Dean Smith, Lifetime Master Coordinators,
    Shaklee, Illinois

Georgette Coniglio, data processor, Massachusetts
Pat Coniglio, owner, Coniglio's photography studio,
    Massachusetts

Karen and Minoru Yahara, owners, Sasuga Japanese bookstore,
    Massachusetts

Linda George, administrator, and Chris George, president,
    business brokerage and appraisal firm, Massachusetts

Sarah Linquist, vice president, and Robert Fishbone, president,
    On The Wall Productions, art gift items, Missouri

Peggy Heyman, president, and Bill Heyman, vice president,
    Supreme Audio Inc., New Hampshire

Joan Minchak, vice president, and Robert Minchak, president,
    J.B. Dollar Stretcher magazine, Ohio

Becky Biesel, president, Party Kits and Equestrian Gifts,
    Kentucky
Andy Biesel, architect, Kentucky*

Beverly Patrick, author and public speaker, Virginia
Gordon Patrick, office manager, Virginia

Nonie Linski, registered nurse, Massachusetts
Jerry Linski, president, MetroWest Teleservices, Massachusetts

Pat Zorn, and Sharon Kleinberg, psychotherapists, founders,
    Relationship Resources, New York

Andy Cunningham, president, Cunningham Communication Inc.,
    California
Rand Siegfried, president, RandArts toy design firm, California

Elaine Bograd, administrative support, Massachusetts
Barry Bograd, principal, Strategic Outsourcing Inc.,
    Massachusetts

Liz Curtis Higgs, CSP, author and keynote speaker, Kentucky
Bill Higgs, office manager, Kentucky

Kirsten Lembo, principal, Design Management Corp.,
    Massachusetts
Peter Lembo, principal, Double Eagle Music, Massachusetts

Jamy Faust, psychotherapist and energy healer, Massachusetts
Peter Faust, acupuncturist, Massachusetts

Leslie Levy, vice president, and Don Levy, president, Digipix
    television production company, New Jersey

---

*Represented by spouse at interview.

Ginger Kay, artist, New Hampshire
Bob Kay, social service director, New Hampshire

Joan and Dennis Rusconi, partners, Rusconi Co., investment
    banking, Connecticut

Sharon Strouse, art therapist, Maryland
Douglas Strouse, partner, Betz and Strouse, Maryland

Alicia Larson, treasurer and secretary, and David Larson,
    president, Larson Associates, Connecticut

Eva Friederichs, president, and Dick Bockius, marketing support,
    Image of Success, California

Nancy Shapiro, principal, Back to Health Information, New York
Jonathan Cohen, chiropractor, New York*

Simone Mastroeni and Phyllis Dilascio, partners, Diversified
    Forms and Printing Services, New York

Elizabeth Welpton, psychotherapist, Massachusetts
Dr. Douglas Welpton, psychiatrist, Massachusetts

Judith and Jerry Sudalter, owners, women's retail clothing stores,
    Massachusetts

Ruth Walters, full-time mother and real estate sales,
    Massachusetts
Glenn Walters, president, Advanced Depositions Technology,
    Massachusetts

Janet Parker, training and consulting, Massachusetts
Marty Sussman, executive director, The Cambridge Institute,
    Massachusetts

---

*Represented by spouse at interview.

Kathy Boyle, president, The Boyle Company, Massachusetts
Bill Smith, principal, Smith, Colbert, and Co., Massachusetts

Kari Spriggs, manager and bookeeper of photo studio,
     Massachusetts
David Yawnick, owner, Albert's photo studio, Massachusetts

Leslie Male, vice president, and Bruce Male, chairman,
     TravCorps, health care professional recruitment,
     Massachusetts

Terri Lonier, author, publisher, professional speaker, New York
Robert Sedestrom, professor of art, New York

Peg Erdland, association administrator, Massachusetts
Jack Erdland, president, NEHRA Human Resource Association,
     Massachusetts

Anonymous, president, manufacturing company, Massachusetts
Anonymous, marketing director, Massachusetts

Linda Weltner, author, journalist, professional speaker,
     Massachusetts
Jack Weltner, psychiatrist, Massachusetts*

Olgar Djam, owner, Djam Insurance Brokerage, New York
Nader Djam, banquet captain, New York

Heather Rizzo, owner, convenience store, Massachusetts*
Domenic Rizzo, owner, Brooklyn Bagels, Massachusetts

C. Lea Osborn and Hal Wilson, founders, NewChoices
     Relationship Center, Colorado

J. Dayne Lamb, mystery writer, Massachusetts
Gardner Stratton, J.D., C.P.A., financial counselor, Massachusetts

---

*Represented by spouse at interview.

Jill and Joseph Korn, authors/editors, *Abe's Story*, Holocaust memoir, Georgia

Arminda Bascope, vice president, and Roberto Bascope, president, Guia Hispanic Yellow Pages, Massachusetts

Linda and Alan Carr, chicken and cattle farmers, Missouri

Cindy and Christopher Miller, partners, Innovation Focus, Pennsylvania

Leslie Tayler, Mary Kay distributor, Pennsylvania
Baron Tayler, owner, Journeys End International, Inc., Pennsylvania

Susan Page, writer and professional speaker, California
Mayer Page, antiques dealer, California

Barbara and Michael Jonas, partners, Games Partnership Ltd., California

Helene Stone, president, and Bobby Stone, vice president, Data-Link Associates, New York

Lucie Germer, author and ESL teacher, New Hampshire
Jerry Germer, author and architect, New Hampshire

Azar Dadgar, bank operations officer, California
Jeff Berner, president, Jeff Berner Creative Services, California

Doff Meyer and Robin Brecker, principals, Doff Meyer Corporate Communications, New York

Kellee Harris, president, MarketSpark, sports and fitness marketing, Oregon
Lance Harris, chiropractor, Oregon

Judy Buch, ventriloquist and professional speaker, Connecticut
Ken Buch, computer consultant, Connecticut

Judy and Joe Sabah, partners, Sabah and Company and
    Pacesetter Publications, Colorado

Paula Knowlton, desktop publishing, Oregon
John Knowlton, owner, Home Based Business News, Oregon

Marilyn Kriegel, author, consultant, professional speaker,
    California*
Bob Kriegel, author, consultant, professional speaker, California

Carol Cohen, flight attendant, New York
Larry Kesslin, founder, Let's Talk Business Network, New York

Judith Sherven, Ph.D.; and Jim Sniechowski, Ph.D.; partners,
    The Magic of Differences, California

Phyllis Shacter and Alan Alberts, partners, Alberts and Associates,
    computer consulting, California

---

*Represented by spouse at interview.

Introduction

Congratulations! By purchasing this book you are already better equipped for the rigors of self-employment than most families. Your willingness to pay attention to relationship and family issues that arise on the entrepreneurial journey is a great first step toward achieving the balance you want in your life.

This book is for you if you are in an intimate committed relationship and one or both of you are self-employed or aspire to be. How self-employment will affect your marriage and family is critically important to you.* You understand that your work and personal life are not separate from each other. You are unwilling to sacrifice your marriage or personal well-being to achieve business success, and you don't believe that you have to. I present to you the book I wish Stephen and I had picked up at the beginning of our entrepreneurial journey together. I hope that it's helpful!

Perhaps you are the intimate partner of an entrepreneur—or the spouse of someone who dreams of self-employment in the future. You know that your partner's choice of work will dramatically affect your life together, and you are preparing yourself for the challenges ahead. Your foresight will go a long way toward protecting your relationship. Good for you for taking the lead.

---

*Throughout this book, the term *marriage* or *spouse* is used to describe any committed intimate relationship.

I am self-employed and I have been the supportive spouse of an entrepreneur. As a wife and mother of two daughters and two stepsons, I know firsthand how difficult it can be to nurture a healthy relationship and family, when finances are tight, sleep is deprived, emotional stress is high, and uncertainty is always in the picture. I also know that my marriage is stronger now because my husband, Stephen, and I have learned how to be together, and to thrive, in tough times.

I interviewed more than 125 entrepreneurial couples who said, "It was harder than we imagined, but the rewards made up for the difficulties." I also often heard, "I wish there had been a book like yours when we were starting out." Most couples start their own business aware that they are taking a financial risk. They may be unaware that they are risking their marriage as well. Consider these couples I spoke with.

Joseph and Tricia had a solid marriage of twenty-six years. They weathered the challenges of raising two children, taking care of elderly parents, and moving seven times in a twenty-year period because of Joseph's career. They thought they could handle anything together. Then Joe lost his job at the age of fifty-four. Frightened and angry, he bought a franchise with $20,000 in severance money and all of their personal savings. Joe quickly got in over his head, and Tricia left her profession as a nurse to help him save his floundering business. After six months, she walked off the job, threatening to leave her marriage as well. Joe was a great husband but a lousy boss, and she wasn't going to put up with his abuse anymore.

Paul frightened his wife, Linda, when he announced he wanted to quit his job to start his own consulting practice. Linda didn't want to be unsupportive, so she reluctantly agreed to provide for them on her limited teacher's salary until he got his first paid clients. A year later when his business had earned only $5,000, they reluctantly took a second mortgage on their home to meet their monthly obligations. When she got pregnant, it wasn't cause for celebration as they had hoped; they didn't know how they could afford a new baby. She never wanted to be a working mom, but now she had no choice.

Roger, a fifty-five-year-old dentist, jokes about how his wife,

Sarah, earns more money in an hour with her new business than he earns in an entire day's practice. Behind the hollow laughter, you can hear his jealousy and embarrassment. In his book, the husband should earn more than the wife. Roger has learned how to cook, and he launders his own shirts when Sarah travels two weeks out of every month. He doesn't like it one bit. He fondly remembers when all Sarah wanted to do was stay home and raise their children. He misses the wife he married.

These couples were unprepared and unskilled for meeting the relationship challenges of entrepreneurship. The circumstances that arose were more than they had bargained for. You wouldn't dream of taking your family on a dangerous white-water rafting trip without proper training and preparation. Yet millions of entrepreneurs are bringing their families on an entrepreneurial journey with little planning, inadequate resources, and no map. Instead of bringing a knowledgeable guide along, they follow a leader named "crisis management." Soon after the journey begins, the family is in jeopardy of capsizing, and no one is enjoying the ride.

With the right guidance and support, and a lot of hard work on your part, you and your partner can successfully meet the challenges of entrepreneurship. You can join thousands of entrepreneurial couples who are celebrating the greatest joys that life can offer—doing work they love, reaping financial rewards, enjoying the freedom and creativity of entrepreneurial life, raising their children, having fun, and falling deeply in love with their lifetime mate.

The path of self-employment holds great promise for you and your partner. Use this book as a helpful guide along the way. Build a life raft solid enough to carry you, your partner, and your children safely through the white waters of entrepreneurship.

Part 1

Creating a Family Plan

1

Exploring
Self-Employment
Alternatives
Considering Family Issues

One day I dragged myself home from a really bad day at work and I said to my wife, "Honey, I want to quit my job." She took a deep breath, and then she said, "OK, Charlie, what do you want to do instead?" I told her I didn't know, but we'd figure it out together.

Former middle manager

When I decided to buy the sporting goods store, my wife, Jill, said she was all for it. But then she started giving me all sorts of grief when I had to work long hours and when we couldn't take our normal vacations anymore. I wish I had known how she really felt before I bought the store.

When David decided he wanted to buy the sporting goods store, I thought it sounded great. I wanted him to be happy, but I didn't know that the store would consume his every waking moment. Ever since he opened the store, I feel like a widow. What's the point of working so hard, if we're never together to enjoy the benefits?

David and Jill, a couple in their mid-fifties

After twenty-seven years of marriage, David and Jill found themselves on different paths. David dreamed of several prosperous stores and Jill longed for a comfortable early retirement with her husband. If they had discussed the questions necessary for entrepreneurs to create a mutual family plan, then they might have discussed their differences *before* investing their savings in the sporting goods store.

"Honey, I want to quit my job," or, "Honey, I want to start my own business." How many times have you or your intimate partner blurted out one of these two phrases? It can be an emotionally charged moment. After all, you've heard the gruesome statistics. Over half of all marriages will end in divorce. The chances of succeeding in a small business are about one in ten. If you are considering starting your own business, or purchasing a business with your spouse or intimate partner, or you are already committed to entrepreneurship as a lifestyle, you've probably bought this book to help you beat the odds against divorce and business failure. Business experts stress the importance of creating a thorough business plan before starting a new business. Now learn how to prepare a family plan as well.

WHY CREATE A FAMILY PLAN?

When I was a single entrepreneur, my only family issue was who would walk and feed my dog when I worked late. Now, as a wife and mother of four children, neither my husband nor I can make any major business decisions without considering our family's needs. When you live with people who are important to you, business decisions are no longer entirely yours to make. What you do for a living, and how you shape your workday, affects all who live with you, or rely on you, each day.

The most common mistake married entrepreneurs make is to

rush into business decisions without careful thought and discussion of how their business dreams will involve and affect their family. Consider several reasons why this happens:

- *Blind enthusiasm*: The entrepreneur, so excited about the prospect of a new business, doesn't want to consider any possible negative resistance.
- *Running away*: The entrepreneur is rebounding from sudden job loss, job dissatisfaction, worries about finances, or the failure of another business. The need to move quickly into a new alternative takes precedence over careful planning.
- *Egocentricity:* The entrepreneur assumes that his or her spouse and family will make the necessary adjustments to support him or her.
- *Fear or inability to communicate*: The entrepreneur isn't accustomed to discussing openly with a spouse issues that will affect their relationship and lifestyle. Act first, talk later (only if necessary), is this entrepeneur's motto.
- *Blissful naivete*: The entrepreneur is completely unaware of how the prospective business will affect marriage and family life. He or she can't imagine potential concerns and questions until they actually arise.

The most common mistake partners of entrepreneurs make is to offer unconditional support from the beginning—in concept—without thinking through the implications of such a lifestyle change. Their support wanes when the actual hardships of self-employment rub up against their fantasy. Consider several reasons why this happens:

- *Well-intended support*: They want to champion their partners' dreams. They don't want to throw cold water on their mates' enthusiasm.
- *Starstruck*: They share their partners' romantic vision for great prosperity and an improved relationship and family life. They are as excited as their partners about the entrepreneurial opportunity ahead.
- *Lack of knowledge or awareness*: They don't really understand

the demands of self-employment and how their partners' self-employment will affect their life.

- *Fear or inability to communicate*: They have great reservations but are afraid to voice their opinion. They don't want their partners to think less of them, be angry with them, or feel unsupported by them.
- *It's better than nothing*: Their partners' job loss or lack of meaningful work frightens them. They are anxious for their spouses to find their right livelihood or to earn some income, even if family sacrifices may be necessary.
- *They weren't asked*: Though their partners' worklife affects them, their partners don't invite their involvement in the planning process or ask for their opinion.

Some entrepreneurial naivete is par for the course. Self-employment always involves risk and unknowns. To muster the courage required to start a business, entrepreneurs and their spouses must view their entrepreneurial prospects with a certain amount of romantic illusion. It is not unlike getting married or raising a child.

When we make a deep personal commitment to a relationship, "for better or worse," we know on some level that those worse days will come. We focus initially on positive dreams for the future and the deep love we feel for our partners. Imagine if we had a crystal ball and on our wedding day we could see some of our worst days ahead. If we knew what was ahead we might not be willing to commit to our partners for a lifetime. We might not even be in a relationship. Rosy-colored, romantic illusion encourages us to embark on an unpredictable difficult journey.

The family plan is a map as well as a compass for your entrepreneurial adventure. Creating a family plan will not eliminate your romantic vision or throw cold water on your entrepreneurial dreams, but it will ensure that you are at least traveling with your mate on the same path, in the right general direction. Thoroughly discussing your business dreams and planning with your family will help you choose the entrepreneurial path with the most potential for satisfying your long-term individual, couple, and family goals.

Before you choose to commit to your mate for a lifetime, you ask and answer at least some basic questions. Do you want children? Where do you want to live? What religion will you observe? How much money and sex do you need to be happy? Though aware of differences, when the answers to enough basic questions are in sync with each other, you are able to envision building a life together. The same goes for business. This chapter provides discussion points so that you can involve your mate as early in the business planning process as possible. A family plan complements your business plan as a measure toward protecting your relationship and family from unexpected hardships of small business ownership. You can construct a family plan in any format that suits you, written or verbal, formal or casual, as long as it answers your most important couple and family questions and concerns.

FIFTY QUESTIONS TO ASK YOURSELF AND YOUR MATE WHEN CREATING A FAMILY PLAN

Think of creating a family plan for your business venture as the equivalent of those late-night discussions you had with your partner when you were first courting. Remember when you shared your dreams with each other in detail, when you wanted to know everything about each other? You would visualize how your life would look and feel after you took the plunge to live together, how you would share your living space, where you would live, even questions as simple as who would get the bigger closet!

When you meet your life partner, you answer questions big and small in order to merge your lives. The longer you are with your mate, the less likely you may be to communicate with each other in the same kind of depth characterized by your dating years. Yet, the consideration of self-employment alternatives deserves that kind of discussion with your life partner, no matter how long you have been together. Setting aside private time from your busy lives to answer the following questions about any self-employment alternative that either or both of you are considering will save you much heartache and financial woe down the road.

DISCOVERY EXERCISE ONE: CONSIDERING FAMILY ISSUES
Completion time: 60–120 minutes.

If you are exploring a particular self-employment option, set aside at least an hour or two with your spouse to consider the answers to the following questions. Answering these questions will help you evaluate how well a self-employment option suits you, your spouse, and your family.

Important Note: These fifty questions are designed to launch you and your partner into *initial* discussion of some of the larger issues related to self-employment. These questions are a good start toward thinking about family plan issues, but *not* all questions to be considered. The chapters that follow in this book will lead you into discussion of family plan issues in more depth and enable you to prepare a more thorough family plan. For example, refer to chapter 2, "Combining Marriage and Entrepreneurship," for deeper consideration of how involved you and your spouse will be together in business; chapter 3, "Financial and Family Planning," to prepare for the financial and family life impact of self-employment; chapter 4, "The Joys and Challenges of Working at Home," to evaluate whether a home-based business will work for you and your family. Each of these chapters will provide opportunities for you to discuss, prepare, and communicate how self employment will affect your intimate relationship and family life. While chapter 1 helps raise the family plan questions for you to be considering, chapters 2 through 4 will help you answer those questions in detail.

You may wish to write down your answers to these questions in a journal or to discuss them with your mate.

FINANCIAL CONSIDERATIONS

Initial Investment
1. How much initial capital will be necessary?
2. Will you need to borrow capital to invest?

3. What proportion of your total assets will you need to invest?

4. Major purchases required.

Ongoing Investment

5. How much cash is required monthly to support the business?

Length of Time Before Positive Cash Flow

6. What is the learning curve in this business? How much time will it take before you can expect to be profitable?

Income Projections

7. What are reasonable expectations for positive cash flow in three, six, and nine months, one year, two years, five years?

Transition Options

8. Can you test the waters while keeping your current job?

9. Can you work the business part-time?

10. How long will the initial purchase or setup process take?

Insurance and Taxes

11. How will insurance needs for your family be cared for? What are the tax implications of the business?

Perceived Risk

12. Considering the norm in the industry, what are the likely odds for success?

13. What do you risk if the business fails?

TIME CONSIDERATIONS

Total Time

14. How much time every day and week is required to operate the business successfully?

Working Schedule

15. What will your working hours be?

16. Are there seasonal, daily, or monthly cycles to the business?

Vacations, Weekends, and Holidays

17. Will the business allow for vacation time—how much?

18. Will the business require weekend work or working on holidays?

TRAVEL CONSIDERATIONS

Travel Required

19. Will your business require any travel?
20. Will travel be local, national, or international?
21. Will the travel require overnight absence from home—for how long at a stretch? How much of an issue will that be for your spouse and/or children?
22. How long will the daily commute be? How will that impact your family life?

HOME OFFICE CONSIDERATIONS

Home Office

23. Will you work out of the home? Full-time or part-time?
24. What are the zoning regulations in your town?
25. How conducive is your home and family to a home office?
26. Does the business have to be located in any particular place? How does that mesh with the current location of your home?

PERSONAL CONSIDERATIONS

Right Livelihood

27. How does the business fit in with your natural personal inclination, what you love to do and do well at, your skills and abilities?
28. How excited are you about the product or service you will be delivering?
29. How will this business option help you achieve your business and family goals?
30. How does this business option integrate with your values?

Perceived Emotional Stress

31. How stressful for you would this business choice be? Are there aspects of the business you expect to find difficult?
32. How demanding will the working schedule be? Will you have to sacrifice anything important to your physical, emotional, and spiritual health in order to succeed in this business?

RELATIONSHIP CONSIDERATIONS

Spouse or Partner Involvement

33. To what extent will your spouse or partner be involved in the business operations?
34. To what extent will your spouse or partner be involved in the initial decision-making and setup process?
35. How supportive is your spouse or partner about this business option?
36. To what extent does this business option require your spouse's cooperation or support to succeed?

Couple Goals

37. How does this business option support your short- and long-term goals as a couple?
38. How is this business option synchronous with your mission and values as a couple?

Synergy

39. How does this business option mesh with your partner's work and livelihood? Is it synergistic, harmonious, and complementary? How will it conflict?

Relationship Maintenance

40. How much intimate time will you be able to devote to your partner?
41. Will you be working together? If so, what relationship issues are you concerned about?
42. How will this business option improve, solidify, or sustain your relationship?
43. How could this business option jeopardize or deteriorate your relationship?

CHILDREN CONSIDERATIONS (if applicable)

Family Support

44. What kind of family support do you need to be successful?
45. Will the children help in the business? How and when?

Family Needs

46. How will this business option allow you to care for your children's or other family members' daily needs?
47. How will this business option interfere with caring for your children or other family members' daily needs?

Long-Term Family Goals

48. Do you hope to pass the business along to your children?
49. How does the business support long-term financial goals for your children?
50. Will this business option prevent you from being able to meet your short- or long-term goals for your children?

CONSIDERING THE FAMILY PROS AND CONS OF SELF-EMPLOYMENT ALTERNATIVES

A business plan provides the framework for discussing and planning business activities and outcomes; it cannot prevent all business problems from happening. A family plan functions the same way. Your answers to the preceding questions will not eliminate challenges to your relationship and family. Every choice has its unique consequences, both benefits and hardships. The question at hand is not "How can we avoid all stress?" but rather, "What kind of stress am I and my family willing to bear?"

Entrepreneurial couples report common positive and negative family experiences with a variety of self-employment options. Consider the following summary as warning signs, as well as coming attractions, and not as predictions of how your individual choice of business will turn out.

Starting Your Own Manufacturing Business

The good news is:	The bad news is:
You can take a great idea, turn it into a finished product, and make a fortune.	The risk may be higher, and the financial investment greater, than you or your spouse had bargained for.
You can develop a company to be sold or passed along to children.	The hours can be exhausting and family/relationship time may suffer.
You can build a company of several hundred or thousands of employees and have a critical impact on their life. Your employees can become a part of your extended family.	You may not want the headache or liability of managing other employees.
You can work with your spouse as a full partner. If your skills are very different from each other, all the better.	Changes in the economy, competition, or other external factors can suddenly put you out of business.
You may have the opportunity for world travel.	You may have to travel extensively from home.

Starting a Service, Professional, or Commission Sales Business

The good news is:	The bad news is:
Start-up investment can be relatively low.	It can be a lot harder to get paying clients than you had bargained for.
You may be able to work out of your home.	Income is limited by what you can do with your time, unless you partner with someone or add staff.

Starting a Service, Professional, or Commission Sales Business *[continued]*

The good news is:

You can work flexible hours, depending on who your clients are and how much income you want to earn.

You may never have to manage an employee other than yourself.

Depending on your service, you may be able to work anywhere in the country.

The bad news is:

You'll have to cope with your fair share of rejection.

As a sole proprietor, you'll need to do tasks you may not be very good at, or like to do, unless you partner with someone who complements your strengths.

You can have a great idea, a useful product, and still not be able to get the product to market or make a profit—even after years of work.

Buying a Franchise

The good news is:

You are buying a product or service with a proven track record, so the chances of success are higher.

You will receive training and support from your franchisor so you're not alone.

The learning curve is reduced, since you are provided with the systems to follow.

The bad news is:

You'll have to give up some control to your franchisor.

The working hours of some franchises, particularly retail ones, can be exhausting.

The initial capital investment can be sizable.

Buying a Franchise *[continued]*

The good news is:

You can sell the franchise when you are ready to move on.

Some franchises are ideally suited for working with your spouse and family.

The bad news is:

The process for being selected as a franchisee can be time-consuming and very competitive.

You'll probably have all the headaches associated with hiring and managing staff.

Buying an Existing Business

The good news is:

You will have a good sense of the cash flow you can expect from the beginning.

You may be able to purchase good will and reputation in the community.

You can be profiting from day one if you buy the right business.

The seller may be willing to extend purchase terms that lower the initial capital required.

You can turn the right kind of business into a family business.

The bad news is:

It can be as difficult to find a good business to buy as it is to find the right marriage partner.

You may have to spend sizable dollars renovating or improving the business.

Depending on the business, the working hours can be extremely demanding.

You may discover negative aspects about the business after you have bought it.

Selling a business can be a difficult, time-consuming process, if you decide you want to sell.

Multilevel Marketing (network marketing businesses like Amway or Shaklee)

The good news is:

You can launch one of several MLM businesses, selling a product you use yourself and believe in, for less than $100.

You can easily moonlight or work the business part-time.

Company-sponsored trips rewarding sales performance can provide family vacations.

You have a shot at six-figure income, without exhausting hours, once your downline is well established and you are collecting residual income.

Many husbands and wives enjoy working an MLM business together.

The bad news is:

It can be harder to build an established downline than it appears.

Many people have negative perceptions about "pyramid schemes" and multilevel marketing approaches. That could include your spouse.

As with any sales, be prepared for plenty of rejection.

Since you are selling a product you don't manufacture, you lose a great deal of control.

MLM products cannot be advertised or sold in traditional ways, challenging your sales efforts.

CONCLUSION

Congratulations! By taking the time to buy this book, and at least read this chapter, you have taken an important first step toward protecting your relationship and family on the entrepreneurial journey! Ideally, you will read the rest of this book, alone or with your spouse, *before* launching into any major self-employment decision. You are about to embark on a journey that promises to change your relationship and family life dramatically. Are you willing to devote ten to twenty hours to preparing yourself for these challenges, so that you don't sacrifice your personal foundation for business success? I hope so! If you've already immersed yourself in the entrepreneurial journey, then use this book to build some new knowledge and skills that will help you communicate with your spouse and sustain your relationship more effectively. Besides, whatever employment scenario you and your spouse are in right now is always subject to change over your lifetime together!

RECOMMENDED RESOURCES

Books

Country Bound! Trade Your Business Suit Blues for Blue Jean Dreams by Marilyn and Tom Ross. Communication Creativity, 1992.

Country Careers: Successful Ways to Live and Work in the Country by Jerry Germer. John Wiley & Sons, 1993.

Do What You Love, The Money Will Follow: Discovering Your Right Livelihood by Marsha Sinetar. Paulist Press, 1987.

Enterprising Women: Lessons from 100 of the Greatest Entrepreneurs of Our Day by A. David Silver. AMACOM, 1994.

Finding the Hat that Fits: How to Turn Your Heart's Desire into Your Life's Work by John Caple. Plume, 1993.

For Entrepreneurs Only: Success Strategies for Anyone Starting or Growing a Business by Wilson Harrell. Career Press, 1994.

How to Buy and Manage a Franchise: The Definitive Resource Guide If You're Thinking of Purchasing a Franchise or Turning Your Business into One by Joseph Mancuso and Donald Boroian. Fireside, 1992.

How to Open Your Own Store: Everything You Need to Know to Succeed in the Retail Marketplace by Michael Antoniak. Avon, 1994.

How to Start, Finance, and Manage Your Own Small Business by
    Joseph Mancuso. Fireside, 1992.
*How to Start a Service Business: The Essential Tools for Success
    in the Fastest Growing Industry of the Future* by Ben Chant
    and Melissa Morgan. Avon, 1994.
*Inc. Your Dreams: For Any Woman Who Is Thinking About Her
    Own Business* by Rebecca Maddox. Viking, 1995.
*Making a Living Without a Job: Winning Ways for Creating Work
    that You Love* by Barbara J. Winter. Bantam, 1993.
*Making It On Your Own: Surviving and Thriving the Ups and
    Downs of Being Your Own Boss* by Paul and Sarah Edwards.
    Jeremy P. Tarcher/Perigee, 1991.
*Making It Work: Practical Solutions for Balancing the Needs of
    Your Career, Marriage, Children, and Self* by Victoria
    Houston. Fireside, 1991.
*Mid-Career Entrepreneur: How to Start a Business and Be Your
    Own Boss* by Joseph Mancuso. Enterprise, 1993.
*MLM Magic: How an Ordinary Person Can Build an Extra-
    Ordinary Networking Business from Scratch* by Venus
    Andrecht. Ransom Hill Press, 1993.
*Our Wildest Dreams: Women Entrepreneurs Making Money,
    Having Fun, Doing Good* by Joline Godfrey. HarperBusiness,
    1992.
Running a Family Business by Joseph Mancuso. Prentice-Hall
    Press, 1991.
*Shifting Gears: How to Master Career Change and Find the Work
    That's Right for You* by Carole Hyatt. Simon & Schuster,
    1990.
Surviving the Start-Up Years in Your Own Business by Joyce S.
    Marder. Better Way Publications, 1991.
The Complete Guide to Buying a Business by Richard Snowden.
    AMACOM, 1994.
*The Family in Business: Understanding and Dealing with the
    Challenges Entrepreneurial Families Face* by Paul Rosenblatt
    et al. Jossey-Bass Publishers, 1985.
*The Working Parent Dilemma: How to Balance the Responsibilities
    of Children and Careers* by Earl Grollman and Gerri Sweder.
    Beacon Press, 1986.

Tips and Traps When Buying a Franchise by Mary Tomzack. McGraw-Hill, 1994.

Wave 3: The New Era in Network Marketing by Richard Poe. Prima Publishing, 1995.

When You Lose Your Job by Cliff Hakim. Berrett-Koehler, 1993.

Working Solo: The Real Guide to Freedom and Financial Success with Your Own Business by Terri Lonier. Portico Press, 1994.

Working Solo Sourcebook: Essential Resources for Independent Entrepreneurs by Terri Lonier. Portico Press, 1995.

You Can Start Your Own Business by Jeffrey Davidson and Arnold Sanow. Washington Publications, Inc., 1991.

Zen and the Art of Making a Living: A Practical Guide to Creative Career Design by Laurence G. Boldt. Penguin, 1993.

Magazines

Business Start-Ups, 2392 Morse Avenue, Irvine, CA 92714, 1-800-274-8333.

Inc.: The Magazine for Growing Companies. P.O. Box 54129, Boulder, CO 80322, 1-800-234-0999.

Nation's Business: The Small Business Advisor, 1615 H Street, N.W., Washington, D.C. 20062, 1-800-352-1450.

Success: The Magazine for Today's Entrepreneurial Mind, P.O. Box 3038, Harlan, IA 51537, or call 1-800-234-7324

Consulting Organizations

Franchise Consulting. Mary Tomzack, author, *Tips and Traps When Buying a Franchise*; 50 Law Road, Briarcliff, NY 10510, 914-347-3530.

Franchise Spectrum. William Moore, president; consulting free of charge to prospective franchisees; 65 Boston Post Road West, Suite 106, Marlboro, MA 01752, 508-460-6787.

Key Resources. Jane Hilburt-Davis, family business consulting; 40 Middlebury Road, Lexington, MA 02173, 617-861-0586.

Richard Snowden, author, *The Complete Guide to Buying a Business*, Box 5491, Portsmouth, NH 03802, 603-436-2240.

2

Combining Marriage and Entrepreneurship

Three Models of Joining Together on the Entrepreneurial Journey

- We'd kill each other if my spouse and I tried to run the same business together.
- We can't relate to couples who hardly see each other all week. We spend twenty-four hours a day together and we love it.
- We could never handle the risk of both of us being self-employed.

Which of these statements applies to you? What works well for one married couple may be disastrous for another. Every marriage and business is unique, and each couple has to search for the right path for them.

Some couples, like Stephen and me, move through all combinations of marriage and entrepreneurship as life circumstances change. Other couples plant themselves squarely in one model for their entire marriage. Each paradigm has its unique challenges and rewards. The question isn't which model is less stressful. The question is what *kinds* of stress do *you* choose to take on? One path isn't more rewarding than another. Rather, what outcomes would *you* find the most rewarding?

Let's begin by looking at three different models for combining entrepreneurship and relationship.

1. *Full partnership:* Full and equal partners in the same business. For example, Kyle and Alex run a chain of franchise stores together.
2. *Dual entrepreneurship:* Each individual operates his or her own separate business. For example, Adrian is self-employed as a desktop publisher, and Joe is a chiropractor.
3. *Spousal support:* One spouse supports the entrepreneurial efforts of the other but does not work as a full partner in the entrepreneur's business. For example, Elaine works a salaried job and takes care of the children. Her husband, Robert, founded and heads up an engineering firm.

What can you expect in each of these scenarios? What are the primary challenges and rewards of each, and how can you tell which one is best for you and your marriage? This section walks you through each model with three assessment tests designed to predict your chances for success in each of the three. You'll also find recommended strategies for solving common problems that entrepreneurial couples like you have successfully faced.

Let's begin by looking at the first model, full partnership. Whether you are currently working with your mate, considering the possibility, or curious about what it takes to make this model work successfully, read the next section.

FULL PARTNERSHIP

Full partners may have started the business together, or one spouse may join the first spouse after the launch of the business.

Both individuals are equally dedicated to the business, although their roles may be very different from each other.

Some examples:

- Co-owners of a restaurant
- Professional speaker and office manager
- President and vice president of a manufacturing company
- Partners in a computer consulting company
- Joint upline in a multilevel marketing organization
- Dairy farmers

Are You Cut Out for Working with Your Spouse as a Business Partner?

A preference for the lifestyle benefits of full partnership does not necessarily mean that this arrangement suits your partnership.

The following assessment test will help you evaluate whether becoming full business partners will strengthen your marriage and your business. Created from my research and interviews with successful couples, this test highlights those elements found in solid, rewarding business and marriage partnerships or missing from those partnerships that failed.

No test is entirely predictive. You may beat the odds and create an outstanding business partnership, even with a low score on this test. Or, you can score high on this test, but then stumble through particular challenges, resulting in a counterproductive partnership.

Take the test separately from your spouse. Or else do the test yourself and verbally quiz your spouse. Then get together to share the results.

DISCOVERY EXERCISE ONE: ASSESSMENT TEST FOR JOINT PARTNERS

Place the appropriate number next to each question, and then total your score.

1 = That doesn't describe us at all.
2 = That describes us somewhat.
3 = That describes us frequently.
4 = That describes us completely.

1. We have worked successfully on joint projects many times in our marriage. We enjoy the process and get good results.
2. We value each other's opinion and respect and admire each other's skill. If I were looking to hire a business partner, I would consider myself lucky to acquire my spouse's talents.
3. I can freely express my opinions to my spouse, even if we disagree. My spouse listens to what I have to say and respects my involvement. We have learned that the best decision is one that considers both of our points of view.
4. We understand that no one is perfect. If one of us makes a mistake, the other is generally forgiving. We apologize to each other when it's appropriate.
5. We consider ourselves equal business partners in ability, dedication, and contribution. Since we have complementary skills, we're stronger as a team than we are separately.
6. Our motivations for starting the business are similar or in harmony with each other. We hold the same values and want the same results from our business.
7. We always knew we would go into business together, ever since we got together. We talked about it even when we were dating. We were just waiting until the right time in our life to follow our dream.
8. Spending more time together strengthens our marriage. I can spend hours with my spouse without feeling bored or irritated.

9. When conflict arises, we don't let problems and resentments build between us. We communicate anger and criticism productively, taking responsibility for our own part of the problem.

10. Neither of us needs to be in control all the time. We can share responsibilities and delegate when appropriate. We aren't competitive with each other or jealous of each other's success. Neither of us has difficulty sharing the credit for our success.

11. We cope well with stress, individually and as a couple. We don't lose our sense of humor for long, and we keep perspective in the difficult times. We've come through hard times with an even stronger relationship.

12. We know what our expectations of each other are, both at work and at home. We agree on how to divide household, child-care duties, and business responsibilities. Both of us are willing to pitch in and do tasks we don't like to do, just because they have to get done.

13. If we need to find a compromise, we are flexible and willing to discuss the issue until we find a solution that satisfies both of us. Neither of us has to be right all the time. We enjoy collaborating with each other, and willingly sacrifice total control for the benefits of our team approach.

14. We have complete trust in each other to make sound and well-reasoned business decisions. We don't feel threatened by any personal relationships that may form as a result of our business.

15. Our commitment to a lifelong marriage is complete and total. We will seek outside help if necessary to prevent our relationship from deteriorating. We wouldn't continue working together in business if it meant sacrificing our marriage.

16. We both have compatible tolerance for financial risk. We have discussed where our comfort zone is for financial risk. We commit to not going beyond the safety level of either of us.

17. Before we even considered working together in business, we had a great relationship. We believe that the foundation of our marriage is strong enough to withstand the pressures of starting a business together. We look forward to how working together as business partners could strengthen our relationship.

18. Both of us prefer a lifestyle that closely meshes together our business, relationship. and family life.

SCORE

56–72: **Destined for Success.** Your foundation is strong. Success as full partners is likely, as long as you keep doing the things that work so well for you. You'll still experience challenges along the way, but the rewards could be enormous.

37–55: **It Could Go Either Way.** The potential for success or trouble depends on how you respond to the aspects of working together that challenge you and your partnership. If you capitalize on your strengths and work hard to improve your individual and couple weaknesses, you could strengthen your marriage as well as your business if you go into partnership together.

18–36: **Look Out! Trouble Ahead.** Be forewarned of the potential risks of partnering together in business. Work to strengthen your marriage before you risk a full business partnership. Seek the advice or counsel of an objective third party before embarking on this journey.

Now we'll review the common challenges and rewards of full partnership.

Primary Challenges of Full Partners

Financial Risk

"Putting all your eggs in one basket" is an apt phrase for one of the primary drawbacks of the full-partner model. Investing all your money, time, and effort as a couple into one endeavor can reap substantial rewards. If the venture fails, you may lose everything including your relationship. There is no other job or business in the household to fall back on if the venture doesn't work. You may forgo pension, life insurance and disability benefits, subsidized health insurance, and paid vacations. You may pay a premium to maintain those benefits as a self-employed person.

Financial risk for full partners extends beyond the money lost if the business fails. It also permeates such common life events as buying a house or medical insurance. Mortgage companies disdain self-employed individuals. Unless you establish your business for several years and are profitable, borrowing money to purchase a home, a car, or any other major purchase may be impossible or expensive. Mortgage brokers will charge you a premium for mortgages that carry titles like, "Nonverifiable income."

> When we decided to go into business together, our greatest worry was how we would get medical insurance to cover Karen. No insurance plans for the self-employed would cover a preexisting condition like cancer. We had to squirrel away enough money in our savings account to pay for her treatments out of pocket. If she needs any type of intensive cancer treatment in the future, it could bankrupt us.
> *Franchise owner*

You may not be able to predict all trouble spots, but you can prepare for some of the bigger known issues. Have a contingency plan for paying the bills if the business isn't profitable in your projected timeframe. Full partnership may be your model of choice; but if one or both of you think that the financial risk is too great, then you must be open to taking another path temporarily. Flexibility is critical.

Relationship Challenges

Full business partnership telescopes such complex relationship issues as shared power, joint decision making, and managing differences in work style. You may fear or even experience some of these common challenges.

Loss of sexual attraction: Do you compartmentalize your life? Is there room in your vision for a sexy business partner? Not for some. One gentleman couldn't turn his sexual energy for his wife on or off, depending on the setting. She was either his partner or his lover, but she couldn't be both:

> When my wife and I started a business together, I lost the desire to make love to her. We were always talking about the

business, even in bed. I couldn't imagine having sex with my business partner.

Small business owner

Learning to celebrate difference: The power of your complementary skills can become a source of conflict as you learn how to accept your workstyle differences. Learning to celebrate and embrace your complementary characteristics, rather than negatively judging your partner, will be one of your greatest challenges as a couple. Every couple must learn how to manage their differences. When you work with your spouse, this can become a daily issue:

> She's the detail person, I'm the big picture guy. She enjoys dealing with the customers and I prefer to focus on business operations. She works best late at night after the kids are asleep, and I work best first thing in the morning. She needs daily business meetings and frequent communication with me and I'm happier if we just meet weekly. We're so different, it's amazing that we can work together at all.
>
> *Manufacturing company president*

Negative judgment: Beyond accepting your differences in work style, you may also witness a side of your spouse's personality you hadn't seen before you began working together. If your spouse works at an outside job, you may never know that she gets snappy with her employees or he spends two hours a day on personal calls. When you work together, you expose yourself to unattractive work habits in your partner that you will need to accept. Talk with your partner frequently about how your relationship is faring. Staying current will help you manage any challenges that come your way:

> The first time I watched my wife flirt with a male customer to get an order, I flipped my lid. I calmed down when I realized she had landed our biggest account yet. Later on, when we had some private time, I told my wife how I felt watching her flirt with that customer. She reassured me that I had nothing to worry about. It was just a sales technique to her.
>
> *Magazine publisher*

Loss of Personal and Family Time

Most small businesses, especially in the start-up and growth stages, require an all-consuming commitment of time and energy. You may have to sacrifice personal space and time with the children and each other. Working partners often go several years without taking any vacation. If you choose a retail or service business, you need to be there for the customers and clients until you can afford to hire someone who can back you up in your absence.

> After three years of working together I demanded that my husband and I take at least two weeks of vacation to travel where there are no booked gigs, no potential clients, and no tax deductions!
>
> *Professional speaker*

I interviewed one couple who were leaving after our interview for the first vacation they had allowed themselves in four years—and it was only for a four-day getaway! The woman was noticeably anxious about the trip. My mom and dad, who partnered in business for several years, solved the problem of not being able to get away for vacation. They bought a condominium on the beach only a forty-minute drive from their primary home.

The likelihood of bringing work home will also crowd your personal time. If your business partner is available to you twenty-four hours a day, you may not wait until the office opens the next day to discuss a hot new idea. Children may suffer from neglect as their parents become consumed in the business, and even dinner conversations circle around business.

If you and your partner operate a retail business outside the house, the freedom you sought as entrepreneurs may elude you. You can find yourselves jailed to the retail location for ten to fourteen hours a day, six or seven days a week. You may be too cash poor in the early stages to hire a manager or assistant to relieve you, requiring both of you to practically move into the store.

I interviewed a couple who started an independent Japanese bookstore open seven days a week. They were each in the store fourteen hours a day. The only holiday they closed was Christmas, so this couple took one day off work a year. Luckily they loved their work and working together, but that kind of schedule could strain even the best of marriages.

The loss of personal space can impede your physical, emotional, and spiritual well-being. You may commute with your partner to the office, lunch with your colleagues, and devote yourself to your family's needs in the evening. You may feel too guilty or pressured to take time out for exercise, meditation, reading a book or magazine, or talking to a friend. If you do, then your partner may resent you. When you drop off to bed exhausted, the last thing you want to do is relate to your mate.

The key is to set boundaries around personal, relationship, and family time when you need it. Get creative. If you wait until the "right time," it may never happen. Drive to work in separate cars. Schedule an aerobics class twice a week. Plan a "no business" Saturday night date. Read chapter 7, "Keeping the Romance Alive," and pick out a few suggestions. Treat creating balance like an important problem to solve and you *will* find solutions that work for you.

Preserving Your Individual Identity

When cocreating a business, you may struggle to maintain individual identity within the couple partnership. When you operate as one unit at work and at home, there is a pervasive element of "we-ness" in every aspect of your life. When the world thinks of you as "Joe and Judy," you may yearn to develop an aspect of your life entirely your own.

The desire for autonomy within a committed relationship is natural and healthy. Find activities outside the business that you can partake of by yourself. Segregate an aspect of your joint business that is yours alone. For example, a woman I interviewed who has worked with her husband for years in the publishing and speaking business, recently started a coaching practice that is an offshoot of their business together. Her coaching practice doesn't involve her husband at all.

Finding Work that Suits Both of You

Imagine you and your partner share a mutual love for exotic parrots. A business opportunity selling parrots might be a perfect match for both of you. But what if one of you loves parrots and the other merely tolerates their screeching and constant stream of bird poop. You may still go into business together if working together suits your lifestyle choice. Couples don't always start a business that perfectly suits the career aspirations and passions of each individual in the relationship.

The challenge comes if each partner doesn't find an aspect of the business personally exciting. I interviewed a nurse who gave up her nursing career to assist her husband in running a MailBox Etc. franchise. After two years, they sold the profitable business; she was planning to return to her nursing career. Although she loved working with her husband, she missed her profession.

If you miss your former profession, then consider remaining in a part-time job or working as a volunteer to maintain your connection. Look for creative ways that your current business can meet the same needs or interface with similar customers. Expand into a new business service that uses your former skills. Break out of the box and look for ways to fulfill the work aspirations of each partner.

You may have different goals and desires related to the business. What motivates you to work every day may be different from your spouse. Perhaps your partner dreams of selling the company for a big profit but you would be happier with a business that didn't demand as much time and effort, even if the profit potential is less. You may dream of opening up a chain of stores and building an empire, but your partner prefers to limit the number of employees and locations. Idealistically, you and your partner will always be on the same wavelength. Realistically, as the business progresses and your family circumstances change, your needs and dreams may differ.

Look for creative alternatives that honor both partner's needs and visions. Stay flexible and change the structure of the partnership as needed. Your business motivations will fluctuate, depending on your family concerns, health, age, spiritual values, and other interests. Let go of convincing your partner that you are right, and look for a win/win solution.

Expanding to Include Your Spouse

If you evolved into a full partnership, you will meet with different issues than couples who began their business together. Often one spouse works a straight job until the business is profitable enough to allow that spouse to quit the job and join the family business. One spouse may join the other spouse's business after losing a job, rather than searching for new employment. Here are some examples.

> I used to run a department and make my own decisions. Suddenly my wife was my boss. She said she wanted me as her business partner, but what she really wanted was an employee who would do what she ordered.
>
> *West Coast businessman*

> My business was my baby. When my husband joined me in the company, it was hard for me to begin sharing the credit for our success. I wanted him to do the work, but I wanted to keep all the credit.
>
> *Midwest entrepreneur*

The most important step you can take toward dealing with this challenge is to communicate about it openly with your spouse. Discuss regularly how each spouse is experiencing the evolution to full partnership. Acknowledge the effort each is making toward making the transition work. Above all, be patient. It can take a year or more to evolve into a true partnership.

Losing Your Escape Valve

Where do you go to complain when you're having a bad day at work? Often your mate. What if your spouse had the same miserable day, is part of the problem, or is too busy working to be available? When you work full-time with your intimate partner, you may miss the best friend who used to be available to you with an objective ear and unconditional loving support. Your vested partner may move immediately into problem solving, reacting defensively, or judging you for the problem.

Create outside support systems available to you when you have an emotional need your spouse can't fill. Be clear with your partner—if all you want to do is vent, and you aren't looking for a solution, say so. Later on in the book you'll learn more effective ways of communicating your needs and getting them met.

Significant Rewards of Full Partnership

Greater Intimacy

Working toward a common goal: United by a joint purpose and vision, your business partnership can expand and solidify your personal relationship. For some couples, cocreating a business provides the same satisfaction as raising a family.

> Since my partner and I are gay, we never had the opportunity to raise kids together. When our bed and breakfast opened its doors for the first time to the public, we felt as if we had given birth after a long year of labor!
> *Bed and breakfast owner*

Sharing a business with your spouse gives you more in common to discuss and experience. You understand each other's work intimately, and your social life can evolve around shared friends and colleagues. When you experience business success, you celebrate together; when you confront business hardship, you fight it as a team.

> We've completely woven together our personal and business lives. Divorce for us is out of the question. It would destroy every aspect of our lives, not just our marriage.
> *Entertainer*

Quicker resolution of issues: When you work with your intimate partner, you get to know *all* aspects of each other. You work to resolve your most troublesome relationship issues, so that you can work together effectively. The average overworked couple of the nineties spends only a few hours a week with each other. By substantially increasing your time together and communicating frequently, you can advance your relationship to entirely new levels.

> We're so tied together personally and in business, it forces us to deal with issues sooner, and keeps us reassessing our life goals.
> *Chiropractor*

Improved sex life: Contrary to the individuals who lose their sexual attraction for their spouse and business partner, some individuals report that their sexual energy improves dramatically after going into business together. When you work together, there can be more time available for sex. Couples may celebrate business success or take a break from a hard day's work by making love in the office. This element of romance and forbidden lust adds some juice to their marriages as well as their businesses!

> When my wife started working in my office after thirty years of marriage, I discovered she was not just the mother of my kids and a good hostess to my business associates; she was also a brilliant sexy woman, filled with creative energy and drive. I fell in love with her in a whole new way.
> *Professional speaker*

Couples who thrive as working partners love to spend time together and appreciate having a best friend as their business partner and spouse. They welcome the challenges to their relationship as an opportunity for personal growth. They have fun together, and their respect and love for each other deepen the longer they work together.

It's Better for Business

Complementary skills: The greatest challenge to your relationship also offers the greatest opportunity for strengthening your business. No entrepreneur is an expert in sales, marketing, operations, finance, and human resources. If you start a manufacturing company because you have a great product idea, chances are you won't excel in ordering office supplies or writing policy manuals. You will need a staff to care for the details for you. Often your mate possesses just the work style that anchors and balances you, with job skills that strengthen your business.

> My husband is the creative one always coming up with crazy ideas. I'm the perfect office manager since I'm very methodical, organized, and detail-oriented. George has learned not to make any commitments to anyone until he checks with me. Even if he doesn't always like what I say, he's learned to listen to me. Nine times out of ten, I'm right!
>
> *Office manager for professional speaker*

Immediate feedback: Full partners relish taking advantage of a creative spark, whenever and wherever it may occur. A twenty-four-hour-a-day business partnership can be extremely productive and fun.

> If I have a brilliant idea at 3:00 A.M. I don't have to wait until the staff meeting tomorrow to discuss it with someone. My business partner is sleeping right next to me.
>
> *Partner in an employment agency*

Family Rewards

Child- and elder-care flexibility: When one of the kids gets sick, your spouse is likely to be more empathic and forgiving than a boss if you need to be with your child. When a baby is born or adopted, you can devise a schedule that works for you as a couple, rather than the wife fitting into the constraints of her job's maternity policy and the husband taking a week's vacation from work. You can schedule time to be present when the children are home from school, when a school assembly begs your presence, or when after-school transportation is necessary.

In family crises where one of you must remain home for an extended time, your business might suffer; but you have more flexibility than if you were working in a job.

Some working couples bring their young children to the job, from the time they are born. As the children get older, you can invite them to pitch in, teaching them valuable lessons about business and family teamwork and the effort required to buy groceries and school clothes. The role model of a successful full partnership may influence your children's career and marriage choices as adults.

The Evil You Know . . .

The evil you know may be better than the one you don't. When you choose a business partner who is not your intimate partner, you don't always know what you're getting and how trustworthy the new partner will be. If your spouse sleeps late in the morning, or argues stubbornly, then you can decide if those traits will prohibit a successful business partnership. A new business partner may have an obnoxious trait or two, but you won't know until you've already signed your partnership agreement.

Your Partner Accepts the Sacrifices

Starting a business can demand tremendous sacrifices by your spouse and family. If you jointly commit to a business, your partner is more likely to accept the hardships. If you unite in front of the children, then they will less likely resist. One couple I interviewed decided to relocate from two corporate jobs and a midwest upper-class lifestyle to a dairy farm in the South, because they wanted to spend more time together and with their children.

> When we sold our custom-built 3,800-square-foot home, we moved into a rundown 1,800-square-foot farmhouse. We gave away all of our fancy things, since there was nowhere to put them. I wouldn't have asked my wife to make this kind of radical change in her life if she wasn't behind it as much as I was.
> *Dairy farmer*

The Seesaw

Full partners bring each other's mood up and are cheerleaders in hard times. Usually one partner is feeling more optimistic at any one time than the other. Like a seesaw, as one partner goes down, the other goes up to return the partnership to balance. In most partnerships, the roles of the optimist and pessimist shift.

> Our business slows down every summer. I always panic that we're going to go out of business. My wife calmly reminds me that we've made it through every summer for the past eight years, and we will again.
>
> *Retail store owner*

All Efforts Benefit the Family

Dual career couples often work 90 to 180 hours a week between their two careers. If a company employs one or both of you, much of your service is going toward increasing corporate profits. Entrepreneurial couples value knowing that their joint effort contributes directly to their own material wealth and to their children's inheritance.

Summary of challenges for full partners:	Summary of benefits for full partners:
The financial risk of putting all of your eggs in one basket.	Your relationship will probably become more intimate.
Your business relationship becomes a forum for working out your most complex problems conflicts as a couple.	The business will benefit from your complementary skills.
Personal and family time can be scarce.	Increased flexibility to meet your family's needs.
You may have to fight to maintain your individual identity.	You are choosing a business partner who is a known entity.
The business may not suit both of your right livelihoods.	Your intimate partner is more likely to accept the entrepreneurial hardships.

Summary of challenges for full partners:

It can be difficult to expand an existing business to include a spouse.

You could lose your spouse's ability to serve as an escape valve at the end of the day.

Summary of benefits for full partners:

You can help bring each other up on a down day.

All of your efforts benefit your family.

DUAL ENTREPRENEURSHIP

Dual entrepreneurship is defined as two self-employed individuals in a committed relationship with each other, where each individual is responsible for running his or her own business. Here are some examples:

- Dentist married to a professional speaker
- Writer in committed relationship with president of a manufacturing company
- Multilevel marketing distributors who maintain separate downlines
- Sales trainer and public relations specialist
- Franchise consultant and franchisor

You can combine dual entrepreneurship and marriage in four different ways:

1: Each individual establishes a business before entering the relationship. The businesses remain entirely separate. Personal and business money is not merged and each individual maintains sole control over the operation of his or her own business.
2: When the relationship begins, one individual is self-employed and the other works in a company or at home raising children. At some point in the relationship, the second individual

decides to start a business, placing the couple into the dual-entrepreneurship model.

3:   Both individuals are self-employed in the same business or industry. They choose not to work together as full partners because they do not wish to give up full control or the full-partner model would strain their marriage. They may consider themselves "side-by-side" business partners.

4:   Both individuals are self-employed in businesses that provide synergy, like a shared office suite, client referrals, combined travel, or joint projects. The public views them as two distinct businesses or practices.

Is Your Relationship Cut Out for Managing Two Entrepreneurships?

The following assessment test will evaluate whether your intimate relationship is well suited for dual entrepreneurship. Created from my research and interviews with successful couples, the elements in this test were frequently present in solid, rewarding dual-entrepreneur marriages or absent in those marriages not favorably inclined toward this model.

DISCOVERY EXERCISE TWO:
ASSESSMENT TEST FOR DUAL ENTREPRENEURS

Take the test separately from your spouse. Or else do the test yourself and verbally quiz your spouse. Then get together to share the results.

1 = That doesn't describe us at all.
2 = That describes us somewhat.
3 = That describes us frequently.
4 = That describes us completely.

Place the appropriate number next to each question, and then total your score.

1. We both had established separate businesses before we got together as a couple.

   or

   My spouse already has his or her established business. I have passions of my own I'd like to pursue with my own business.

2. My spouse and I are both strong-willed. We each need to be the boss of our own business. It would never work to share control and decision making.

3. We love each other, but we would find it too suffocating and boring to be together all day and evening. Sharing the experiences we gain from our own separate businesses enhances our marriage.

4. My partner and I have very different interests. It would be hard for us to find one business that excites us equally.

5. We wouldn't be willing to take the financial risk of full partnership in one business. With two separate businesses, at least if one of the businesses fails, we have the other business to fall back on.

6. We have very different work styles and approaches. We would fight too much if we ever tried to work together.

7. Our kids are independent enough to handle the absence caused by both of our businesses.

   or

   One or both of our businesses are well suited for being available for the children.

   or

   We have the hired help necessary to take care of our children when we both need to be away for business.

   or

   We don't have any children at home.

8. We prepared for the financial risk of two entrepreneurships, rather than suffer the drawbacks of one of us working in a nine-to-five job.

9. We have enough emotional and physical energy to devote ourselves to two separate businesses and still have energy available for our relationship and family.

10. I like it when my spouse travels for his or her business. Our brief separation adds some spark to our marriage and helps keep the romance alive. I enjoy my time apart from my spouse and don't find it a threat to our marriage.

or

My spouse and I both travel for our businesses. We can coordinate our travel schedules to be together at times while on business,

or

Neither my spouse nor I travels overnight for business.

11. There is synergy between our businesses. We generate business referrals and advice for each other. My business is stronger because of my spouse's business knowledge and connections.

12. We have the best of both worlds. We each have the freedom of entrepreneurship, and the benefits of a business partner to collaborate with when we choose to ask for advice. We don't have the hassles of a formal business partner to share decisions with.

13. Healthy competition between us motivates me to work harder at my business. When my spouse is successful in his or her business, it inspires me to generate the same level of success in my business.

or

My spouse's cynicism regarding my ability to succeed in my own business challenges me. I take the attitude, "I'll show him or her!"

or

I'm completely self-motivated for business success; how successful my partner's business is is irrelevant to my drive.

14. We cope well with stress, both individually and as a couple. We don't lose our sense of humor for long, and we keep perspective in the difficult times. Our relationship has come through hard times even stronger.

15. We acknowledge the potential stress of managing two businesses within our marriage. We will seek outside help if necessary to prevent our relationship from deteriorating. We will consider other work options if this one threatens our relationship.

SCORE

48–60: **Dual Entrepreneurship Suits You.** This model of combining entrepreneurship with your significant relationship either ideally suits you or is the only viable option that makes sense at this time, given your business interests. You are likely to try hard to make this lifestyle work.

29–47: **Dual Entrepreneurship Could Be Difficult.** The potential is there for success or trouble, depending on how you respond to the challenges of combining two entrepreneurships with your marriage. Be prepared for some bumps along the road. With effort and open communication you have the potential for two successful businesses and a thriving relationship at the same time.

15–28: **There May Be Better Options for You.** Your low score on this test indicates there are other models for combining marriage and entrepreneurship that may make more sense for you. Working together as full partners, or limiting entrepreneurial activity to just one of you, might be more suitable. Review other options available to you before pursuing this avenue.

The Primary Challenges of Dual Entrepreneurship

The wide spectrum of dual-entrepreneurship options suggests that the challenges can vary widely depending on the nature of the businesses combined, the maturity of the businesses and your relationship, and whether you have children. A significant portion of dual entrepreneurs frequently experience the following challenging situations.

Limited Personal and Relationship Time

Two self-employed businesses can consume most of your psychic and physical energy. During start-up and growth phases, the business tends to come first, the children second, personal space third, and your intimate relationship last.

Human beings have a limited capacity to relate intimately when they aren't taking care of themselves first. Without personal space, you have less energy to give to your relationship. Couples I spoke with saw the danger signs when they put their relationship on the backburner or only spent a few hours a week with each other. Most accepted this condition as the inevitable trade-off for combining two self-employments into one relationship.

It takes a tremendous amount of psychic energy and self-absorption to create a business. Once we've handled the kids, we have nothing left over for each other and our relationship. It's hard for me to be available for a sex life. Most of the time I would rather sleep at the end of the day.

East Coast entrepreneur

Scheduling time together can be tricky if your businesses operate at different hours. Perhaps one business sees clients primarily during the day, and the other business sees clients at home on weekends and evenings. This arrangement may be ideal for child care and household chores but problematic for finding time with your spouse. Vacations may also be nonexistent for long periods of time if you can't put one or both businesses on hold or in someone else's care for a week or more.

I work 140 hours a week. I start making bagels at 3:30 A.M., and I don't usually leave until 10:00 P.M., seven days a week. My wife, Jerry, works at her convenience store about 55 hours a week. Last year we took off Christmas day—that's it.

Bruce, a bagel shop owner

Most of us couldn't fathom a work schedule this demanding, or imagine keeping a relationship solid with so little time to give it attention. Yet this couple conveys that they are doing well together. How do they do it? They have employed several of the strategies below.

Feel connected by your long-term vision: Bruce and Jerry dream of retiring in ten years. A young couple, they are postponing children until they can be home to rear them. They expect to work this grueling schedule while the bagel shop goes through a franchising phase, but they know it won't last forever. They are *both* willing teammates, sacrificing short-term intimacy and time together to achieve financial independence as a couple at an early age.

Have realistic expectations: Bruce and Jerry talked a lot about what the bagel business would demand *before* Bruce bought the business. They knew they would see little of each other as a result. *They made a conscious decision to accept the sacrifice.* With *mutual* agreement that the potential benefits outweigh the difficulties, they have realistic expectations of how much energy is available to nurture their relationship.

Appreciate quality time: Bruce and Jerry describe themselves as independent, apart for extended periods without feeling disconnected from each other. They are grateful for the moments they grab together and make the most of them.

Create time to nurture yourself: Creating even a few moments daily to nurture yourself will make you more emotionally available for your relationship. Some entrepreneurs find exercise, reading a nonbusiness book, lunching with a friend, or meditating for ten minutes to be relaxing and nurturing.

When Only One Business Is All-Consuming

Two writers I interviewed became reclusive for months at a time in the writing process. Their entrepreneurial spouses owned more established businesses that didn't require more than a forty-hour workweek. These partners learned to connect with their children and to establish hobbies and friends outside the marriage, to fulfill their needs for intimate connection. Their stories illustrate creative strategies for managing the discrepancy between their working hours and their spouses'.

> When my husband's first book was going to press, he disappeared in his den for fourteen hours at a time, seven days a week. I felt rejected and ignored. After a year of arguing about it, I enrolled in a professional training program for my field that demanded a lot of time and ocassional travel. When I had something exciting to focus on, it was OK that he was unavailable.
>
> *Service professional*

> My husband feels better if I'm just in the room with him, so I've learned to do my paperwork sitting with him while he watches TV. I'd rather be working in a quiet place, but I make the sacrifice so that he won't be so unhappy.
>
> *International entrepreneur*

The theme that connects all dual entrepreneurs successfully meeting this challenge is the willingness and ability to develop an individual work and social life outside their marriage, and accepting "quality time together."

Financial Risk

A new state law reducing insurance coverage for chiropractic care slashed a chiropractor's income by 40 percent. This drastic change in his practice happened the same year that his wife quit her salaried executive job to pursue her dreams of self-employment. This couple transitioned from relative middle-class comfort to financial crisis in a few months. Dual entrepreneurship may not be the road for risk-averse couples who need financial predictability and security. Unforeseen business disasters, or a family crisis, can dramatically alter either business's profitability or solvency.

> Ricardo joined a new start-up just when my business was unstable because of the economy and a new Republican administration. Three weeks before my husband's company had final approval of their product, a new federal law caused the venture capital investors to pull out. They bounced my husband out on the street within a few days. We racked up twenty-five thousand on our charge cards and came close to losing the house. We would never go the route of two self-employments again.
>
> *Grant writer*

Often, the financial demands of two businesses can strain a household. Sometimes one profitable business will subsidize the other, making two entrepreneurships possible.

These are some questions that can help you determine financial difficulty or relative comfort.

- Are the businesses profitable and able to cover current expenses with cash flow from the business?
- Do either or both of the businesses require sizable capital investment?

- Do either of the businesses rely on the profits of the other business for subsidy? What happens if the profitability of the established business diminishes?
- Does either of the businesses have to meet a payroll?
- How cyclical and unpredictable is the cash flow of either business?
- Is either of the businesses large enough to provide paid benefits?
- Are there any major family expenses, like college tuition or medical bills?
- Is either business indebted to venture capitalists or investors?

Dual entrepreneurs who manage financial challenge well usually have one, if not two, profitable businesses, a cushion of cash in savings and investments, sound financial planning, and a flexible lifestyle that can adjust to fluctuating business performance. They also have a detached attitude toward money—if it's there, terrific, if it's not, we'll manage. "We'd both rather deal with financial risk than be chained to a desk every day in a dead-end job."

Another financial risk is particular to dual entrepreneurs. A woman described to me what happened to her business's profitability when her husband's business got in trouble. With a salaried job, this woman would have brought the same income home every week, even if working every night in her husband's business distracted her. Dual entrepreneurs are particularly vulnerable to being impacted by upheaval in their partner's business.

> A lawsuit caused a third of my husband's clients to pull out. What was happening to *his* business stressed me so completely, I couldn't concentrate on my own business. He had to lay off his office manager so I was working two-three hours a night for him, when I should have been working on my own business. We kept his business from going bankrupt, but my income diminished by half.
>
> *Consultant*

Taking Care of Children

Dual entrepreneurs with kids are constantly juggling scarce resources—time, money, and energy—to devote to multiple conflicting priorities. Exhaustion and burnout are likely without support systems to help. Taking care of household, child-care, and business responsibilities stretches a couple thin, unless they can recruit a nanny, housekeeper, network of friends and family, or older children to help.

The households of dual entrepreneurs are either in comfortable, familiar chaos or carefully orchestrated to handle the many activities of the day. Most entrepreneurs have a daily planner on their wall at the office. Dual entrepreneurs often have one on the wall in their kitchen.

One of the questions that dual entrepreneurs must answer is "Who will take care of the children when they are sick and transport them after school when necessary?" Some women reported to me that their husbands assumed that their wives would take care of this responsibility, even though both parents had demanding businesses.

Competition and Scarce Resources

Two businesses operating parallel to each other can breed rivalry or insecurity. Instead of acting like a team, supporting each other's efforts, the couple's energy diverts to sabotage, resentment, and jealousy. When this phenomenon is present it can be destructive enough to warrant finding another way to work or entering marriage counseling. A little bit of healthy competition can be inspiring. Too much can be disastrous.

> I celebrated my wife's business success until she started earning more money than me. Her achievements as a business woman magnified my ineptitude as an entrepreneur and my self-worth went down the tubes. I went back to a corporate job to save our marriage.
>
> *Vice president of engineering*

With scarce financial resources and time, dual entrepreneurs must negotiate who gets an upgraded computer first or takes care of the kids on Sunday, so that the other can meet a work deadline. Each person is likely to feel strongly about his or her own needs and to react defensively to any implied message: "My business is more important than yours." Scarce resources prompt the need to search for a solution that helps both individuals in the partnership feel as though their needs are being met. Resolving these questions takes patience and thoughtful communication.

Primary Rewards of Dual Entrepreneurship

Empathy and Support

No one knows the challenges of entrepreneurship better than another entrepreneur. When you marry someone who has experienced the same middle-of-the-night terror or the stress of prospecting for new clients, then you have an intimate partner who can empathize in the deepest sense, translating into emotional support and practical advice.

> A few years into my business, one of my employees left to start a competitive business, recruiting away my best employees. I would have gone bankrupt without my wife's financial expertise. She spent nights at my office giving me the straight scoop on how bad it was, and then she helped me put the business back together again.
>
> *Business consultant*

Emotional support can range from reassurance in a crisis to tolerating long hours or mood swings. Practical advice can take the form of brainstorming solutions to business problems, recommending a resource you discovered in your business, or teaching a technique you learned for getting clients. Many dual entrepreneurial couples I interviewed treasure the resources available to them in their seasoned entrepreneurial spouses.

Synergy Between Businesses

Dual entrepreneur couples I interviewed shared the following examples of how they linked their businesses to help each business grow.

- I have connections with the chamber of commerce. I told my husband, the owner of a specialty advertising company, whenever a new company joined the chamber.
- My husband, the owner of a picture frame store, placed a display advertising my Shaklee products on his front counter.
- My husband and I are both therapists, but we specialize in different kinds of clients. We refer clients to each other regularly.
- My wife owns a desktop publishing service. I recommend her services to my clients, who are entrepreneurs and often in need of marketing materials.
- Through my connections at Rotary, I was able to put my wife in contact with a nonprofit organization that became her biggest client.

One dual entrepreneur couple I interviewed have well-established consulting businesses both in high demand. They book their clients up to a year in advance, coordinating commitments with a joint calendar, so that they can travel together often. They have turned down clients or requested rearrangements if the booking would interfere with their planned time together. Their efforts haven't negatively affected their ability to grow their businesses. Clients perceive they are of even higher value since it is so hard to book them, so they've been able to raise their fees!

We're Both Doing What We Love to Do

When you are miserable in your work, you will likely project your dissatisfaction onto your spouse, demand that your relationship fulfill more than is reasonable, or numb out entirely. Though dual entrepreneurship can be overwhelming at times, some of the happiest couples are those where both individuals are pursuing their right livelihood.

We have less money and we work harder than we used to, but we each love what we do, so we're a lot happier. We're kinder and more generous with each other, since we're each getting our needs for self-expression met in our work. We're not asking our relationship to compensate for an unrewarding worklife anymore.

Artist

A woman I interviewed wanted for years to pursue her true passion—providing a service to women. Her self-employed husband discouraged her because of the anticipated stress of bringing two entrepreneurships into their marriage. Years later, she gave her husband an ultimatum: "I pursue my passion, or we get a divorce." She could no longer tolerate the emptiness she experienced in her worklife, and the resentment she had built toward her husband was destroying their marriage.

We Inspire Each Other

The contrast to destructive rivalry is healthy competition that inspires each entrepreneur to perform even better in his or her work.

- When my husband gets a new client, it spurs me on to get a new one too. It's become kind of a game between us.
- I get up earlier in the morning than I would normally because my wife does. I feel like a lazy bum when she's getting dressed for work at 7:00 A.M. and I'm still sleeping.
- My wife and I bring in about the same income from our businesses. I would feel uncomfortable if she started making more money than me, so I make sure that I'm keeping up with her.
- My husband knows the best way to motivate me is to tell me that he doesn't think I can pull something off. It's as if he's daring me, and I work twice as hard to prove him wrong.

These couples credit their relationship with an entrepreneur as a prime motivating force in their business pursuits. Although most entrepreneurs are self-motivated, there's nothing like a friendly rival to inspire you to run faster to the finish line.

Freedom of Schedule

Depending on your businesses, you may both have more flexibility in your schedule than most corporate employees. These dual entrepreneur couples find that to be one of the greatest benefits of their lifestyle.

> My wife travels all over the world on business. Since I control my own hours, I will often work a four-day workweek and fly to meet her wherever she is. We're in our fifties and married twenty-four years. There is still something romantic about meeting my wife in a hotel room on a Thursday night!
>
> *Salesman*

> My wife is the president of a $15 million company. She works long hours and travels at least one hundred days a year. We have small children who need attention, so I work my business on a part-time basis. I could make a lot more money if I tried to grow my business, but one of us needs to be available for the kids.
>
> *Retail consultant*

Summary of challenges of dual entrepreneurship:	**Summary of rewards of dual entrepreneurship:**
Limited personal and relationship time.	You have greater empathy and support for each other.
One spouse can feel ignored if the other's business is all consuming.	There may be synergy between your businesses.
You bear the risk of dual self-employment.	Hopefully, you are both doing what you love to do.
You'll have to negotiate who takes care of the children.	You can inspire each other to greater success.
You may have to compete for scarce resources.	You both have the freedom and flexibility of self-employment.

SUPPORTIVE SPOUSE

There are millions of unsung heroes working every day to support the entrepreneurial dreams of their spouse or significant other. Their contribution may be apparent or entirely hidden from public view. Regardless, the business could not thrive, or perhaps even function, without their support.

Spousal support can take many forms:

- My wife takes care of the children and the house so that I can concentrate fully on my business.
- My husband does my business books and pays my taxes.
- My life partner works at the store nights and weekends, above and beyond his regular full-time job.
- My girlfriend has been an emotional anchor during the worst of business times. I would have given up without her support.
- We're using my wife's inheritance to live off, since my company isn't bringing in any income. She's agreed to cut back on her spending, to live within our new budget.
- My husband is working a straight job with medical benefits for the family, so that I can start my own business. He'd love to quit his job too, but he sticks it out because we depend on his income and benefits.

A supportive spouse is an intimate partner who provides the emotional, financial, or practical support that enables the other partner to be successfully self-employed. Supportive spouses may work part-time in their partners' business or offer advice and consult for the business, but they are not full working partners in the business. Every intimate partner of an entrepreneur is a supportive spouse to some extent, even if he or she also falls into the model of full partner or dual entrepreneur. Much of the guidance in this section could apply to the other marital models equally well.

Are You Cut Out for the Role of Supportive Spouse or Partner?

If you are the intimate partner of an entrepreneur or you may become one, take a few moments to complete the following assessment test.

DISCOVERY EXERCISE THREE: ASSESSMENT TEST FOR SUPPORTIVE SPOUSES

The following assessment test evaluates whether you have the emotional makeup and the kind of marriage that will help you thrive as the supportive spouse or intimate partner to an entrepreneur. Created from my research and interviews with successful couples, the elements in this test were frequently present in solid, rewarding supportive spouse partnerships or absent from those partnerships that struggled or failed.

1 = That doesn't describe me at all.
2 = That somewhat describes me.
3 = That describes me most of the time.
4 = That describes me completely.

1. I am fully behind the entrepreneurial pursuits of my partner. I support my partner's choice of business and efforts to be successful without reservation.
2. We financially prepared for my partner to be self-employed. I can handle the financial risk without being too distressed by financial worries.
3. I'm eager to help my partner be successful in the business, but I have no desire to be his or her full business partner at this time.
4. I may work in my partner's business on a part-time basis, take care of the children while he or she is working, be available for emotional support and practical advice, and/or work a straight job with steady salary and benefits to reduce our financial risk. My partner and I view these contributions as essential to his or her success and I feel valued.
5. My partner regularly expresses appreciation for my contribution and tells other people about it as well. My partner rarely takes me for granted.
6. I am doing what I want to do with my time. I'm not playing the role of supportive spouse only because I have to right now—I genuinely prefer this arrangement to any other.

7. I don't resent the amount of time and energy my partner has to give the business, even if my partner isn't as available to me or our family. I know the short-term sacrifice is ultimately for our family's benefit.

8. I like being asked for my advice, but I don't need to have control over my partner's decision making in the business. If my partner made a business decision I disagreed with, I could express my feelings and opinions and then let it go. What my partner does with the business is up to him or her.

9. I have the energy and strength to handle the multitude of responsibilities that fall on my shoulders, while my partner is busy with the business.

10. People help me to support my partner. I have a support system of friends, family, and coworkers to rely on when my partner is physically or emotionally unavailable.

11. My partner gives me full authority within my areas of responsibility and respects my abilities. That might include work I do in the business, or household and child care responsibilities.

12. I may be "behind the scenes" of my partner's business and not getting any public credit for my contribution. It's enough for me to know that my partner couldn't pursue a dream or achieve business success without my help.

13. My partner shares with me as much information about the progress and daily happenings in the business as I care to know.

14. My spouse and I make the time weekly for personal space and intimate relationship time so that I am reenergized to meet my partner's needs.

15. When we met, I knew that my partner would be an entrepreneur. I prepared from the beginning of our relationship to be a supportive spouse.

16. The pattern we have in our marriage now is very similar to what I experienced growing up in my family. It's a role that is very familiar and comfortable to me.

SCORE

51–64: **Well Suited for Supportive Spouse Role.** You appear to be the perfect candidate for the supportive spouse role. Your partner is lucky to have you behind the scenes, or by his or her side, and he or she knows it!

You'll have your hard days, as anyone would, but you won't spend too much time wishing you were doing something else with your life.

35–50: Some Aspects of This Role Could Be Challenging. The potential is there for success or trouble, depending on how you respond to the aspects of being a supportive spouse that challenge you and your partnership. It will make a big difference if your partner gives you the recognition and appreciation that you deserve. Make sure you create support systems that will help you take care of yourself.

16–34: You'll Need All the Support You Can Get! Maybe you have no other choice right now, so you're going to make the best of it. You may want to support your partner's entrepreneurial dream even if it will be difficult for you. Regardless of your motivation, you are stepping way out of your comfort zone, and you will find the role distressing at times. Get coaching or counseling if you need it, and communicate your feelings and needs to your spouse when you're struggling. If you don't think you're up to the challenge, negotiate another arrangement with your spouse.

Primary Challenges for Supportive Spouses

I Do a Lot of the Work, but I Don't Get Any of the Credit

If you need public recognition for your contribution to the success of the business, then you'll find the supportive spouse role difficult. Appreciation from your spouse may be your only recognition. The supportive spouse of a fast-track entrepreneur shared this analogy:

> It's as if my husband is in the army and I help prepare him for battle every day. I wouldn't want to be on the fighting lines with him. I'd rather be on the sidelines making sure he has the right ammunition, and enough food and water. I know he couldn't win the battle without my help, and that's enough for me.
>
> *Supportive spouse of manufacturing
> company president*

Every day my husband goes out on the road meeting new people and eating in some of the best restaurants in town.
Meanwhile, I'm home taking care of two toddlers and doing his
filing. When we go to social functions, people treat my husband
as if he's some kind of hero and talk to me as if I don't do anything worth mentioning.

Supportive spouse to salesman

The salesman couldn't serve his customers as effectively without his wife's organizational skills *and* her agreement to care for
their children full-time. He acknowledged her during our interview, but his wife then said, "This is the first time I've heard him
say thank you." She resented her unrecognized role in supporting
his success.

Supportive spouses need to find satisfaction in the work itself
or share in their spouse's long-term vision for how the business's
success will positively affect their marriage and family. To be
happy, they must feel as if they are working with their spouse as a
teammate, toward a mutual goal, and receive regular expressions
of spousal appreciation.

Little Control Over Business Decisions that May Affect You

If you trust your mate completely to make business decisions
on your behalf, and you have no desire to shape directly the direction of the business, then this challenge may not apply to you. If,
on the other hand, you need control over events that will change
your destiny, then you'd better fasten your seat belts for a challenging ride!

When you are a supportive spouse, rather than a full business
partner, you can advise, criticize, or question your spouse's business decisions, but you do not have the authority to insist that
your opinion be regarded. (Unless you and your spouse have an
agreement that you must approve certain financial investments or
changes in business operations that would affect you significantly.)

I found this aspect of being a supportive spouse so painful that
ultimately I left the role. When my husband, Stephen, started his

consulting business and struggled with the usual start-up difficulties, I had very strong opinions about what he should and shouldn't do to improve the situation. Since his business success had a direct impact on the quality of my life, watching silently while he made some decisions that I wouldn't make was really tough. Since I was not his business partner, I could frequently register my opinion, but I had no control over his actions. I was in an untenable situation for me—unable to fix a problem affecting me.

Supportive spouses struggle with this challenge most often if any of the following conditions is present:

- The business isn't doing as well as projected, directly affecting your quality of life.
- You haven't been married long enough to trust your partner's business abilities completely.
- You think you know more about how to solve your spouse's business problems than your spouse does.
- You are controlling by nature and find it difficult to let your spouse do his or her own thing, especially when it affects you.

When the supportive spouse worries about finances or is anxious about having some control over the entrepreneur's business, the entrepreneur may suffer as well. This entrepreneur shared her negative experience when she started a consulting business.

> My husband constantly interrogated me about how many billing days I was doing each month. All he seemed to care about was how much money I was making. He didn't want to hear how difficult it was for me to get clients.
> *Consultant*

An entrepreneur already fighting the demons of self-doubt and fear may be unable to cope with an unsupportive "supportive spouse." If you are in the supporting role, you might increase your understanding of the business in some ways, especially if you form your opinion in a vacuum. Consider all aspects of the business, to enable you to accept your spouse's point of view. Ask your spouse to help you understand the rationales behind each decision.

You might also distance yourself from the business, ask fewer questions, be less nosy. Catch yourself if you are asking, "How are things going?" when what you really mean is, "Are things going the way I think they should?" If you start to interview your spouse like a boss, then you need to keep your questions to yourself and look for evidence in your marriage that your spouse can make wise decisions, even if you don't agree with them. Establish clear ground rules with your spouse regarding when you have the right to influence, and even provide permission for, business decisions. Then learn to leave your spouse alone when he or she isn't asking for or appreciating your advice.

Time for Connection Is Scarce

When you spend the workday apart from your spouse, you have limited time for connection. You may have some private time in the early morning, at the end of the workday, or before bed if you are on the same schedule. With children, intimate time becomes even rarer. You are operating in separate universes for most of the day. Although you may touch base during the day to share an update or two, it will never be possible to capture the subtle nuances and details of each day.

> My husband travels at least two weeks a month. I'm home with our three children full-time. He's great about calling me from the road, but sometimes I just feel angry after he calls. He gets to check in and then hang up, leaving all the difficulties for me to handle.
>
> *Female supportive spouse*

The distance that can develop between business owners and their supportive spouses can range from mild and somewhat sad to severe and threatening to the marriage. Traveling away from home, working separate shifts, or working in jobs or businesses that are entirely different from each other increases the challenge. Maximize your opportunities for real sharing and connection no matter how short they may be. If your partner is willing to listen, talk to him or her about the small nuances of your worklife.

Don't just portray an overall picture with no detail. ("My boss is a jerk"; "The customers are driving me crazy.") Attend business functions together whenever possible. Cross into each other's universes every now and then. Take an afternoon off with the kids and give your stay-at-home partner a break. Help your business-owner partner with a work project. Listen with real interest to your partner's concerns and stories of the day, even if they sound alien to you. Research shows what your spouse probably wants from you more than anything is a best friend.

I Want Space and She Wants Connection at the End of the Day

When Stephen started working in a corporate job, and I was working at home self-employed, we had difficulty finding a level of intimacy that met both of our needs. Stephen arrives home from work burned out from being with people all day long. His corporate job leaves him no personal space, so he has little desire for intimate connection with me when he comes home after a long workday. If he has any opportunity for free time later in the evening, he craves either sleep or being by himself.

I talk by telephone with people in my coaching practice or with colleagues related to my research, but in-person contact during my workday is rare. Most of my day is spent alone, in front of a computer. When Stephen arrives home from work, I look forward to intimate connection and am disappointed and lonely when it is absent.

My experience with Stephen is typical for partnerships where one individual is working mostly alone and the other is interacting with people all day. Similar issues reported to me in my interviews were:

- I'm on the road most of the month, eating out at restaurants. When I come home, all I want is a home-cooked meal. My wife has been home with the kids and she's dying to get out to a restaurant.
- I travel so frequently, I don't want to go away from home for a vacation. My husband, who works a corporate job, is eager to

get away from the same old routine as often as he can.

- I miss my kids when I'm working all day, so when I'm home on weekends I want to be with them. My wife has been with them all week, and she needs a break. She'd rather be alone with me.

- My husband wants to spend most of our evening time entertaining clients. I miss having just a private date with him every now and then.

John Gray elaborates on male/female differences in the need for space and connection in his book, *Men Are from Mars, Women Are from Venus.* Generally, if a man gets even fifteen minutes of the private space he needs, he can be much more open for connection. When a woman has the opportunity for just ten minutes of talking, if she's really being listened to, it can be enough to satisfy her. Small shifts can make a big difference. Occasionally, instead of compromising, give your partner exactly what he or she needs. Every marriage has to consider the different needs of each partner. If you want everything your way, all the time, don't get married or have children. It's easier to have complete control when you are single and childless! The supportive spouse model often requires meeting each other halfway.

The Supportive Spouse Grows Unsupportive

You can provide the emotional, financial, or practical support that enables your partner to be successfully self-employed and still feel unsupportive to your entrepreneurial partner's business.

I supported our family financially, and helped Stephen in his business marginally, while he was starting his business. When Stephen's business failed to meet income projections in its first year, and we discovered how difficult it was for him to find clients, my emotional support for the business began to wane. Over time, I came to hate his business and what it was doing to our relationship, our bank account, and Stephen's sense of self-worth. As I became more unsupportive about this particular business venture, I began to resent my role of supportive spouse.

My wife and I hired a consultant to take an objective look at the business. The consultant came back with bad news—I needed to overhaul my business completely if I wanted to turn it around. It was easier for me to hear that from him than from my wife.

Entrepreneur who went bankrupt

One of the hardest things you may have to do as a supportive spouse is to pull the plug on your support or deliver an ultimatum to your partner. If the business is draining your financial resources, negatively impacting your family life, endangering your partner's health or your own (for example), you may reach a point where you no longer can support your partner's business.

You can pull your support away in a number of ways:

- Refuse to support the family with your paycheck.
- Set limits on your willingness to single-parent your children.
- Refuse to listen to complaints about the business anymore.
- Refuse to allow joint money to be invested any further into the business.
- Give an ultimatum—the business must be profitable within a designated time, or else . . .
- Quit your part-time and unpaid assistance to the business.

Coping with the Entrepreneur's Mood Swings

Your entrepreneurial partner will probably experience moods of elation, despair, anxiety, and discouragement. From time to time, you'll be drawn in, like an insect caught in a spider's web.

When my husband got hit with a lawsuit, he was hardly ever home. When he was home, he was either grouchy, depressed, or sleeping. I tried to cheer him up, but there wasn't anything I could really do for him except wait for him to recover.

Female supportive spouse

In the supportive spouse model, the entrepreneur is not alone in his or her experiences, even though you don't share ownership of the business. How the entrepreneur feels about him or herself, and how the business is performing, will directly affect the quality of how he or she relates at home. Supportive spouses may advise, comfort, or encourage their entrepreneurial partners, but they often can't solve the problem.

It is usually more difficult for a woman to detach from her male partner's mood swings, than vice versa. Men will generally try to help their wives solve the problem, and they may get angry at the source of their wife's trouble. Men usually find it easier to shield themselves from emotional codependency. Women find it more difficult to be in relationship with an angry or despondent partner while maintaining their own sense of well-being.

The serenity prayer comes to mind:

> God grant me the serenity to accept the things I cannot change, courage to change the things I can, and the wisdom to know the difference.

Supportive spouses need to find their own unique way of supporting their partners through a myriad of business ups and downs, without losing their own sense of well-being and integrity. They also need to identify the kind of support that is really effective for their partners. (Perhaps you would like a hug when you're feeling down, but your partner needs to have more personal space.) Give what your partner needs, within your abilities, and then find ways to take care of yourself.

Male Supportive Spouse Role—A Unique Challenge

In my interviews with couples in the supportive spouse model, some male supportive spouses and female entrepreneurs experienced a difficult adjustment, summarized well by this man who now earns half the income his wife is earning as a successful business woman.

> When we got married, I took care of my wife and the kids and she was dependent on me for everything. Now her business has

made her independent. She doesn't really need me anymore. If she needs someone to mow the lawn, she can hire a landscaper.

Male supportive spouse

This challenge normally arises when the man is somewhat insecure and measures his self-worth by his ability to support his family. His wife's success, independence, or business contacts with other men may threaten his ego. She may feel stifled by his jealousy and resentful of his lack of support.

The assistance of a marriage counselor or coach can be crucial to handling this challenge. Each partner needs to do his or her part. The man needs to work on developing his self-esteem and ability to support his partner's success without feeling threatened. The woman needs to find effective ways to reassure and include her husband in her success. When she can approach him with compassion for his vulnerability, rather than resentment for his lack of support, she will find this challenge easier to deal with.

Primary Rewards of the Supportive Spouse Model

Care for the Children: The Traditional Model

Millions of families still prefer a traditional model of marriage, where the husband supports the family entirely, and the wife is a full-time mom and housewife. The couples I interviewed who thrived in this model had chosen their roles. For example:

> We both knew that we wanted a traditional marriage, with my wife home full-time with our children. We were each raised with our moms home, and we wanted the same for our children. Our wedding song was Michael Bolton's "Soul Provider."
>
> *Franchisor*

Many of the male entrepreneurs I spoke with remarked they were better able to focus on their work because they knew that their wives were taking good care of their kids at home. Their wives felt great satisfaction in their role of running the home, while their husbands ran the business. They understood that their husband's ability to provide income for the family depends on not being distracted by home details. Husband and wife worked together as a team in a well-choreographed dance, with each role separate and defined and vital to the whole performance.

Care for the Children: Entrepreneurial Flexibility

The other supportive spouse model, where one individual is an entrepreneur and the other is working a regular job, also has its advantages for raising children. Entrepreneurs with flexibility over working hours may be more available for taking care of the children's needs during the day. Stephen and I experienced this when my stepson enrolled in his new school in Pennsylvania. The school required several meetings. It was easier for me to work these appointments into my schedule than it would have been for Stephen. We often remarked that we didn't know how we would have managed moving into our new home and establishing ourselves in a new community, if I hadn't been home to make the hundreds of phone calls required.

Enhanced Social Life for Supportive Spouse

We frequently entertain foreign businessmen in our home. My husband's business contacts have expanded my horizons and introduced me to many different cultures. By traveling to conventions and trade shows with him, I've been able to see the world.

> *Supportive spouse of international*
> *entrepreneur*

Entrepreneurs who travel or have a social component to their work often involve their spouses in the social end of the business. Their partners may develop longstanding friendships with the partners of other entrepreneurs in the same industry. The business may pick up the tab for a host of cultural events related to entertaining out-of-town business associates. Wives and husbands often accompany their entrepreneurial spouses to business functions whenever possible or appropriate.

Greater Freedom and Personal Growth for the Supportive Spouse

> My husband travels for business most weekdays, returning to our home only on weekends. We have very happy reunions when he comes home, but I don't get upset when he leaves again Monday. We're happily married after forty-five years of marriage because we've spent so much time apart!
>
> *Supportive spouse of international manufacturing executive*

> Because my partner works so many hours, I've taken up gardening, improved my golf game, and joined the local men's club. I've created a satisfying life that doesn't depend on him.
>
> *Carpenter*

Full partners in the same business credit spending *more* time together for creating intimacy in their relationship. In contrast, many couples in the supportive spouse model believe that spending *less* time together promotes individual growth and encourages greater sexual desire and appreciation for each other's company. They see their daily separation from each other as an advantage to their relationship.

Rewards for the Entrepreneur

The benefits for the entrepreneur of having a supportive spouse model of partnership can be numerous. Many entrepreneurs view it as the best of two worlds. They have a business partner who offers advice, encouragement, and assistance, without the legal hassles of sharing control with a formal business partner. They are better businessmen or women because of the contribution of their spouses, and all the profits of the business return to the family. Their spouse's support of their dreams enables them to do the work they love to do. Pulling together to fight the challenges of entrepreneurship deepens their love and respect for their life partner.

In virtually every interview, entrepreneurs spoke with gratitude about how their spouses had made it possible for them to follow their dreams. These are just a few examples:

- My wife took care of the kids like a single parent while I worked over ninety hours a week for ten years. I think she had the harder job of the two of us!
- My partner was really there for me when my business was crumbling. I learned that she wasn't with me for my money or my prestige. She stuck it out with me because she loved me.
- My home was like an oasis for me. When I came home dog-tired from the office, my husband was waiting for me with dinner on the table—often at ten o'clock at night!
- My thriving MLM business is only what it is because I had an incredible husband backing me every step of the way. If he hadn't been willing to support our family for the year my business wasn't making much money, I would have given up a long time ago.

Summary of challenges of supportive spouse model:	**Summary of supportive spouse rewards:**
You may do a lot of the work, with little credit.	You may be able to care for the children at home if you choose.
You don't have control over your partner's actions.	Your partner's business may enhance your social life.
Time for connection as a couple is scarce.	The role of supportive spouse gives you personal growth and freedom.
The supportive spouse may grow unsupportive over time.	The rewards for the entrepreneur of having a supportive spouse are numerous.
You'll have to cope with the entrepreneur's mood swings.	
Being a male supportive spouse has unique challenges.	

3

Financial and Family Planning

Planning Ahead to Avoid Disaster

When the business didn't earn what we projected, we invested $30,000 more than I had originally agreed to. After two years, we still weren't profitable. I gave my husband an ultimatum: turn a profit, or close the business down. I'm not willing to invest one more nickel in this business.

> *Elaine and Tyler, a couple in their mid-forties, who purchased a franchise with severance pay Tyler received after a layoff. Poor financial planning devastated their bank account and their marriage.*

When I encouraged my wife to start her own business, I didn't realize that our house would fall apart. She stopped cooking, cleaning, and caring for the kids. Suddenly the only thing that was important to her was her business.

> *Disgruntled husband of business owner*

When you are single, you endure entrepreneurial hardships alone. When you are a married business owner, your spouse and children bear the personal and financial risk as well. If you haven't solidly prepared your family for the financial and personal sacrifices inherent in starting a new business, you put your marriage and the well-being of your family on the line.

The first three chapters have one purpose: to help you create a solid family plan that will support your relationship and family goals while growing your business. Chapter 1, "Exploring Self-Employment Alternatives," guides you to choosing the best small business option for you and your family. Chapter 2, "Combining Marriage and Entrepreneurship," guides you to choosing the best small business option for your relationship. Once you have selected the type of business most suitable for you and your family, chapter 3, "Financial and Family Planning," guides you on how to plan for the financial and family impact of entrepreneurial life. Following, in chapter 4, "The Joys and Challenges of Working at Home," is a guide for managing the unique challenges of working at home.

The "Ten Guidelines for Financial and Family Planning" and the exercises provided in this chapter, will help you and your partner prepare your family plan. You will learn how to:

1. Acknowledge the existence of risk.
2. Identify your risk personality and that of your partner's.
3. Clarify how much you and your spouse are willing to risk materially to be self-employed.
4. Form mutual agreement about material risk.
5. Hope for the best, but plan for the worst-case scenario.
6. Establish guidelines for money management and decision making.
7. Allow the differences between how you and your partner handle money to work to your advantage.
8. Discuss money issues at a time and place that will be productive.
9. Define your boundaries for personal sacrifice.
10. Plan for the details of entrepreneurial family life.

Guideline exercises: The exercises contained within each guideline will help you and your partner build a strong foundation of mutual understanding to guide you through the journey. You may choose to do the exercises with your partner, separately from your partner, with discussion at a convenient time, or even entirely on your own, if your partner refuses or is unable to participate. You may choose to do all the exercises or only the ones that appear to be the most relevant and important for your present circumstances.

At the end of every exercise you will have an opportunity to record any agreements you make with your spouse. Some couples find the process of formalizing their agreements reassuring and satisfying. If you lean toward the formal side, you may even want to consult your family attorney before or after constructing any financial agreements. Other couples prefer a looser approach— jotting down ideas on a piece of paper, or even talking into a tape recorder. Do what works for you, provided that it helps you clarify and express your expectations of and agreements on financial management and family planning. Your relationship and family will benefit enormously from the few hours of preparation this chapter requires.

GUIDELINE ONE: ACKNOWLEDGE THE EXISTENCE OF RISK

> Our best friends warned us we were moving too fast when we decided to quit our jobs to go into business together. It was hard listening to their negativity, but it's a good thing we did. When we researched the new business more carefully, we realized that the financial risk was much greater than we were willing to take. I went back to my former job, and my husband worked the business alone for two years before I joined him.
>
> *Husband and wife MLM partners*

It takes enormous courage to become self-employed, especially when family and business associates express great concern. Enthusiasm and optimism are essential for success in life and any entrepreneurial venture. To protect your family, you *must* balance optimism and positive visualization with thorough preparation and sound business advice. After all, dreaming is safe. But some dreams are not meant to be actualized! Acting out one's dreams, especially when your family is involved, can be quite risky.

Dr. Victoria Felton-Collins, psychologist and certified financial planner, counsels, "There is a difference between prudent risk and wild gamble. Before you put one dime of partnership funds into any investment, know that difference" (Felton-Collins, *Couples and Money*, page 120).

My husband, Stephen, decided to leave his corporate job as an accountant to set up a consulting business, focusing on lowering clients' overhead expenses. Since Stephen planned to sell his consulting services to company owners on a contingency basis, paid only through the savings he could find for them by reducing their operating costs, we expected clients to be knocking down Stephen's door for service. After all, he could potentially save them thousands of dollars a year, with no up-front consulting fee. We invested $12,000 to get Stephen the training and office equipment he needed. We thought we were taking a prudent financial risk.

My father and father-in-law, both experienced businessmen, saw potential difficulties in the sale of this service to business owners. They cautioned us about the risk of basing a consulting business on contingency sales. Stephen could donate his time and expertise with no income to show for it. They predicted problems collecting accounts receivables, since Stephen would have to wait until the company experienced savings before being paid for his services. The wait for full payment could be as long as a year. They warned us that company presidents may not be as open to change as we expected, even if it could save them some money.

We heard our parents' warnings, but interpreted their advice as the caution of overly concerned family. We wanted this business option to work, so we listened instead to the enthusiasm of a few people successfully selling these services in other states. We figured if they could do it, so could Stephen. We were so sold ourselves on the value of this business service, we didn't test the market. Our parents' predictions ended up coming true in all respects, and contrary to our intention, we turned a prudent risk into a sizable gamble.

Our experience is typical of many entrepreneurs who rush *toward* entrepreneurial dreams or *away from* confusion, distress, or miserable jobs. If you are in the early stages of exploration, don't let your initial excitement blind you to the risks. Face the risk squarely, honestly, and with your spouse. If you and your partner go white-water rafting, at least know the level of difficulty of the river before you leave the riverbank so that you can better prepare yourself.

GUIDELINE TWO: IDENTIFY YOUR RISK PERSONALITY AND THAT OF YOUR PARTNER

> When the needle on my gas tank is on empty, and the red light is flashing, I worry about getting more gas. My wife fills up her gas tank when it's still a quarter full.
>
> *Jim, a manufacturing CEO*

If you are risk averse, marriage to an entrepreneur will be a formidable challenge for you. Your entrepreneurial spouse may drag you reluctantly from your comfort zone into your idea of a nightmare. In contrast, if you are an entrepreneur who thrills in trading risk for reward, and you marry someone who doesn't feel the same way about risk, then your spouse's lack of support may frustrate you, or even prevent you from achieving entrepreneurial success all together.

Where are you and your spouse on the vast spectrum of risk tolerance?

> I quit my job without telling my wife in advance, risking everything we had, including our marriage, to start my company. Material security is meaningless to me, but it was hard on my wife. She doesn't feel the same way I do about money.
>
> *Alan, a forty-year-old CEO who put his family $1 million in debt to capitalize his start-up business.*

When I lost my job, we had three kids in college, paying out 50K tuition a year. When the perfect business opportunity came my way, I took the gamble. It nearly killed me when my daughter called home from college and said it would be OK if she had to take a semester off.

Donald, a high-tech executive, who started his own company after losing his job in a company downsizing.

Chances are you and your spouse feel differently about the financial and personal risk that accompanies self-employment. To thrive in marriage, you must consider both sets of feelings when you are making major financial decisions. With few exceptions, risking joint assets should be a joint decision. As one woman expressed to me: "It may be *his* business, but it's *our* money so it's *my* business too!"

The Origins of Your Risk Personality

Let's call your attitude toward risk your "risk personality." The following section explores four sources that influence the formation of your risk personality—family messages, adult experiences, friends and colleagues, and the media.

Family Messages

How your parents raised you to think about money influences how you perceive risk in your adult life. According to psychotherapist Olivia Mellan, memories from your childhood have a tremendous influence on your adult money personality (Mellan, *Money Harmony*, page 34). Most of your money behavior as an adult probably reflects either following in your parents' footsteps or rebelling against them.

Childhood upbringing strongly influences your comfort with an entrepreneurial lifestyle, as one business consultant admits:

My dad was extremely security conscious. He worked for the telephone company for thirty years. When I quit my salaried job and started my own business, his disapproval rang in my ears all day long.

Business consultant

When my husband's company was just getting started, we had to sell stock I had inherited to pay the bills. My parents taught me "never touch the capital" and "money in the bank equals security." I panicked when I saw my inheritance begin to dwindle.

Wife of entrepreneur

If you had positive experiences as the child in an entrepreneurial family, as I did, you may naturally seek out an entrepreneurial life as an adult. If your experiences were negative, you may be risk averse as an adult, vowing never to let that happen to your family.

Adult Experiences

How have you experienced the consequences of financial risk as an adult? Once you begin taking risks as an adult, the outcome of your decisions, and your attitude toward success or failure, will influence your risk personality.

We invested everything we had to buy our business. Filing bankruptcy when we couldn't make it profitable devastated us. Once is enough. We both went running back to our corporate jobs.

Onetime business owners

My wife and I have started four businesses together. Our first business was a secretarial service. The landlord sold the building to someone who didn't want the service, so the business closed. Our second business was a computer company. We did well for three years, but then the market changed and we had to close down. Then we bought a continuing education program at a local college. Opening day of classes, the big earthquake hit—there went our third business. Now we're starting our fourth business together. We'll never give up!

Career entrepreneurs

DISCOVERY EXERCISE ONE: FAMILY INFLUENCE ON RISK PERSONALITY

Completion time: 15 minutes.

Discuss the following questions with your partner to understand better the family influence on your risk personality. Note your similarities and differences. Also record any new insights you gained from thinking about these questions.

1: *What were the messages you received about risk from your family?* Was it "Nothing ventured, nothing gained," or "A bird in the hand is worth two in the bush"? What were the actual expressions about money and risk you heard in your house, at the dinner table, or in conversations between your parents? What kind of risk-taking in employment did your parents role-model? Were your mom or dad entrepreneurs, corporate career types, or full-time homemakers?

2: *What was your actual experience with money as a child?* Did you worry about the family having enough money? Did you get what you needed as a child? Could your family afford family vacations or school clothes? Did you have enough food to eat? What kind of condition was the house you lived in? How did you finance your education beyond college?

3: *How did your parents manage their money (if you know)?* Did your parents invest in the stock market, mutual funds, or savings bonds? Did they ever lose a significant portion of their assets? What did they believe about savings accounts? What kind of assets do they have now, as a result of their financial decisions, or what did they leave as an inheritance? Did your parents ever argue about money?

4: *What messages about risk did your parents learn from your grandparents?* Were your grandparents immigrants who risked everything to come to this country? Did your grandparents work together in a family business, such as farming or shopkeeping?

Friends and Colleagues

A business owner who lost his shirt in a poor business decision or ran into some bad luck can dissuade you from taking a risk. If you are risk averse by nature, you may interpret another business owner's difficult experiences as evidence to support your decision to avoid financial risk. On the other hand, successful friends, neighbors, or colleagues may inspire you to follow their lead.

> We were making jewelry as a hobby. We met someone who was making a great living as a jewelry maker for the wholesale market. We thought if he can do it, why can't we? I quit my day job, and when the jewelry business was successful enough to pay the bills, my husband joined me full-time in the business.
>
> *Jewelry maker*

Media

Radio, newspapers, and magazines love to report the drama of business success and failure. We've all read about how WalMart put the mom-and-pop store out of business when it moved into town, or how the California earthquake destroyed hundreds of uninsured small businesses. We also love to read about how an ordinary guy or gal down the street achieved the American Dream and made it big. The stories you read, hear, and pay attention to influence your perception of risk. You will filter in or out the positive stories of risk and reward, or the tragic stories of loss, depending on your frame of mind regarding risk.

Your Daily Money Behavior

DISCOVERY EXERCISE TWO: IDENTIFYING YOUR DAILY MONEY BEHAVIOR

Completion time: 15 minutes.

Are your styles of spending money different? Is this a source of conflict for you as a couple? You may perceive your partner's way of handling money differently than they perceive it themselves. You will need to take daily spending and purchasing habits into account when planning for a new business, so it's important to start with an understanding of how each of you typically handles money.

1: *What are your purchasing habits?* Do you buy the floor model to get a great deal, even if you risk quality? When you are shopping for a big-ticket item, like a new television, do you comparison shop in several different stores?
2: *What are your investment habits?* Do you prefer long-term conservative investments, choosing lower yield as a trade-off for safety? Do you enjoy playing the stock market? Do you prefer to have a balanced investment portfolio?
3: *How long does it take you to make a financial decision?* Do you make decisions impulsively? Do you weigh all the data carefully before making a commitment? Do you reach decisions intuitively, or do you demand substantive information to guide your decision?
4: *How do you and your partner differ in your answers to questions 1 through 3?* Are you two peas in a pod, or is it amazing you can reach agreement on any financial decision for the home? Do you balance each other well, or do you both tend to lean toward one direction? Are you comfortable with how you currently compromise to reach agreement?

Your Money Philosophy

Victoria Felton-Collins states four primary motivations that determine how people use money: freedom, security, power, or love (Felton-Collins, *Couples and Money*, page 76). The primary motivator for you will drive your daily choices about what you spend money on, how you interact with your spouse about money, and your preferences for the type of business or work you choose. No motivation is more right or honorable than another, and what you think is motivating someone may not at all be the case. A person may spend a great deal of discretionary income on family members, but this generosity could be a clever disguise for a need to feel self-important or to manipulate relationships. The entrepreneur who appears motivated by ego may actually want to achieve power so that he can provide well for his family.

DISCOVERY EXERCISE THREE: UNDERSTANDING YOUR MONEY AND RISK PHILOSOPHY
Completion time: 15–30 minutes.

These questions help you identify what money means to you.

1: *Are you basically optimistic or pessimistic when it comes to your relationship with money?* Do you have confidence in your ability to make money? Do you trust in the benevolence of the universe? Do you worry incessantly about financial harm befalling you? Do you believe that money is a fluid resource that may come and go many times in your lifetime? Or, do you view money as an asset that isn't easily replenished once it is lost?

2: *Do you consider risk taking a necessary evil, like going to the dentist, or an exciting adventure, like mountain climbing?* Do you get a sick feeling in your stomach, or a pleasant adrenaline sensation when you are taking risks? Is the absence of risk boring to you or comforting? When you look back on your life, are the times you took your biggest risks your best memories or your worst?

3: *How does money represent freedom to you?* Do you dream of earning enough money so that you won't have to work anymore? So that you can hire housekeeping staff and a gardener? So that you will not be indebted to anyone? If you were able to achieve the wealth you long for, what privileges would be available to you now that you don't have?

4: *How does money represent security to you?* Does the provision of material needs give you peace of mind? Have you ever had enough money, and still felt poor, or afraid of loosing it all? Is there ever enough money for you to feel secure? How much is enough? Is money meant to be spent or do you prefer to save for a rainy day? Do you save twenty years away for retirement or only five years ahead, because anything can happen?

5: *How does money represent power to you?* Do you aspire to be managing a company with several employees working for you? Do you appreciate the status money provides? Is it important to you to influence people's actions with your money? How have you felt more powerful when you have had money, compared to when you haven't?

6: *How does money represent love to you?* Do you expect your partner to take care of you financially, as a demonstration of love for you? If you have discretionary money, do you prefer to spend it on loved ones? Do you ever attempt to buy love through giving? When you receive a gift from a loved one, what does it mean to you? If you don't receive a gift when you expect to, how much importance do you give the oversight?

7: *Who are your role models, the people you admire the most when it comes to financial success?* Do you wish you were the one who thought of "Mrs. Fields Cookies," or would you just as soon have the comfortable retirement of a corporate CEO? Who in your family, neighborhood, or circle of friends has achieved the kind of financial success you dream of?

How you and your partner answered the questions in Discovery Exercises One, Two, and Three will help you understand your orientation toward risk, and why your partner's viewpoint may differ.

GUIDELINE THREE: CLARIFY HOW MUCH YOU AND YOUR SPOUSE ARE WILLING TO RISK MATERIALLY TO BE SELF-EMPLOYED

By now, you have acknowledged the risk inherent in your decision to become self-employed and determined your risk personalities. Now let's get specific. You may be assuring yourself and your partner that you accept the risks of your entrepreneurial endeavor. But beware! Another form of denial is to avoid articulating exactly where your risk boundaries are. What precisely are you willing to risk? Your entertainment expenses? Your kids' college tuition? The house? Are you willing to file for bankruptcy? Exactly how far will you go?

Perhaps these questions seem to you like a form of negative thinking. You expect the business to be profitable within the first few months, so why worry about what you might lose? That's what Stephen and I thought. We never discussed what we were willing to invest in the business beyond our initial capital outlay. We never considered what would happen if the business wasn't as profitable as we had hoped. When money got tight, we were unprepared to handle the crisis in a constructive way. Tension between us escalated, compounding financial woes, and making everything feel even worse.

Remember as a child experiencing the ritual of a fire drill at school? You may have even prepared for a potential bomb scare. I remember crowding down on my knees under my hall locker, wondering how this action would save me from anything. The uprooting of the school day was considered a small price for adequate preparation in case of a real disaster. Here are four reasons it is critical to identify your risk boundaries and discuss them with your spouse *before* you need to worry about them:

1: Neck deep in a financial crisis is the worst time to argue about what you are willing to risk. You are emotionally invested in the business, frustrated that the business isn't performing according to plan, and scared about impending financial disaster. You aren't emotionally neutral enough to have a calm reasoned discussion.

2: You will feel safer when you identify your risk boundaries and receive a commitment that your spouse will not cross those boundaries.

3: We often take our possessions and material comforts for granted until they are gone. If you know what your most important material values are, and those of your spouse, it will be easier to construct a sound financial plan that makes sense for your business and family needs.

4: Your spouse will feel reassured and supported when you share how far you are willing to stretch out of your comfort zone if you need to. You will both realize that in a worst-case scenario, if you need to cut back on expenses to support the growth of the business, you can manage. You will gain strength and courage from realizing that your material attachments are more negotiable than you might think.

The following is an example of what can happen to you if you don't clarify expectations and agreements up front.

My husband didn't want to face that his business wasn't making it, so he kept pumping *our* money into the business, trying to make it work. We worked for twenty years to build our nest egg, and he destroyed it in one year. I don't know if our marriage is going to survive this disaster.

Frightened and angry spouse

DISCOVERY EXERCISE FOUR: IDENTIFYING YOUR BASIC ORIENTATION TOWARD RISK
Completion time: 5 minutes.

First circle the number that most applies to you. Then circle the number you believe best applies to your spouse. Ask your spouse to do the same exercise. Do you find any differences in perception of each other? (It would not be unusual for you to rate your spouse as more extreme than you see yourself.)

HUSBAND

Risk Averse		Risk Tolerant			Risk Inclined	

1	2	3	4	5	6	7	8	9	10

WIFE

Risk Averse		Risk Tolerant			Risk Inclined	

1	2	3	4	5	6	7	8	9	10

DISCOVERY EXERCISE FIVE: RISK ASSESSMENT TOOL
Completion time: 30 minutes.

The following risk assessment tool will help you identify what you and your spouse are willing to risk materially to reap the rewards of entrepreneurship. The assessment provides the basis for discussion about the allocation of cash if a business venture causes money to be scarce. It asks you to differentiate between events that would cause you discomfort and events that would cause you such distress that you would want to avoid them under any circumstances.

For the assessment tool to be effective, you must be willing to suspend all predictions and assumptions about the projected risk of your business venture. Imagine for the purposes of this assessment that anything is possible.

Complete the following assessment by yourself and ask your spouse to do the same. Place the appropriate number in the space before each risk event. Circle any questions with the answer 5.

After completing the assessment, follow the instructions at the end of the assessment for sharing your responses with your spouse.

0 = not applicable
1 = no big deal, hardly uncomfortable
2 = somewhat disagreeable and uncomfortable
3 = very disagreeable, uncomfortable, and embarrassing
4 = extremely disagreeable, humiliating, way out of my comfort zone
5 = under no circumstances—would violate my sense of safety and stability

Rate your willingness to risk the following events.

SHELTER
take a second mortgage or home equity loan
postpone home repairs, like plumbing, and upkeep, like painting
postpone replacement of old appliances when needed
move to a smaller home or rent instead of own
rent a smaller home than you are renting now
lose your second home
shut off utilities (heat, light, telephone)
foreclosure and eviction from primary home
move in with in-laws, parents, or other family members
other:_____
comments:_____
_____
_____

DEBT

Need to borrow money from . . .

parents
in-laws
other family, friends, private investors
banks
venture capitalists
other:_____
comments:_____

_____

Credit card debt:
up to $5,000
up to $10,000
up to $15,000
more than $15,000

Unable to make monthly payments on current debt (estimate amount):

mortgage
alimony and child support payments
school loans or other personal loans
auto loan
credit cards
need to declare personal bankruptcy
other:_____
comments:_____

_____

FINANCIAL CUSHION

Savings account falls below . . .

$1,000
$5,000
$10,000
$25,000
$50,000
Where is your savings account now?
comments:_____

_____

Mutual funds and other short-term investments fall below . . .

$1,000
$5,000
$10,000
$25,000
$50,000
What are your balances now?
comments:_____

_____

Long-term investments and IRA fall below . . .

$1,000
$5,000
$10,000
$25,000
$50,000
What are your balances now?
other sources of financial cushion: _____
comments:_____

_____

FOOD
curtailing eating out at fine restaurants
curtailing eating out at family/casual restaurants
cut back on junk food
cut back by 25 percent on expense of meals at home
cut back by 50 percent on expense of meals at home
cut back by 75 percent or use food stamps
other: _____
comments:_____

_____

AUTOMOBILE
postpone car repair and maintenance
increase car insurance deductibles
lose car telephone
reduce gasoline budget by 50 percent

trade in current car for used or less expensive car

postpone purchase of new car

lose use of second car

lose use of only vehicle

other: _____

comments: _____

_____

INSURANCE

lose health insurance

keep catastrophic medical insurance only

lose disability insurance

eliminate life insurance

reduce life insurance premiums by 25 percent

reduce life insurance premiums by 50 percent

lose dental insurance

other: _____

comments: _____

_____

LOSS OF PLANNED SAVINGS

for retirement

for college

for life-cycle events (weddings, etc.)

for new car

for taxes

other: _____

comments: _____

_____

CHILD EXPENSES

Unable to pay for . . .

religious school education

summer camp

new clothes

private school tuition

school expenses—supplies, field trips
orthodonture or other uninsured medical expenses
other: _____
comments: _____
_____

ELDER-CARE EXPENSES
Unable to pay for . . .

travel to visit elderly parents
supportive services for elderly parents
renovation of home to allow elderly parent to live with you
other: _____
comments: _____
_____

CHARITABLE DONATIONS
donate less than 5 percent of earnings
donate less than 10 percent of earnings
donate to church or synagogue only
eliminate donations entirely
other: _____
comments: _____
_____

ENTERTAINMENT EXPENSE SIGNIFICANTLY REDUCED OR ELIMINATED
curtail or postpone vacations
reduce expenses for couple dates
reduce expenses for kids—iceskating, sports events, circus
eliminate or reduce entertaining guests
eliminate or reduce cable TV and movies
reduce the purchase of magazines and books
limit the purchase of alcohol and drugs
other: _____
comments: _____
_____

GIFTS
unable to leave sizable inheritance for children/grandchildren
unable to give significant birthday, Christmas, or Hanukkah presents
unable to support adult children who need financial support
other: _____
comments: _____
_____

FAMILY PET
sell family pet(s)
go to veterinarian on emergency basis only
purchase cheaper food; reduce toys and treats
other: _____
comments: _____
_____

PERSONAL DEVELOPMENT
Eliminate or cut back for one or both of you . . .

therapy or counseling
personal growth workshops and seminars
books and magazines
fitness center membership
hobby expenses
chiropractic, acupuncture, massage
vitamins and nutritional supplements
regular haircut
other: _____
comments: _____
_____

If both of you are self-employed, complete the one applicable to your business.

PROFESSIONAL DEVELOPMENT FOR FIRST PARTNER

Eliminate or cut back . . .

office rental and utilities
travel
national conventions
membership in professional organizations
educational classes, workshops, seminars
journals, books, newspapers
business supplies
public relations, advertising, business communications
professional clothes
entertainment expense
professional services—accountant, lawyer
other: _____
comments: _____

PROFESSIONAL DEVELOPMENT FOR SECOND PARTNER

Eliminate or cut back . . .

office rental and utilities
travel
national conventions
membership in professional organizations
educational classes, workshops, seminars
journals, books, newspapers
business supplies
public relations, advertising, business communications
professional clothes
entertainment expense
professional services—accountant, lawyer
other: _____
comments: _____

Discussion of Risk Assessment Tool with Your Spouse

The risk assessment tool provides an objective means for evaluating how far into debt you can go if you wish to keep your marriage secure while you are building your business.

Ground Rules for Using the Results of the Risk Assessment Tool Effectively

1: Don't judge your spouse for any of his or her number 5s. Each of you has your own truth, formed by your life experience and training. You are each entitled to your own boundaries without fear of criticism or denigration.
2: Be as flexible as possible, and look hard at whether you can renegotiate any of your own 5s, if necessary. Reserve 5 for those circumstances that you would find intolerable, not just uncomfortable. Could you move a 5 category to a number 4, if circumstances demanded it?
3: Remember: Boundaries related to risk and financial management are most effective if they are flexible. Ironically, if you give your partner permission to establish firm boundaries, he or she will often become more willing to turn those boundaries into gates and windows, rather than solid barricades. First he or she needs to feel safe.

Use the insight the risk assessment tool provides you for completing guideline four, which follows.

GUIDELINE FOUR: FORM MUTUAL AGREEMENT ABOUT MATERIAL RISK

Whether it's his or her business, or you share the business as full partners, you must form a mutual agreement about how much material risk you can bear. After completing the risk assessment tool, you and your partner may need to negotiate a compromise to avoid triggering a catastrophic (5) loss for either of you. You each may be quite similar in your orientation toward risk, needing to negotiate only one particular issue. You may be dramatically different from each other, requiring the negotiation of several financial decisions. According to Victoria Felton-Collins, "Love/money partnerships that work always honor the risk threshold of each partner" (Felton-Collins, *Couples and Money*, page 117).

I spoke with two individuals whose entrepreneurial partners were not sensitive to the need to "honor their partner's risk threshold." These spouses suffered greatly when they were forced out of their risk comfort zones. In each case, the stress almost destroyed their marriage.

> When my wife pledged the house to raise capital for her business, I didn't sleep for months. I would wake her in the middle of the night and scream at her, "What have you done? We're going to be out on the street!" She was angry at me for not believing in her, but my anger had nothing to do with her. I didn't believe in her *product* enough to take that kind of risk. Eventually her business became profitable and I calmed down, but it was six months of hell for both of us.
>
> *Panicked husband of female entrepreneur*

Appreciate your spouse's sacrifice: If you are the one who is asking your partner to step out of his or her comfort zone, convey your gratitude to your spouse on a regular basis. Just when your spouse needs your appreciation the most may be the time you find it hardest to provide support. The stress of your new business has you preoccupied. You may feel guilty, frustrated, embarrassed, or even humiliated because you are causing your spouse great discomfort. Instead of acknowledging your spouse's gift to you and expressing your gratitude, you may prefer to avoid the subject altogether. Step out of your comfort zone, as your spouse has stepped out of his or hers, and express your appreciation regularly.

Be as flexible as possible: Before I met Stephen I was single for many years and in total control of my own money. I was for the most part debt-free and preferred it that way. I thought that having less than $20,000 in the bank was risky. I worked hard and saved a lot of money to ensure that I had a comfortable financial cushion. When Stephen and I married, we merged our finances completely. Even though he carried more debt than I, and many new monthly expenses would now be mine, keeping our money separate was inconsistent with our view of marriage.

Before I met Stephen, I said that I would *never* let my checking account fall below a certain level; I would *never* carry charge card balances; I would *never* be willing to pay someone else's debt with my hard-earned money. I have done all of those things in our marriage, and guess what—it was difficult, but not as tragic as I had always imagined. I stretched beyond my self-imposed absolutes. Using the Risk Assessment Tool, my 5s became 2s and 3s. Some of the losses I once felt "I could not endure under any circumstances," became losses I learned to view as only disagreeable and uncomfortable. If I had been inflexible with Stephen about my risk threshold, I would have missed the opportunity to develop strength and courage and to redefine my relationship to money and security.

Be willing to compromise: What should you do when, with one item on the Risk Assessment Tool, you score a 2 and your spouse scores a 5? How do you "honor your partner's risk threshold"? The answer is compromise. You must be willing to accommodate your partner's needs. Compromise about financial risk can take a wide variety of forms. A compromise with your spouse could mean that you need to do something like this:

- Move faster on a business decision than you are comfortable with, trusting the intuition or wisdom of your partner, or move more slowly on a business decision than you would like to, to accommodate your more risk-averse partner.
- Create financial safeguards to satisfy the security needs of your partner. For example, pay down the mortgage, or obtain life or disability insurance.
- Keep your day job while you test out the new business idea part-time.
- Put aside a predetermined amount of money safeguarded from risk.
- Invest more money in the business for now than you are comfortable with, or accept less money invested in the business than you would like.

- Allow a business decision to be made without enough information to satisfy your need for data, or postpone a business decision until your partner can gather enough information to be satisfied.

Few compromises are completely equal. At any one time, one of you may be giving more than the other. In a true equal partnership, it all "evens out in the wash." Sometimes it's your turn to do the bending, and then at some later time in your marriage, it will be your spouse's turn. Sometimes, you both bend toward the middle enough that each of you can stay within your comfort zones.

CLARIFICATION EXERCISE SIX: FORM WRITTEN AGREEMENTS ABOUT RISK, DEBT, AND SPOUSAL SUPPORT
Completion time: 30 minutes.

If you choose to, you may wish to create written agreements with your spouse, derived from the Risk Assessment Tool, regarding the level of financial risk each of you is willing to experience. You can write a joint agreement or two individual agreements for each other. Consult your family lawyer if you are concerned about making these agreements legally binding, or if, in fact, you want to ensure that they would *not* be considered legally binding in the event of an unplanned and unfortunate divorce.

RISK BOUNDARIES AND DEBT (USING THE RISK ASSESSMENT TOOL)
What are your agreements about risk boundaries and debt? Here are some alternatives:

1. We should close down the business or find another alternative if continuing the business would require transgressing a number 5 risk boundary for either one of us.
2. I agree to do everything I can to avoid transgressing a number 4 or

5 risk boundary for either one of us. I will do so only with your permission.

3. No matter what, we won't, for the sake of the business, _____. (Describe the number 5s for each of you.)
4. Let's revisit the Risk Assessment Tool on a quarterly basis.

Example: I agree to honor your risk boundaries, and I will not take any actions or make any decisions with my business that would require you to feel unsafe or unstable. To that end, I promise you that in no circumstances under my control will we lose the house, borrow money from your parents, or cancel our medical insurance. I will find another alternative before any of those things happens. I agree to negotiate with you about any business decisions that might result in taking you out of your comfort zone concerning the loss of our material possessions or financial stability. Let's revisit the Risk Assessment Tool once every three months.

_____

_____

_____

PROFITABILITY OF THE BUSINESS

What are your expectations and agreements about the profitability of the business? Here are some alternatives:

1. We agree that if the business is not earning money by this date, we will cut our losses and look for another alternative.
2. As long as you can find a way to bring money into the household each month, it's your decision how long to keep the business operating.
3. When the business is earning money, on a part-time basis, then I will quit my full-time job.
4. When the business is earning $_____, then you can quit your job and join me in the business full-time.
5. We understand that the purpose of this business is not to make a profit or a living wage for us. We'll keep the business operating as

long as it does not require more than $_____
(or _____ percent of our assets) over time.

6. We agree to reinvest $_____ (or _____ percent of profits) back into the business for _____ (period of time).

Example: We are starting this business expecting prosperity and success. We intend to earn a pretax profit of $40,000 during the third year. We accept that it will likely take two years of development before we can expect profitability. We expect to invest $50,000 in the first year, and $40,000 in the second year to accomplish that. We agree that if the investment required in total exceeds $100,000, or if the business is earning less than $20,000 pretax after the first two years, we will reevaluate the feasibility of ongoing operations.

_____

_____

_____

SPOUSAL SUPPORT

Sometimes the only way to start a new business is to depend on one spouse to provide income and benefits for the family. If that's the case for your family, which approach suits you best?

1. I have no problem with being the primary breadwinner for this family. We can rely on my income and benefits. We do not need your income to survive financially.
2. I am willing to be the main breadwinner for the family for the time being, but these are my limits: _____(not longer than a certain amount of time, not expecting more than a certain level of income).
3. I am willing to support the family while you are starting your business until _____(fill in date). At that point, it's my turn to have you support the family, because I want to _____(quit my job, go back to school, start a business, have a baby).
4. I am willing to support your business emotionally and to help in whatever way that I can part-time. I am not willing (or able) to sup-

port the family financially. I expect you to continue to fulfill that role, one way or the other, even if it means supplementing income from your new business with a second source.

Example: We can make it on Lisa's salary without any income from George for about a year if we cut way back on expenses and stick to our financial plan. Lisa is willing to support the family for a year while George grows his business. After a year, we hope to have a child. If Lisa is able to get pregnant, neither of us wants her to work full-time. We need the business to support the family within two years. If it doesn't look as if that will be possible, we will revisit our commitment to the business.

_____

_____

_____

GUIDELINE FIVE: HOPE FOR THE BEST, BUT PLAN FOR THE WORST

Heading into a new venture, you can only estimate financial and personal risk. Most business owners will tell you: "If I had known how much risk I was taking, I might not have been willing to start." Visionary entrepreneurs may enter a state of semidenial to summon the courage to move forward. It's a bit like having children. We focus on the positive rewards of raising children when we are planning to have a family, because if we focused on the predictable hardships, we might never be willing to give it a try!

Financial advisers and seasoned business owners will tell you the dangers of wishful thinking, rather than careful planning. They will say things like, "Create a business plan, and then double the expenses you are planning for," or, "Keep six months of liquid assets available, not pledged to the business, if possible." Take an honest look at your business plan. Is it a wishful fantasy or a solid realistic guide?

Talk with your partner about how you will handle potential

difficulties. Describe your worst-case scenario, and imagine how you will handle it if it should happen. What are the warning signs that will let you know you are headed in that direction? Don't base your financial planning on the assumption that you will be wildly successful or that your partner will be faithful to your dream no matter what the cost. Hoping for the best, but planning for the worst isn't negative thinking—it's smart business and family planning. Some small businesses won't survive in the long run, and every supportive spouse has limits.

GUIDELINE SIX: ESTABLISH GUIDELINES FOR MONEY MANAGEMENT AND DECISION MAKING

From the beginning of your relationship, you had to decide whether to pool your money or keep it separate, how the bills would get paid, and who would reconcile the checking account. When one or both of you is self-employed you may not need a new conversation about money management. For example, if you established your businesses before you married and you handle all the financial transactions of your business individually, or if you maintain separate bank accounts and don't merge your finances in any way. Under most circumstances however, when you are starting a business of your own, you will need to create new understandings with your spouse about money management.

Joint or Separate Checking Accounts

I interviewed several couples who swore the key to their successful relationship was keeping all of their money separate. These marriages were frequently second or third marriages, marriages with no children or grown children, and marriages in which the partners established businesses before they married. Sometimes couples in first-time marriages decided to keep money separate because they recognized significant differences in their spending patterns, or each individual wanted to maintain control over his or her own money. Separate accounts worked for these couples:

We never have money issues to deal with as a couple, since we keep our finances completely separate except for mortgage and utilities. My girlfriend has her ways of dealing with money and I have mine.

Male entrepreneur in mid-twenties

My husband came to our marriage with sizable alimony and child-support payments and $40,000 in student loans. We have a joint account for household expenses, but everything else is separate. I wasn't willing to take on his debt.

Female entrepreneur in late fifties

I also interviewed several couples who insist that a total merger of finances is the source of their relationship's strength and intimacy. They view themselves as one financial unit and can't conceive of marriage with separate checking accounts. For these couples, when there is a decision to buy or start a business, the decision is always a joint one. These couples exemplify this attitude:

It was hard for me to merge our money when we got married. My husband was $60,000 in debt and I came to him with practically no debt at all. But what was I going to do? I'm the old-fashioned sort. To me, marriage means merging everything, for better or worse.

Supportive wife of bakery shop owner

Financial Decision Making for the Business

When you introduce entrepreneurship into your marriage, clarify the extent that joint money will fund one or both businesses. Is the business "my" business, "yours," or "ours?" If the business is yours, but funded in part by joint funds, then a certain level of joint decision making comes with the privilege of using joint money for capital. If your business is self-sustaining and funded only by your money, decision making about financial purchases or business expenses may not be shared with your spouse.

You may consult your spouse for advice, but his or her lack of endorsement may not stop your actions.

In some traditional marriages, wives are still expected to seek permission from their husbands to spend joint money, but their husbands make financial decisions without consulting their wives. Other couples make virtually every financial decision together. What are the decision-making ground rules you and your partner will operate with on a daily basis? For example, this is the agreement that Stephen and I formed regarding financial decisions for his business.

> Stephen will consult with Azriela about nonrecurring business expenses over $100. For any nonbudgeted expense over $300, Azriela must concur with Stephen's request before he will spend the money. All major changes, like moving Stephen's office, will be a joint decision. Azriela expects Stephen to consult her as if she were a full partner in his business, even though she won't be working with him in the business full-time, since a significant portion of Azriela's savings is being used to capitalize his business. If he finds sharing decisions with her unacceptable, he will find another way to fund his business.

Entrepreneurial couples who operate a business together may divide decision making by function—"He handles operations and she handles marketing," or agree to joint decisions over a set dollar amount. Some insist on joint decision making for all decisions, and other couples give each other wide latitude for unilateral decision making. Establish the decision-making ground rules optimal for you in your situation. Clarify which business decisions you will make jointly and unilaterally. For example, who will decide:

- How much to pay the employees and how much to spend on benefits (human resource issues).
- When to buy office supplies, and how much to spend (office management).
- When a customer should receive a refund and when to negotiate price with a customer (customer service policies).
- How much money to spend on advertising and promotion (marketing and sales).

- How much to charge for the merchandise, product, or service (product pricing).

Example: Sherry is in charge of day-to-day operations. She will make all decisions related to operations expenditures. She will consult with Mike if she wishes to spend more than $500 nonbudgeted expense. Mike is in charge of all marketing, sales, and promotion. He will make all decisions related to those expenditures. He will consult with Sherry if he wishes to spend more than $500 nonbudgeted expense. Mike and Sherry will meet weekly to keep each other informed of financial issues.

Resolving Disagreement

In a corporate hierarchy, "the buck stops here" reflects an understanding that, though democratic consensus may be ideal, a particular individual is ultimately responsible for any one problem needing resolution. Entrepreneurial life doesn't always provide a simple hierarchy to follow. Regardless of the type of business you and your spouse engage in, you must agree on a framework for negotiation when you disagree on a decision requiring joint approval. Establishing guidelines in advance will help you avoid trouble. When you reach stalemate, who or what will break the tie? Some couples agree that one of them will ultimately have authority over a certain functional area in business or in the home if they reach an impasse. Other couples use this simple rule of thumb: "The one with the stronger feelings gets his or her way."

CLARIFICATION EXERCISE SEVEN: MONEY MANAGEMENT AND DECISION MAKING
Completion time: 15 minutes.

With your partner, articulate verbally or in writing your understandings of personal and business money management and responsibility for business decisions. Here are some alternatives:

1. All our money is joint. Therefore, we will share all money-related decisions.

2. Although we will fund the business with joint money, we agree that I must check with you only if the business goes over budget.

3. I agree to consult with you on any business or household decision requiring more than $_____ (fill in the blank).

4. Since our money is separate, I will check with you only if my financial decisions will affect our lifestyle or joint personal possessions.

5. I agree to handle the bookkeeping for all of our household bills and for the business.

6. I will take care of paying my personal and business bills. I expect you to do the same.

7. Although we operate this business as full partners, I leave the daily financial management to you. However, I expect you to involve me in financial decisions requiring additional investment over $1,000 as a one-time expense or $500 monthly.

8. We agree that I will make financial decisions related to operations, and you will make financial decisions related to marketing and sales, as long as the decisions are consistent with our business plan, and not more than 5 percent over budget.

Example: We agree to consult with each other for any household decision involving more than $100 expense, and any business decision that will require an unplanned expense of more than $200. Susan will take care of paying all of our household bills, and Frank will take care of reconciling our monthly household bank accounts. We will hire someone to do the business books.

_____

_____

_____

INVESTING MONEY IN THE BUSINESS

How much will the business be capitalized by personal money? Here are some alternatives:

1. My business will never use joint money. It's my business completely, and I take full responsibility for supporting the needs of the business.

2. I won't use joint money beyond the initial investment. You are will-

ing to invest $_____ (fill in the blank) up front. I understand that my business must be self-sustaining to continue.

3. Even though you quit your job, I expect you to continue to pay half of our living expenses.

4. Although we normally contribute equally to living expenses, I agree to pay _____ (fill in the blank) percent of them until you can contribute your fair share, which is normally_____.

5. I will invest up to $_____ (fill in the blank) in the business over time. If the business requires more than that, we will close it down or seek outside investors.

6. I will invest our joint money into your business until I hit one of my number 3s on the Risk Assessment Tool.

Example: As we agree, we will take $10,000 from our joint savings account to fund the start-up of our business. For the next year, while the business becomes profitable, we agree to fund the business with our joint savings and investments, as long as we do not exceed $40,000. If we need to cut back on expenses, we are willing to cut back on any of the 3s on the Risk Assessment Tool. Neither of us is willing to endure any 4s or 5s on the Risk Assessment Tool for the sake of the business.

_____

_____

_____

GUIDELINE SEVEN: ALLOW THE MONEY STYLE DIFFERENCES BETWEEN YOU AND YOUR PARTNER TO WORK TO YOUR ADVANTAGE

If you are like many couples, your most volatile fights concern money. Money conflict is the most frequently cited reason for divorce and the hardest issue for couples to resolve effectively. Chapter 6 on conflict resolution offers you some helpful approaches. This guideline encourages you to view the differences in money style between you positively.

> My wife, Joy, and I have the "stop and go" approach to spending money. I'm the driver and Joy's the brakes. I'll call her from the field and tell her I want to buy something. She'll tell me I can't because money is too tight this month. She has a better handle than I do on how much money we have, so I've learned to listen to her.
>
> *Arthur and Joy, husband and wife*
> *franchise owners*

Arthur has learned from experience to trust Joy's system for evaluating financial purchases. Frequently one partner is the big dreamer with ideas and chutzpah to act. If lucky, this person will team up with a partner who injects a regular dose of reality, a knack for details, and cautious money management—a complementary partnership.

Look what happens when you don't have a complementary partnership:

> We both started our business because we are creative people. It never occurred to us that bookkeeping could be such a big deal. Our accounts receivable are getting out of hand, and we can't afford to hire a bookkeeper. It would be easier if one of us were the more administrative type.
>
> *Husband and wife seminar leaders*

Polarization

A common block to couples working out money style differences is called polarization. Polarization occurs when couples become argumentative and opposites in reaction to each other. For example, the freewheeling spender's behavior becomes even more exaggerated in reaction to a tightwad saver.

Suppose Arthur reacted to his wife Joy's insistence that he stop spending money by spending even more, just to prove to her that she can't control him. That would of course lead Joy to react to his overspending by trying to control him even more. Quickly they are in a vicious cycle. Polarization moves your behavior to extremes.

Here are two ways to move from rigid polarization (Mellan, *Money Harmony*, page 141):

1: *Exchange appreciation for the part of your partner's behavior that you can admire or appreciate.* Even if all the manifestations of your spouse's behavior don't thrill you, you can usually find a small part of his or her money behavior that you appreciate. Don't worry: admitting that your partner has a strength you admire doesn't give him or her license to manifest the frustrating behavior even more.

2: *Role-play your partner for a day, or a week, to deepen your understanding of his or her perspective.* See the world through your partner's eyes long enough to appreciate his or her positive intentions, and how your partner's actions make sense from that perspective.

Another way to break out of negative blaming behavior is to call in outside advisers. Build an objective feedback system that may include an accountant, financial planner, lawyer, and couples counselor, and use their neutral feedback to help you make decisions.

One of the greatest challenges of your married life will be to come to *celebrate* the differences in money style between each of you. Stephen and I wrote the following into our marriage vows in recognition of such a challenge: "I will strive for tolerance and acceptance of our differences, with the hope of coming to celebrate them." Make it your goal to move from annoyance, to tolerance and acceptance, to celebrating the differences that make you a stronger partnership.

SKILL-BUILDING EXERCISE EIGHT: APPRECIATING MONEY STYLE DIFFERENCES

Complete the following exercise by yourself, and then share your responses with your partner.

1. When it comes to money management, my greatest strength is
    _____.

2. When it comes to money management, your greatest strength is
    _____.

3. We recognize these money style differences between us:
    _____.

4. We're lucky those differences exist. We complement each other in the following ways, making us a stronger team: _____
    _____.

5. When we get polarized and rigid about our differences, this is what I do that contributes to the problem: _____
    _____.

6. When we get polarized and rigid about our differences, this is what you do that contributes to the problem: _____
    _____.

7. I want to come to celebrate the differences between us. To that end, I agree to_____
    _____.

GUIDELINE EIGHT: DISCUSS MONEY ISSUES AT A TIME AND PLACE THAT WILL BE PRODUCTIVE

Our worst money arguments are usually unplanned, triggered by some small event that takes the top off a volcano already poised to erupt. A reaction to your spouse's peculiar money habits puts you over the edge, or his or her failure to deliver on an agreed-upon task infuriates you. Whatever the event may be, it occurs at a lousy time when you aren't able to deal with it as an adult in a reasonable way. Tension mounts quickly, and before you know it, you and your spouse are discussing whether you should close down the business, get a job, or even get divorced.

Here's an example: A check bounced from Karen's business account. Karen's husband, Roy, is her bookkeeper. Karen discovered the problem when she opened her mail and saw the notice from the bank. Roy is at his full-time job, but she is so furious she can't wait until he comes home to discuss it. She calls him at work.

Roy: I'm right in the middle of an important meeting. Can it wait?

Karen: No, it can't! You told me you were taking care of reconciling my checkbook. Obviously I should have hired someone to do it. You bounced a check to one of my most important vendors!

Roy: Well, if you weren't spending so much money on that business of yours, we wouldn't be bouncing checks. When are you going to start bringing in some money?

Karen: That's not the problem and you know it. The problem is you promised to keep my books up to date and balanced, and you haven't done it for the last two months. If you had kept your end of the bargain, we would have known we needed to transfer money and I wouldn't have bounced this check.

Roy: Where do you think we're going to get the money to transfer? I'm working sixty hours a week to support this family, and there still isn't enough money to take care of our bills. We're going to bounce the check for the mortgage this month!

Karen: Why didn't you tell me things were this bad? I wouldn't have printed my new brochure if you had warned me. What do you want me to do? Shut down after putting in all this effort? If you would help more with the kids, I'd have more time to work on my business.

Roy: Look, I told you this wasn't a good time to talk. We'll talk about it later.

Karen and Roy violated guideline eight in several ways. They talked about a serious money issue at the wrong time (interrupting Roy's meeting), in the wrong place (on the telephone), and in a very unproductive way. They are speaking to each other with blame, defensiveness, and overreaction. Both Karen and Roy are unable to discuss the problem fruitfully, the way they are approaching it.

The saddest thing about this scenario is that Karen and Roy are battling each other, rather than joining to problem-solve their current financial crisis as one team.

Ground Rules for Productive Discussions About Money Issues

Use these ground rules to discuss a decision as significant as closing your business down, or a problem as major as being unable to make the mortgage payment.

Discuss Money Concerns Only in a Designated Meeting Scheduled at the Right Place and Time for Both Parties

If your money concern could be an emotionally hot one, ask your spouse for a meeting at a mutually convenient time, preferably in a place that allows you to talk face to face and uninterrupted. For example, Karen could have waited until Roy came home from work and said, "I received a notice in the mail today that my check to the advertising agency bounced. I'm really angry about the possibility of losing an important business relationship. Can we talk about it before dinner?"

If possible, a meeting should take place within twenty-four hours of the request. If Roy didn't want to discuss the problem before dinner, he should suggest an alternative time before the end of the next day. With a family, it is often difficult to get uninterrupted time, but that is the ideal.

Agree that You Will Make No Significant Money Decisions as a Knee-Jerk Reaction

Avoid asking for any major changes to your current financial circumstances until the appropriate time for discussion with your spouse. If you make a decision or demand based on an argument, cancel the agreement or request made in haste, and discuss it at a more appropriate time.

For example, this is how Roy might have handled his outburst more effectively:

> I'm sorry, I didn't mean to snap at you. I know you are working hard on your business. Our checking account balance has me really worried. I would like to set up a meeting to talk with you about how we can bring in some money quickly to help us get out of this jam. Can we talk about it this evening, after the kids are in bed?

To the Best of Your Ability, Discuss Money Concerns Before They Become a Crisis

When you are in the midst of money difficulties, sometimes it is too painful or frightening to look at the reality of your situation. Procrastinating discussing the problem until it is at a crisis level is not an effective way to solve the problem.

Roy gave Karen only a few weeks notice about their inability to make the mortgage payment. Yet signs of the problem were there for a few months. By the time he told Karen about it, there was little they could do to respond effectively. Another option would be for Karen to be equally involved in maintaining the checking account, so she knows the status of the account herself.

In every entrepreneurial venture, unpredictable money crises arise. Employees quit, accidents happen, customers fail to pay, or the cost of supplies increases. It may not be possible to prevent all crises ahead of time. Manage the crises you can control with proper planning, awareness, and discussion.

Use Conflict Resolution Techniques When Trying to Resolve Money Conflicts

When battling over an issue as hot as money, you will need your strongest communication skills to express your concerns and negotiate effectively. With practice, you will learn how to have a fruitful and calm discussion about your greatest money concerns. Chapter 6 provides specific techniques you and your spouse can use to resolve your money conflicts effectively.

These ground rules encourage the ideal environment for resolving your money conflicts. If you can't follow all of them all the time, that's OK. Start gradually, practicing with the money issues that aren't as charged for you. Work your way up to using these rules for all of your money discussions.

GUIDELINE NINE: DEFINE YOUR BOUNDARIES FOR PERSONAL SACRIFICE

So far, we have focused on the financial planning necessary to ease the pressures of entrepreneurship on your marriage and family. Now we move family planning to a deeper level than financial investment by exploring what you and your partner will sacrifice personally to be self-employed. Any experienced entrepreneur will tell you that business success comes with a personal and family price. Are you willing to pay that price? Is your spouse?

> We quit our jobs to buy our own business so that we could have control over our time. It hasn't worked out that way at all. Both of us have to be at the store six days a week, ten hours a day. Instead of giving us freedom, the business feels like a jail. It's gotten so bad, we've put the business up for sale.
>
> *Husband and wife retail store owners*

> Before I started my own law practice, I used to swim three times a week at the local club. Now I'm so busy, I feel guilty if I take the time out to swim. Since I stopped swimming, I am more irritable and I've gained a few pounds. I know I should return to working out regularly, but it's hard to make the time.
>
> *Lawyer*

DISCOVERY EXERCISE NINE: PERSONAL SACRIFICES TO BE SELF-EMPLOYED
Completion time: 30 minutes.

Many couples find out midstream that the personal or family cost of self-employment is greater than they predicted. The next exercise helps you examine the personal sacrifices that you might be willing to make to be self-employed. Take a few moments, alone or with your spouse, to consider the following questions. Keep a journal of your responses if you choose, and share your thoughts with your partner. If you are currently self-employed and feeling burned out, these questions may give you a clue to where your personal sacrifice has become too large.

RELATIONSHIP WITH YOUR SPOUSE

1: What is the minimum amount of time you need to spend with your spouse to maintain an intimate and thriving marriage? Do you need "quality time" daily, weekly, or monthly? What constitutes "quality time" for you? Will your business allow for that? What happens to your relationship when you are unable to devote enough time to intimate connection? What are the warning signs that you need to spend more intimate time together?

2: How much travel will your business require? Do you have any concerns about infidelity—yours or your partner's? How many days a month are you willing to be separated from your spouse? What happens if you go over that limit? How much does travel drain your energy and ability to be present to your partner? Will you consider limiting business growth in order to curtail travel?

3: Is your relationship strong enough to weather financial crisis, exhaustion, the demands of business ownership, or working together? Where is the evidence from your history together that you will be able to manage? Are you both on board and committed to the same dream? Are you willing to close the business down, or seek outside help, if business starts jeopardizing your relationship?

4: Does your business leave you with enough energy to be emotion-
    ally and sexually available to your partner? Does the pressure of
    your work distract you from being able to focus on your partner's
    needs? How are you able to balance personal and work commit-
    ments? What happens to you, and your relationship, when you get
    out of balance?

RELATIONSHIP WITH YOUR CHILDREN

5: What is the minimum amount of time you need daily or weekly to
    develop and maintain a rewarding relationship with your children?
    How will your business allow you to have that? What are the conse-
    quences of absence from your children? Are you willing to miss key
    developmental moments in order to achieve business success? To
    what extent?
6: Will you be able to be present and available for your children in the
    ways that are important to you? (For example: attending little
    league games, school performances, teachers conferences, car
    pooling.) Will your business require your absence in new ways that
    you and your children aren't used to? If so, how have you prepared
    yourself and your children? Do you have the support systems nec-
    essary to take care of your children's needs without your physical
    presence?
7: Do any of your children have special needs that require your atten-
    tion? (For example: help with homework, preparation for Bar
    Mitzvah, athletic coaching, emotional difficulties, trouble with
    drugs or alcohol, physical disability.) Will your business allow you
    to be available for your children's needs? If not, do you have
    resources to help you?

YOUR HEALTH

8: What are the daily and weekly routines you need to maintain in
    order to stay healthy? Consider food, exercise, sleep, hygiene, and
    personal growth. (For example: eating home-cooked healthful
    meals, running twice a week, working out at the gym, playing ten-
    nis, sleeping six hours a night, attending AA meetings.) How much

time alone do you need to recharge, unwind, and keep mentally fit? How will your business allow you to take care of yourself the way that you need?

SPIRITUAL LIFE

9: How will your business enable you to pursue the spiritual exploration that is vital to your centeredness and well-being? Will you be able to attend church or synagogue services, or to observe the Sabbath, if that is important to you? Will your schedule allow for regular daily prayer and meditation? Will travel and eating out interfere with any religious commitments? Are you able to devote time to community service, if that is an important dimension of your spiritual life? How is your business consistent, or inconsistent, with your spiritual values?

FRIENDS AND FAMILY

10: Will you be able to keep up with your current individual and couple friendships? Contact with close family members? How much time, energy, and creativity does that require? How will your business allow or encourage developing new friends or business colleagues? How important is that to you? Does your commitment to entrepreneurship change any of your current friendships or make it more difficult to remain in your current social group or neighborhood? Will your business allow you to get together with family and friends at important holidays or occasions?

HOBBIES

11: Will any of your hobbies require more time and money than you may have once your business is under way? Are any of them essential to your mental and physical well-being? What else might you do instead? How could your business support and involve your personal interests? Are you committed to spending time with other people involved in your hobby? Will any of these commitments have to change as a result of your business demands?

SELF-ESTEEM

12: How will you handle rejection and failure if you have to? How have you handled it in the past? How will you cope with being judged poorly by your spouse, parents, and in-laws, or business colleagues, if the business fails to thrive? How will you confront and overcome your personal weaknesses and fears? Are you willing to face your worst demons? How would a decrease in your social status, as a result of making a career change, make you feel? How will you handle your spouse's greater success or contributions to family support while you launch your business?

OTHER

What other personal sacrifices do you expect to make as a result of being self-employed?

Define the fences you and your spouse will erect around private, relationship, and family time. Articulate your personal boundaries in writing. Commit to those activities essential to sustaining your marriage, your family, and your physical and emotional health. For example:

> Even though I work long hours all week, my wife doesn't complain when I leave the whole day on Sunday to play golf. She realizes that playing golf makes me happy. If I'm not happy, everyone is miserable.
>
> *Professional speaker*

> My wife and I always have dinner together. Since her business is so demanding, we often have dinner at 10:00 P.M., and I'm usually the one who is cooking it. I'd prefer a more reasonable schedule, but it's the time when we catch up with each other, so we never miss it.
>
> *Supportive spouse of company president*

No matter how busy we are, we take Sunday off to be with the kids and to go to church. You have to draw the line somewhere, or the business will eat away everything.

Life insurance salesperson

GUIDELINE TEN: PLAN FOR THE DETAILS OF ENTREPRENEURIAL FAMILY LIFE

I asked a married entrepreneur who works an average of one hundred hours a week for his strongest advice to new entrepreneurs. He said, "Make sure they plan out the details of what each day is going to look like, not just the big stuff that goes into the business plan."

> When Gary and I started our new business, neither of us had any time for keeping up the house. Before we knew it, we were too embarrassed to invite even our best friends over for dinner because the house was such a disaster. One day I wrote HELP in the dust on our living room coffee table.
>
> *President, social service agency*

> When I told my wife Ellen I wanted her to join me in my business, she was enthusiastic. Ellen had always been home with our boys full-time, and she was ready for a change. Unfortunately, it took three months to find reliable day care that we both felt good about.
>
> *Retail store owner*

Business responsibilities place a strain on family life. Interviews with experienced entrepreneurial couples reveal that even those who prepare complex business plans often overlook the *day-to-day* details of caring for a family while running a business. You may have the big picture all figured out, but it's the small stuff that can sometimes cause your business or family to collapse. No detail is too small to prepare for.

Satisfying family life depends on establishing dependable routines. Discuss often with your spouse and children, in advance if possible, and throughout your entrepreneurial journey, how your daily family life will look, feel, and accommodate to the demands of your business. These regular chats bring forth your family's fears and fantasies, which help you better prepare and manage.

Your children will often wonder about the smallest of details, rather than the bigger concerns. (Can I still play with Johnny after school? Who will give me my lunch money in the morning?) Your spouse may be supportive of the *idea* of your being self-employed, but need reassurance that you'll still get the grass mowed. You may be gung ho about starting your own business, but need to resolve how your elderly mother will continue to get the biweekly visits you have been providing her. Don't underestimate the importance of asking and answering these kinds of questions.

CLARIFICATION EXERCISE TEN: PLANNING THE DETAILS OF FAMILY LIFE
Completion time: 30 minutes.

Listed below are activities of family life to consider. Jot down as many daily concerns for each category as you can think of, and a way to care for these details.

INTIMATE RELATIONSHIP
Example: We like to walk together every day to stay connected.

Plan: Walking together three times a week, in the early morning, is all that is likely, given our new schedule. We'll get up extra early on those days to fit it in.

_____

_____

_____

_____

CHILDREN

Example: Molly needs to be transported to Girl Scouts two afternoons a week.

Plan: We'll take the evening shift in the car pool if someone can bring her in the afternoons.

_____

_____

_____

_____

EXTENDED FAMILY

Example: Someone needs to look after Mom during the day.

Plan: We'll arrange for a home health aide to visit her daily.

_____

_____

_____

_____

PETS

Example: Someone needs to walk the dog in the late afternoon, before we get home from the shop.

Plan: We'll hire one of the neighborhood kids to walk her.

_____

_____

_____

_____

HOBBIES, PERSONAL GROWTH, AND EDUCATIONAL PURSUIT

Example: Russel plays golf every Sunday, and Cheryl plays tennis twice a week.

Plan: One of us will baby-sit our daughter, while the other is at the club.

SPIRITUAL EXPLORATION

Example: Maude has a Bible study class every Tuesday night.

Plan: We'll cover the store with Suzanne on Tuesday nights, so Maude can attend.

HOUSEHOLD

Example: Someone needs to make dinner every night.

Plan: Larry and I will alternate cooking meals for the family. We'll eat out every Saturday night.

THE FAMILY CALENDAR

Simple tools for managing daily communication are a wall calendar and a dry erase board. Stephen and I keep our own personal agendas, we have a family calendar in the kitchen, a large dry erase board in the kitchen for family communication, and a small dry erase board in our bedroom for leaving private messages. On the family board go instructions for the kids, reminders to put the garbage out, grocery shopping lists, important phone numbers, phone messages, and sometimes, just a note of greeting. Everyone in the family checks the board when they enter the house.

Depending on the complexity of your family life, you may wish to create a weekly schedule to be posted on the wall, reminding each of you of your daily responsibilities and commitments. Children appreciate having a reference to remind them of where everyone in the family is, even if they have already been told, and what they are supposed to do every day. You can get quite creative and involve your entire family in the creation of the family calendar. Check out an office supply store with a selection of tools for keeping employees informed and prepared. Many of these tools can be used for your family as well.

CONCLUSION

You have learned about setting boundaries, assessing risk, defining your needs, communicating proactively with your spouse, and planning for hundreds of family details. If you have completed the nine exercises in this chapter, you should have all the information you need to prepare a thorough, considerate family plan. These guidelines won't prevent all hardship or distress, but they will support you and minimize family hardship. When your foundation remains strong, you can handle entrepreneurial pressures with greater agility by remembering the following ten guidelines.

Summary of the Ten Guidelines for Financial and Family Planning

1. Acknowledge the existence of risk.
2. Identify your risk personality and that of your partner.
3. Clarify how much you and your spouse are willing to risk materially to be self-employed.
4. Form mutual agreement about material risk.
5. Hope for the best, but plan for the worst-case scenario.
6. Establish guidelines for money management and decision making.
7. Allow the different ways you and your partner handle money to work to your advantage.
8. Discuss money issues at a time and place that will be productive.
9. Define your boundaries for personal sacrifice.
10. Plan for the details of entrepreneurial family life.

Review these ten guidelines with your spouse occasionally, when money troubles have gotten you down, when you need a gentle reminder to get back on track, or when you are considering a change in direction. Revisit the Risk Assessment Tool and the other exercises you completed as your journey progresses. Your family plan, like your business plan, is a living document. Plan to update it continually, so that it will remain useful.

Congratulations! By taking the time to read this chapter, you have demonstrated that you take seriously how your entrepreneurial pursuits will affect your marriage and your family.

RECOMMENDED RESOURCES

Books

Couples and Money—Why Money Interferes with Love and What to Do About It by Victoria Felton-Collins, Ph.D. Bantam, 1990.
Money Demons—Keep Them from Sabotaging Your Relationships—and Your Life by Dr. Susan Forward and Craig Buck. Bantam, 1994.

Money Harmony—Resolving Money Conflicts in Your Life and Relationships by Olivia Mellan. Walker and Company, 1994.
Your Money or Your Life by Joe Dominguez and Vicki Robin. Viking Penguin, 1992.

Newsletters

More Than Money is a unique quarterly publication that explores the blessings and dilemmas of having more than others. Each issue is peppered with personal stories, practical ideas, and humor, placed within a wider political and spiritual context. Themes include: Money and Couples; To Spend or Not to Spend; Money, Work, and Self-esteem. $35/year; free sample on request. Contact: MTM, 2244 Alder Street, Eugene, OR 97405, 503-343-2423.

Organizations

The Impact Project: Nonprofit organization with national programs offering counseling, workshops, and literature to people with wealth and the professionals who serve them. Wealth counseling includes: taking charge financially, resolving family or work issues, fulfilling dreams. Contact: IP, 21 Linwood Street, Arlington, MA 02174, 617-648-0776.

The New Road Map Foundation: Nonprofit dedicated to educating Americans in practical tools for shifting to low-consumption, high-fulfillment lifestyles. Cofounded by Joe Dominguez and Vicki Robin. Box 15981, Seattle, WA 98115, 206-527-0437.

Advisers

Robin Bullard Carter, Money $ense, money counselor and educator providing practical and emotional empowering of people around money issues. Offers seminars, workshops, individual and couples counseling. 17 Graham Avenue, Newbury, MA 01951, 508-465-3282.

Victoria Felton-Collins, Ph.D., and Certified Financial Planner, advises individuals and couples on practical and psychological issues related to financial planning. Phone consult as well as in-person consultation. Keller, Coad, and Collins, 18300 Von Karman, Suite 640, Irvine, CA 92715, 714-476-0300.

Institute of Certified Financial Planners, 1-800-945-4237.

International Association of Financial Planners, 1-800-945-4237.

Olivia Mellan, psychotherapist with practice devoted to assisting individuals and couples with money issues, conflict resolution, and business therapy (periodic seminars and workshops offered on a variety of topics). Olivia Mellan and Associates, 2607 Connecticut Avenue N.W., Washington, D.C. 20008-1522, 202-483-2660.

National Association of Personal Financial Advisors—fee-only financial planners, 1-800-366-2762.

Sharon Rich, Ph.D., and Certified Financial Planner. Fee-only financial planner with practice to help empower women and couples with financial issues. 76 Townsend Road, Belmont, MA 02178, 617-489-3601.

Gardner N. Stratton, J.D., CPA, Personal Financial Specialist and Registered Investment Advisor, provides fee-only counseling to couples, individuals, and small companies on financial and legal issues including financial planning, investments, income and other taxes, capital formation, and estate planning. 116 Charles Street, Boston, MA 02114, 617-523-1757.

4

The Joys and Challenges of Working at Home

How Working at Home Can Work— and When It Can't

My ex-wife couldn't accept that I wasn't available for dealing with home problems when I was working at home. She was always interrupting me to do one thing or another for her or the kids. When I closed the office door and demanded that she leave me alone, she took it personally, as if I was shutting her out.

Multilevel marketing distributor

When I took early retirement, I switched from VP of a $45 million budget, to becoming my wife's assistant in her business. We argued about how to set up her home office to allow me to join her. She wanted me to use her work space as she had designed it. I wanted to reorganize the office entirely. What we were really fighting about was that I wanted her to view me as an equal partner, and she didn't want to stop being in charge.

Retired executive

Perhaps you've heard the famous saying, "I married him for breakfast and dinner, but not for lunch." Years ago that expression referred to a housewife coping with her husband's sudden presence at home upon retirement. Now approximately twelve million self-employed individuals work from home full-time. Couples across America are adjusting to a shift from the tradition of the husband working outside the house, and the wife home full-time. Husbands now work from home and their wives leave for the office in the morning. Business partners manage their business together from a shared home office. Spouses with separate offices at home meet each other for lunch in the kitchen.

Dozens of home office experts have responded to the burgeoning home office market, offering practical guides on how to set up and manage a productive home office. If you need advice on practical business matters, such as what kind of office equipment to purchase, how to maximize the tax advantages of working from home, or how to market your services, then refer to the resources at the end of this chapter.

This chapter focuses exclusively on how working from home affects your marriage, family, you, and your business. No fixed rules exist. The home office environment that delights one couple could be troublesome to another. This chapter will help you answer these six questions:

1. How will a home office suit your marriage and family?
2. How will working at home affect your relationship?
3. What are the challenges and rewards of sharing a home office with your spouse?
4. What house rules will protect both your home and your business?
5. How do you work at home as a parent?
6. When should you move the business elsewhere?

ASSESSING HOW A HOME OFFICE WILL SUIT YOUR MARRIAGE AND FAMILY

If you're not sure how well suited working in a home office would be for your relationship and your business, then complete this assessment. If both you and your spouse will work at home, then do the test separately.

EXERCISE ONE: ASSESSING HOW A HOME OFFICE WILL SUIT YOUR MARRIAGE AND FAMILY

Score each question from 1 to 5, 1 indicating "strongly agree" and 5 indicating "strongly disagree." Then total your points.

1. My significant other is enthusiastic about my working from home.
2. Our home has private office space where I can work uninterrupted.
3. My children understand how they must behave in the house when I work at home. They are cooperative and responsive to house rules.
   or
   No children live with me at home.
4. I don't have children or elderly parents in my care.
   or
   If I do, someone else will care for them during my workday.
5. If I plan to care for my children while working at home, I have realistic expectations about how much work I will accomplish and how much business I can handle.
6. My spouse and I have talked a great deal about how our routines and household rules will change when one or both of us start working from home.
7. I can ignore nonessential household repairs and clean-up when I have work to do. My spouse has reasonable expectations about how much household work I will accomplish while working from home.
8. I can easily set boundaries so that I spend adequate time with my spouse and children. I don't tend toward workaholism.
9. Working at home doesn't exacerbate any personal addictions (for example: overeating, sleeping, watching TV, drinking alcohol).

10. I already have the essential equipment needed to operate a productive business at home, or we have enough capital to buy or lease the essential equipment.
11. I am self-disciplined, well-organized, and a self-starter. The isolation of working from home doesn't scare me—I even look forward to it! Working from home suits my personality.
12. I don't mind family interruptions and distractions when I work, as long as I can get uninterrupted time when I absolutely need it.
13. My spouse and I handle transitions well. We are generally flexible and cooperative, and we work effectively as a team to overcome obstacles.
14. We have no choice other than a home office at this time.
15. Both my spouse and I have active support systems outside our marriage that we turn to if either needs assistance.
16. I'm not reluctant to pay for outside help if I run into trouble.
17. The well-being of my marriage and family is my highest priority, above the success of my business. If working at home seriously troubles my family or my spouse, then I will consider other options, even if it increases my operating expenses.

SCORE

16–36: **Green Light!** You and your spouse appear to have a marriage conducive to making a home office work. You'll still experience some challenge, but if your business and lifestyle choice is to work at home, go for it!

37–58: **Proceed with Caution!** You have some challenges ahead, but with increased preparation, dialogue with your spouse, and a lot of luck and hard work, you can pull it off. Make sure that you *and* your spouse read this chapter in its entirety. Discuss issues as they arise with your partner and your children.

59–80: **Trouble Ahead!** You either haven't thought through the implications of your home office on your marriage and family, or the early signs are that this could be a difficult and risky transition for you. You may want to consider other options. If that isn't feasible at this time, make sure that you and your spouse read this chapter in its entirety. Start talking about how you could make it work. Hire outside help right from the onset.

DISCOVERING HOW WORKING FROM HOME CAN CHANGE YOUR RELATIONSHIP

Working from home will affect your relationship with your spouse in unforeseen and significant ways.

Following are five common challenges to entrepreneurial couples with a home-based business, followed by ground rules for coping with these kinds of challenges.

How Working from Home Can Challenge Your Intimate Relationship

When You and Your Spouse Change Roles

When a woman changes her identity from housewife and mother to a work-at-home entrepreneur, the change can be difficult for her husband. Though he may express his enthusiasm and support for her endeavors, he may reveal his discomfort in subtle, or not so subtle, ways that undermine her home office efforts. He may resent his wife's spending more time in the office and less time being a caretaker. This gentleman, on the brink of divorce, expressed his indignation to me:

> My wife tried to make a profit with her little business for three years. I was working an average of one hundred hours a week to get us through financially. Since my wife was working out of the house I expected her to pick up the house at least and make the meals. I'd come home exhausted and she had done nothing. She said she was too busy working on her business. I said, until she starts earning some money, the least she could do is keep the house clean.
>
> *Disgruntled spouse*

For this couple, the home office became an arena for fighting over marital roles. He was angry about being the sole breadwinner and felt unsupported by his wife. He was angry that she had ceased to take care of the house, and of him, the way that he expected of a wife. She resented her husband's expectations and felt unappreciated. His lack of support for her business hurt her feelings, and she wondered if she might not be better off living alone. (This couple divorced shortly after our interview.)

Another equally difficult transition can be when a husband who normally worked away from the home suddenly comes home to work. He may have lost his job and decided not to return to corporate life, or quit his job to pursue his entrepreneurial dreams. Even if his wife supports the idea of his self-sufficiency, his working at home is unfamiliar to her. If she is at home, she worries that her husband will interfere with the rhythm and routine of her day, or demand more of her. She fears unsolicited advice about how she should care for the kids, keep the house, or run her business. If she works outside the home, she is unaccustomed to coming home to her spouse's presence.

> Before my wife moved in I had been working at home in silence. Suddenly I had to learn how to live with another human being who wanted to listen to the radio, watch TV, talk on the phone, or just talk to me. We lived in a small apartment and I couldn't get away from the distractions.
> *Creative consultant*

Coping with a Judgmental Spouse

The tendency to judge how the home office entrepreneur works is a difficult passage for some couples. When Stephen worked from the house, he cleaned and maintained the house and garden beautifully. I wanted Stephen to focus more on building his business. Stephen quit his job so that he would no longer have to report to a boss. Instead, I became his new boss. When I came home from work and said, "How was your day?" Stephen heard in my tone of voice: "Did you spend your day the way I think you should have?" He resented my intrusiveness and became quite defensive. I wanted Stephen to prospect for clients the way I would have done it. Stephen wanted me to trust him and to leave him alone. Working at home put Stephen's behavior under a microscope for me to see, and it was impossible for me to keep the distance we both needed me to have.

If you have any control issues with your spouse, you may

intrude on a home-based business in an unwelcome way. Couples struggle with this aspect of home office life when trust is tenuous, criticism is prominent, and money is tight.

Setting Boundaries Around Personal Space

A home office infringes on the privacy of both partners. When Stephen started his business in the house, I lost my personal space as a result. He was in our home before I left for work and there when I returned. It was hard to talk to Stephen about how much I missed the few hours of privacy I had when he worked outside of the home. I didn't want him to feel unwanted. Now our roles are reversed. I work from home as an author with plenty of personal space, and Stephen, now employed in an outside job, complains about the lack of personal space in his life. It's hard to achieve the perfect balance for both partners.

> I see clients from noon until 10:00 P.M., four days a week. Before my life partner, Marie, moved in to my small house I used my mornings to meditate, walk, eat, and center myself, to prepare myself for the demands of the day. Now Marie is always around. I can't even get dressed in private. I didn't realize how much I needed privacy to do my work until Marie moved in.
>
> *Psychologist*

> My girlfriend is a different woman in the office than she is in the kitchen. If I kiss her in the kitchen, she loves it, but if I try to kiss her in the office, she takes my head off. When she steps into her office she becomes a whole different person. She's no longer my lover. She's made it very clear: she's off limits when she's at work—even if she's home.
>
> *Boyfriend and business partner of an*
> *MLM executive*

Oil Spill Phenomenon

A home office can take over an entire household, leaving no room sacred. The computer and fax are in the bedroom, materials are spread over the dining room table, clients walk through the kitchen and peek at dinner, and the business phone rings day and night throughout the house. Employees share your living space, know your family affairs, and use your bathroom.

Oil spills are notoriously difficult to contain, once they have spread. They kill what's around them, as the oil oozes into a wider and deeper area. With no boundaries around business in your home, your home office becomes toxic to intimacy and destroys a comfortable living environment for your family. The home office as we think of it—an office in your home—becomes an office where you and your family also live. I spoke to a few couples who laid off all of their staff, or moved their home office out of their home, just to reclaim their home as a personal space.

To clean up the oil spill, consider keeping business paraphernalia out of the bedroom, or at least out of the bed. Let an answering service pick up messages in the evening. Allow clients to visit only during designated hours. Devote one bathroom in the house to employees and customers. Set the boundaries that both you and your spouse need and then enforce them. If your home stops being a private and pleasant place to live and work, then you jeopardize your business success and your marriage.

Tendency to Overwork

Some home office entrepreneurs regularly work eighty to one hundred hours a week. If your business is always in your face, you will need self-discipline to contain work to a reasonable number of hours. Consider your family by reducing the number of hours you work, permitting interruptions at certain times of the day, sharing child-care duties, or even just showing up for dinner. Engage your spouse to help you set limits.

The business obsessed me and became my life. Even though I was working at home, I never spent any time with my wife or kids. When my wife threatened divorce I was angry with her for not being supportive. Now I realize I needed her to set limits for me because I couldn't do it myself. I worried at first that my business would fall apart if I didn't give it the time. To my sur-

prise, our marriage *and* my business both improved after I cut
back on my work schedule.

Entrepreneur who almost lost his marriage

When we began our business a few years ago, we made ourselves available around the clock to our clients. I burned out
after a year of always keeping the house clean, and answering
phone calls until midnight. When I came down with pneumo-
nia, we started setting limits with our clients. I don't think we
lost any business because of it, and I got my health back.

Female partner in a business referral service

You have now learned about five common challenges home-
based entrepreneurial couples confront:

- When you and your spouse change roles.
- Coping with a judgmental spouse.
- Setting boundaries around personal space.
- The oil spill phenomenon.
- Tendency to overwork.

Some or all of these challenges may apply to you. Undoubtedly,
you have also experienced challenges not presented in this section.
Refer to the following ground rules for meeting whatever challenges come your way.

Ground Rules for Coping with Home Office–
Related Tension in Your Relationship

Keep Emotionally Current with Your Spouse

When you withhold feelings of any kind because you fear
hurting or angering your spouse, remember that (1) your spouse
can usually sense your anxiety, even if you don't express it clearly
or directly, and (2) you may emotionally erupt for a completely
unrelated reason, doing far more damage. Be straightforward and
discuss problems openly. Seek outside counsel if you can't work
out your complaints effectively.

Look for Simple, Immediate, and Beneficial Changes

One small adjustment—a "do-not-disturb" sign on the door, an extra computer, or an answering service in the evening—to the way you manage working at home can make the difference between an unworkable and a satisfactory arrangement.

Clean Up the Oil Spill

If the business is oozing throughout your home, then talk with your family about ways to contain it physically (to one or two rooms), in time (no calls taken after 6:00 P.M.), or emotionally (daily activities with family and your spouse).

Get Outside Support

Reach out to build your networks. Join a home office association. Attend a convention and meet other home office entrepreneurs. Vent your frustrations to friends, therapist, and colleagues instead of criticizing your spouse. Find others in the same situation who can empathize. Seek the help of a counselor or coach if you and your spouse are stuck in negative patterns.

Read Books, Newsletters, and Magazines for Home Office Workers

The resource sections of this book list several publications targeting the home office market. Pick up one or two to learn some valuable tips from people who have met similar challenges. Get onto the Internet and chat with other entrepreneurs working from home.

Take Responsibility for Your Part of the Problem

Creating tension takes two. What can *you* do differently to improve your relationship or your attitude? How can you be more cooperative, flexible, forgiving, or patient? Books like *Divorce Busting* by Michelle Weiner-Davis provide creative solutions to relationship difficulties by shifting maladaptive patterns of response—even if you're not close to divorce.

Review Your Priorities

Did you start your own business so that you would have a higher quality of life, more time with your family, a better relationship with your kids? If your life is out of balance, then remind yourself of why you are working so hard in the first place. Success can be empty when you don't have anyone to share it with.

How Working from Home Can Enhance Your Marriage

The home office lifestyle can positively affect your relationship, even with its rough spots. What are the potential rewards for your marriage of working from home? This section brings you the stories of several thriving home-based couples, as well as my own experience, to demonstrate.

Greater Involvement in Each Other's Lives

Stephen and I worked together in separate businesses, in the same shared office for months. We conversed throughout the day about business developments and turned to each other for practical assistance, emotional support, and companionship.

Now that Stephen works outside our home, he tells me about his day in summary fashion. I don't know his work or his colleagues, and a certain kind of distance has developed between us. Connecting deeply to your partner's professional life is easier if you are able to witness or experience it.

More Flexibility for Household Maintenance Leads to Greater Intimacy

Fatigue is the greatest killer of a satisfying romantic and sexual relationship. If you work outside the house ten or more hours a day, then you are ready to sleep by the time you return home from your job and take care of the demands of the household. A home office may afford you the flexibility to do household chores and errands throughout the day, releasing more time and energy for intimacy.

Before I started working from home, I devoted all my free time outside work to child care and cleaning the house. I was too burned out to be interested in any kind of intimacy with my husband. Now that I'm working out of the home, I take time out during the day to take care of some of the household demands. I'm much more relaxed and easier to live with now. Working from home has improved our marriage considerably.

Amway distributor

Greater Opportunities for Romance and Sex

When I was working a corporate job, the only time my wife and I had to make love was late at night after the kids were asleep. If we made love once a month it was a lot. When I started working from the house, one day my wife took a lunch break from work and came home to seduce me. After I got over the initial shock, I was a very willing partner. Now we make "lunch dates" every few weeks. It's one of the unexpected bonuses of working from home!

Home-based entrepreneur

A home business can encourage a more relaxed breakfast time together or a therapeutic neck and shoulder massage in the middle of the day. If you are both self-employed, you can be more spontaneous, leading to creative romantic encounters. Family life often works better when at least one partner has professional flexibility. When family life is running smoother, romance and sex are more likely! If you are both home-based, here are two additional benefits.

Dual Home-Based Entrepreneurs Keep Each Other Honest

My wife, Harriet, and I both work out of the home in separate offices. If I was totally on my own, I would probably sleep late and watch TV. Harriet keeps me honest. When I see her working all day, I feel too embarrassed to let her see me goofing off.

CPA

We See Each Other More Often

The average working couple spends less than an hour a day together, and even that isn't private. You can enhance intimacy between you merely by increasing the time you see each other.

> My husband's corporate career took him away from home so often we hardly knew each other after fifteen years of marriage. We decided to change our life radically. We both quit our jobs, sold our home, and bought a small working farm in another state.
>
> *Farmer*

SHARING A HOME OFFICE WITH YOUR SPOUSE

The next section of this chapter relates to the unique challenges and rewards of sharing a home office with your spouse.

The Challenges of Sharing a Home Office with Your Spouse

The key elements to sharing an office successfully with your spouse are (1) the nature of the relationship and the business, and (2) whether the office space allows each partner to carve out distinct space within it. People are creatures of habit. They work best when they can organize and use their physical space however they please, to be productive.

Sharing Space and Equipment

The most challenging arrangement is sharing equipment, a computer, workstation, and filing cabinet, etc., with your spouse.

> My wife Bridget and I always got along beautifully—until we started sharing a computer and a desk. I decided that buying a new computer for a few thousand dollars would be cheaper than getting a divorce!
>
> *Business consultant*

DISCOVERY EXERCISE TWO: CAN YOU SHARE AN OFFICE SUCCESSFULLY?

Completion time: 15 minutes.

If you are considering sharing a home office with your spouse or are sharing one now, then this quiz is for you. Complete separately and compare your responses.

Score each question from 1 to 5, 1 indicating strongly agree and 5 indicating strongly disagree. Then total your points.

1. My spouse and I have the same need for tidiness, organization, space, and clutter in our work area.
2. I can share a computer or desk space with my spouse, or we have separate workstations for each of us.
3. My spouse and I enjoy being together a great deal. We can work together in close quarters without friction.
4. I don't need private uninterrupted space to do productive work.
5. I work better when I am working nearby my spouse than when I am working alone.
6. My spouse and I are able to negotiate and problem-solve well. We easily resolve conflicts that arise.
7. I really appreciate having my spouse available for advice, encouragement, and constructive comments throughout the day.
8. My spouse and I can share office equipment efficiently and still meet our individual business needs.
9. The only space available is shared office space, so we will make it work one way or the other

   or

   We have other space available, but it's our strong preference to share a home office if possible.
10. Even within our shared space, I am able to carve out my own separate work area.
11. My partner may have work habits that annoy me but even if I feel judgmental, I've learned how not to express it, unless it gets in the way of my work.

12. Both my spouse and I have a sense of humor. We laugh and have a good time together throughout the day.

13. My spouse and I take space regularly from each other, outside the home office, when needed.

14. My spouse and I have learned to keep our business and personal conflicts separate. We don't fight dirty, carry fights over from work to home, or vice versa. When we do fight, we don't stay angry with each other for very long.

15. My spouse and I both work best at different times of the day, so we are able to coordinate private time in our shared office.

16. Sharing a home office is our first choice right now. If doing so begins to jeopardize our relationship, we will look for other alternatives.

SCORE

16–36: **Looks Promising!** You have the potential to share a home office with your spouse quite successfully. You may produce better work and enjoy a more satisfying relationship. There will be some issues to negotiate, but you'll likely work them out over time.

37–58: **You Have Your Work Cut Out for You!** With positive intention, hard work, and regular open dialogue, you and your spouse may meet the challenges ahead. But don't underestimate the potential difficulties and prepare to compromise. You can't always have your way.

59–80: **Danger!** Sharing an office could spell trouble. If you have no other options, prepare for a significant growth opportunity! Your relationship could become stronger, as sharing a home office forces you to learn how to accept each other's differences, to give and take, and to resolve conflict.

Sharing an office when you are both home can be as distracting as working in a large corporate office space divided into cubicles. Your partner speaking on the phone next to you breaks your concentration. It's difficult to have a private conversation without feeling eavesdropped upon. Productivity decreases because of frequent interruptions. Couples who make this arrangement work often schedule private time in the office to respect each other's needs for uninterrupted work time. They make sure that they have space enough and access to their own office equipment when needed.

> My husband and I own eight computers. We each have our own computer at the office outside our home, our own computer in our shared home office, our own laptop computers, and even our own computers in our weekend house. We like to be able to work wherever we are and neither of us can stand sharing a computer. Eight computers may seem excessive, but $25,000 is a minimal investment when you're running a $10 million a year company.
>
> *Retail executive*

Separating Personal and Work Conflict

For most couples, the greatest challenge of sharing a home office is learning how to separate personal and work conflicts. If you fight in the morning about one of the kids and then walk downstairs to begin your business day together, you may struggle to leave the conflict behind. Likewise, an unresolved business conflict can easily spill over to the dinner table. Blurring of boundaries invariably results. Entrepreneurial couples who hope to work together at home for any time must learn how to move through conflict quickly and to separate their work and personal conflicts. Many couples struggle with the process before they find a system that works for them.

I interviewed a couple who fought passionately in their marriage before he lost his job and joined his wife's business as her partner. When they began working together in her basement office, the fights increased and carried into the evening hours. In desperation, the wife devised this strategy to manage the fighting:

I knew we'd never stop fighting completely, but I came up with a new rule: Business fights had to take place in the basement office, and personal fights had to take place upstairs. One day we got into an ugly personal fight in the office. I excused myself, went upstairs, called my husband from the upstairs phone, and yelled all the insults and obscenities that I wanted to say to him in the office. Another day, when we started fighting about work at the dinner table, I grabbed my husband and dragged him down to the basement so that we could finish the fight down there.

Purchasing business owner

Ground Rules for Resolving Conflict in a Shared Home Office

Create the Separation Symbolically Between Business and Personal Conflict

Designate places in your home, like your bedroom, as sacred from business conversation. Identify where business discussion is most appropriate. Refrain from continuing a business argument over the dinner table or a personal fight in your office. The more often you reinforce these boundaries with each other, the easier it will become.

Schedule Business Meetings Regularly to Resolve Business Issues

If you can't tackle something in one session, then plan another session, rather than continuing throughout the evening. You may need daily, weekly, or biweekly meetings to stay current on business issues. The same goes for relationship issues.

Don't Take Advantage of Your Partner's Hot Buttons and Vulnerabilities

Belittling your spouse in anger will never lead to a positive outcome. For example, to bolster her argument for spending more money on a copier for the office, Kim accused her partner of being a tightwad and unreasonably cheap because of his upbringing. Kim sidetracked from a straightforward business analysis of purchasing a specific copier to a personal attack on her husband's spending habits. She hurt her relationship and failed to convince her husband to buy because he was defending himself.

If you use secret emotional weapons to win an argument, you create a toxic environment where your spouse feels angry, exposed, and defensive. To your best ability, speak to your spouse with the same respect given an outside business partner.

Take Time away from Each Other When Necessary

If tension is building, or you are recovering from a personal fight the night before, then structure the day so that you can regroup. Get out of the house. Lunch with a friend, exercise at your health spa. Reschedule business meetings. Create a "no-business" date if business arguments intrude upon personal time.

Keep Your Sense of Humor and Lighten Up When You Can

Marvel at your ability to work together most of the time. The majority of couples would never attempt it! Go insane by working for a day with clown noses on. Play hooky together and let the machine answer your calls while you crawl into bed watching a video. Or take the kids on an outing. Working together at home in your own business gives you an enormous amount of flexibility. Use it occasionally to lighten the mood.

There Are Cycles and Seasons to Everything

Accept that your relationship sometimes bores, angers, frustrates, or annoys you. Some days you will be just plain grumpy. That's life, at home or in a corporation. Working together in a home office is more uncomfortable when you aren't getting along well, but you'll tend to work through fights faster. If your marriage is strong and you keep perspective, "this too, shall pass."

Change the Setup If Sharing a Home
Office Isn't Working

If you've really tried, sought outside help in person or by reading, and your relationship and/or your business still deteriorates, then look for other alternatives. Many couples discover their need for more private space or time from each other to keep their relationship healthy and enjoyable. To thine own self be true.

The Rewards of Sharing a Home Office
with Your Spouse

On a practical level, sharing office space conserves resources. Couples share copy and fax machines, laser printers, and answering services, expensive business investments on a lean start-up budget. For some couples, sharing an office significantly adds to the quality of their life together as well. Couples who enjoy sharing a home office cherish each other's company, the ongoing exchange, the advice, brainstorming, and companionship. They have a low need for privacy or quiet to work productively.

> Working at home was lonely at times. Except for the occasional conversation with a client, I could talk to no one for hours at a time. I gained twenty pounds working at home because I kept going to the refrigerator when I was restless. When my husband decided to work out of the same office, my productivity and creativity increased. Now when I'm bored or lonely I ask my husband for a hug instead of hitting the refrigerator.
>
> *Home-based desktop publisher*

> I can't even relate to couples separated for days at a time. Because I work with my husband at home all day long, I feel really connected to him, and our business and marriage are thriving.
>
> *"Double-Diamond," Cell-Tech*

DEVELOPING HOUSE RULES TO PROTECT YOUR HOME AND YOUR BUSINESS

House Rules

So you've decided together that one or both will work from home. How will you organize the household routines and responsibilities of everyone to work synergistically with your home office? What do we mean by house rules? Who is going to do what when, and who is not going to do what, when? For example, the kids will never answer the business phone, the entrepreneur at home will make dinner four nights a week. Your family operates by implicit social rules all the time, based on your expectations of one another. Do you openly communicate the rules and renegotiate when they no longer apply?

> When my kids entered high school I decided to start my own roommate matching service. My business took off and I was working almost every night and weekend. Since I was working out of the house during the day, my family still expected me to cook every meal, clean the house, chauffeur the kids after school, and do everyone's laundry. I killed myself for six months, playing superwoman. Then one day I lost it on my husband. He told me he had no clothes and he needed his laundry done before he went to work the next day. He's fifty-five years old and he can't even wash his own damn underwear? I dumped the laundry basket out on the floor and told my husband that from now on he could do his own laundry. You should have seen the look on his face!
>
> *Housewife who started her own roommate matching service*

Since this woman failed to communicate her new needs and expectations to her family, they naturally expected that nothing in the household routine would change. If she were single and living alone, she could change her routine without affecting anyone. If the dishes piled up in the sink, the food in the refrigerator turned green, or the laundry didn't get done for a week, who else would care? As a wife and mother she is an integral part of a system that depends on every individual to play his or her role in an established way. When one member of the system changes the routine, then all must adjust.

Most households establish house rules to prevent a situation from occurring. One of my most memorable stepparenting moments prompted me to invent an immediate house rule.

September 1994 brought us an unseasonably sweltering Indian summer. I was eight months pregnant and working part-time out of the house. We lacked central air-conditioning and in desperation, I removed all my clothes and worked naked at our kitchen table by an open window to stay cool. Our kitchen was about ten feet from the front door. I had all of five seconds notice when my teenage stepsons came flying in the door from school, two hours earlier than expected. I raved like a lunatic at them to get out of the house until I dressed. When I allowed them back in, I spontaneously implemented a new house rule: They must tell me when they had a planned half day at school! (I never did have the courage to work at home undressed again.)

This section explores four categories of house rules to articulate if you will work at home with a family.

1. Assigning household responsibilities.
2. Conducting business in the home without intruding on the needs and privacy of household members.
3. Protecting the business from interference by household members.
4. Caring for and supervising the children.

The following exercise should help as you embark on a home office, or if you have a home office already established, but no defined systems to keep your home and business operating smoothly together.

CLARIFICATION EXERCISE THREE: DEFINING HOUSE RULES

Completion time: 60 minutes.

This exercise stimulates discussion about important family issues. Read the questions together with your spouse. Establish a mutual understanding of how you will handle and negotiate each if necessary. If your children are old enough, then involve them democratically in the rule-making process, or, if you prefer, hold an autocratic family meeting to share your decisions with them. Writing down the agreed-upon rules is particularly important with children. Agree to review the rules monthly, quarterly, or even weekly at the beginning.

HOUSEHOLD RESPONSIBILITIES

Cleaning. Who is going to keep the house in order, clean, polish, dust, vacuum, empty the garbage, clean the bathrooms, keep the office clean and straightened? How often will someone complete these tasks? Are children responsible for keeping their rooms straightened? Who does extra work when a client comes to the house, like maintaining any bathroom a client uses? Who decides what the cleanliness standards are? Will you hire a housekeeper?

_____

_____

_____

Meals. Who prepares breakfast, lunch and dinner—how often, what time? Who sets the table, cleans the kitchen afterward, empties the dishwasher? Who grocery shops? Will you designate mealtime as family time, with everyone expected to attend? What exceptions are there?

_____

_____

_____

Laundry. Who does laundry for whom, and how often? Who washes, folds, and puts away the clothes? Are children responsible for their own laundry at a certain age?

_____

_____

_____

_____

Maintenance. Who does household and auto repairs and mainte-nance? How often? When will you hire outside help instead of doing it yourself? What maintenance will you do around the house to prevent breakdowns and repair them?

_____

_____

_____

_____

Clutter. Who's the clutter cop? Who straightens, sorts the mail, keeps the business and household paperwork organized and filed? Who recycles old newspapers and magazines, puts away children's debris, keeps miscellaneous household clutter manageable? Who puts away business materials at the end of a workday?

_____

_____

_____

_____

Pets. Who walks the dog, feeds the cat, cleans the guinea pig cage, buys the bird food, and takes the pet to the vet?

_____

_____

_____

_____

HOW WILL YOUR BUSINESS RESPECT YOUR FAMILY'S NEED FOR PRIVACY, RELAXATION, AND ATTENTION?

Public space. If you locate your work area in the family room or kitchen, where does everyone go to hang out? Is your business area off-limits to the family at certain hours?

_____

_____

_____

_____

Dress code. Do the members of your family have to dress a certain way when clients are in the house? (For example, can your sixteen-year-old daughter parade through the house in her string bikini?)

_____

_____

_____

_____

Client visiting. Can clients drop by unannounced or call at anytime? Is business ever off limits, so you can devote focused, uninterrupted time to your family?

_____

_____

_____

_____

Children's activities. Does your home office restrict your children's music, television watching, or inviting friends over to the house?

_____

_____

_____

_____

Accessibility. How will you respond to your children's requests for attention? What kinds of requests must the children postpone until your work is done? How will your children know when it is OK to interrupt your work? Define an emergency.

_____

_____

_____

_____

HOW WILL YOU PROTECT YOUR BUSINESS FROM INTERFERENCE BY HOUSEHOLD MEMBERS?

Telephone. Who answers the business telephone? With what greeting? Are children prohibited from using the business line to make telephone calls? Will you share a modem line for home computers with your children?

_____

_____

_____

_____

Privacy. How will you maintain privacy in your work area, ensure that your work space is not interfered with, prevent your children from turning your home office into a playpen, keep your office secure?

_____

_____

_____

_____

Client visitors. How will you ensure a positive impression for your clients or customers when they visit your home? Do you expect anyone in the family to answer the door? Will you introduce business visitors to your family? How should your family behave toward clients if they do interact? How will you control unruly or excitable pets, a barking or jumping dog, unattractive smells, sounds, or sights?

_____

_____

_____

_____

HOW WILL YOU CARE FOR AND SUPERVISE THE CHILDREN?

1. Who gets the children off to school or day care in the morning?
2. Who connects with the children when they return in the afternoon?
3. Who chauffeurs the children to after-school activities?
4. How will you supervise, feed, entertain, diaper, or calm infants and very young children if they are home during the workday?
5. Who will supervise, guide, and keep teenage children out of trouble?
6. Any extra household chores you expect of the children?
7. Any new restrictions you would place on the children?
8. Who will help the children with their homework?
9. Will the children help in the business? Will you pay them?
10. Any rules for the kids regarding off-limits business space and materials?
11. How will you minimize interruptions when you are on the phone or visiting with a client? When is it urgent enough for the children to interrupt you?
12. Have you discussed these rules with your children and received agreement?
13. Who gives the kids their bath and puts them down to sleep?
14. Who will take care of sick children when necessary?

Write here any other house rules you can think of that need clarification or discussion:

_____

_____

_____

_____

_____

_____

_____

WORKING AT HOME WHEN YOU ARE A PARENT

Working at Home with Young Children (under school age)

Stephen and I had a plan: During my three-month maternity leave from my full-time job, I would write the book proposal required for publishing this book. Babies mostly sleep in their first three months, right?

Six months later, I finished my proposal, after returning to work, even though I was back at the computer within a few days of Sarah's birth, nursing with one hand and typing with the other. Sarah slept for an hour or two at a time and then was hungry again—day and night, day after day. By the time I diapered, nursed, and cuddled her, I had only a few hours left to write. I sacrificed sleep to do the impossible, getting up with Sarah for her 2:00 A.M. feeding and going to the computer until she awoke at 4:00 A.M. for her next meal. Predictably, after two months, I got very sick, the result of too little sleep and running myself too hard.

When I quit my job to devote myself full-time to writing, we kept Sarah in at-home day care. Some people wondered why I didn't pull her out and care for her at home, now that I was working at home. I had learned my lesson, and I knew what my limits were. When we relocated from Boston to Pennsylvania, I was under contract with HarperCollins, with a deadline to meet, and pregnant again. We searched for the right day-care provider ahead of the move, so that Sarah could start day care the week we arrived. I realistically assessed the effort required to move an entire house, manage my second pregnancy, care for my husband, Sarah, and teenage stepson, and still deliver the manuscript on time. Caring for Sarah full-time at home, even for a month, would have made meeting the HarperCollins deadline impossible.

Give up any fantasy of working *full-time* from home and caring for an infant or small children, unless you have child-care help coming into your home, or you can work at night when your children sleep. You'll set yourself up to feel like a lousy parent, or an ineffective entrepreneur, and you'll wear yourself down to exhaustion.

On the other hand, if your expectations of yourself as a parent and business person are realistic, working at home while raising your babies can go well, allowing both quality time at home with your children and a business of your own.

EXERCISE FOUR: CAN YOU WORK AT HOME SUCCESSFULLY WHILE CARING FOR AN INFANT OR SMALL CHILDREN?

Completion time: 10 minutes.

Answer yes or no to the following questions.

1. Can you complete your business effectively in part-time hours, in short spurts of time, with distractions and interruptions from the children?
2. Can you work fatigued and feeling pulled in two different directions?
3. Will your spouse, parent, or older children share child-care responsibilities with you?
4. Do you plan to hire child-care and/or housekeeping help to come into your home?
5. Are you able to take a sabbatical from your business for a time, without destroying the business?
6. Do you have the financial means to earn less than a full-time income?
7. Do you have the flexibility to set your own pace in your business, so that if your baby gets sick, has a cranky day, is teething, etc., you can let the work slide a bit without jeopardizing a deadline?
8. Does your spouse have a realistic assessment of what you can accomplish while staying home with a young child?
9. Are your children reasonably healthy and even-tempered, not demanding more care than the average child of their age? (For example, not colicky or mentally or physically challenged)
10. Have you spaced out your children in age so that you aren't caring for more than one infant or toddler at a time?
11. Is raising your children at home your highest priority? Will you sacrifice business success, if necessary, to accomplish that goal?

If you can answer yes to all or most of these questions, you may be ideally suited for a home business. If you answered no to several questions, reevaluate your alternatives, rather than feel like a failure because you tried to achieve the impossible.

Working at Home with Children Between Ages Five and Twelve

With your children in school at least part-time, you can usually plan uninterrupted work for at least four to six hours a day. Thousands of parents chose self-employment options that allow them to work "mother's hours" when the children are either at school or asleep. Some parents abruptly stop their work upon their children's arrival from school. Others work through the distractions and interruptions that children bring.

What works for you depends on your business and your children. Children ages five to eleven are normally still too young to leave for a long time without adult supervision. They will get bored and want to be entertained, which translates into interrupting your work, or getting themselves in trouble. You can plant children in front of a television set as a baby-sitter, but not habitually. The television does not substitute for adult interaction. Bickering between siblings is natural and frequent; it won't disappear just because it's inconvenient for you. If your children are bored or miss you, then they will fight just to get your attention.

Paul and Sarah Edwards discuss what you can expect with children at home in their chapter, "What to Do About Children" (Edwards, *Working from Home*, page 443).

> Whatever their ages, kids will be kids. Don't expect your children to act like grown-ups just because you are working at home. Don't expect them, for example, to be quiet. Remember, by nature children are not quiet, and to be so for more than short periods of time is unhealthy for their development. Constantly trying to hush them will be a losing battle for you in the short run and not good for them in the long run. A good rule of thumb, applying to children of all ages, is to "child-

proof" your home office rather than trying to "office-proof" your children. In other words, let your kids be kids. Set up your office and your schedule so that having "normal" children around will not disrupt your work.

Young children may resent your work and act out even more if you force them to constrain their natural behavior and to act like adults when they are too young for those expectations. Even worse, they may act like adults and sacrifice their childhoods to your small business. This is a high price for them to pay. On the other hand, if they receive adequate attention, then they can come to love the fact that you are there when they return from school and available when they need you the most.

Most young children don't know what their parents do for work. When I was in elementary school, I told people that my daddy was an "engineer," whatever that meant. When one or both of you works at home, even very young children can start to understand what your business is for and about. Over time, they will appreciate your effort to make money for what they want. All young children have a fantasy that money just appears when they need it. Twenty-four-hour cash machines increase the illusion. Working at home can help to dispel that myth. One clever woman responded to her daughter's plea for a pair of designer jeans by telling her how many extra hours the family would have to work to buy the item. The child put down the jeans.

My kids grew up helping in the family business from the time they were five years old. Some of our best family times were spent sitting around our large work table, working together to get a mailing out. Our kids have always known that Mommy and Daddy had to work very hard to pay for groceries and movie money, and they appreciate us more as a result.

Partner in a mail-order business

When she was ten, my daughter took a bad fall on her bicycle, requiring several stitches. Since I was working at home, I was only minutes away to comfort her and take her to the hospital.

Bed and breakfast innkeeper

> When we built our new custom home office, I had a special extra wide desk designed that allows my kids to do their homework at my desk in the afternoon. My kids get a kick out of working at the desk like "a big person," and it's easier for me to stay connected with them.
>
> *Midwest psychologist and consultant*

You may elect to bring day-care or baby-sitting help into your home to cover the time during the day that the children aren't in school. Stay flexible and open to alternatives, and be creative. Start a baby-sitting co-op in your neighborhood for other work-at-home parents. Join with other parents to hire a baby-sitter to watch all the children in one place. Either you or your spouse may elect to work second or third shift to have one parent always available to the children. Bring a live-in nanny into your home if you have the financial means and the space.

Working at Home with Teenagers

Children over the age of twelve can entertain themselves and follow and respect house rules, even if they don't like them. Now you may have to contend with normal teenage behavior, like playing the stereo too loud, walking through the house in ragged clothes and a punk hairstyle when your best client is there, expecting or demanding to be chauffeured, cooking up a storm in the kitchen and leaving it a mess, or not doing homework unless supervised. The same children who liked having you home may wish you'd leave, so they can have more freedom.

Depending on your relationship, working at home with teenagers can be a very positive experience. Your children may become even more active in your business as essential assistants. As a trade-off, you may be more available for transporting them to and from after-school activities. You can get to know their friends better, and have a better handle on any worrisome teenage behaviors, such as drug or alcohol use, trouble in school, conflict with other kids, or even depression.

> I noticed that my son Charlie always came home directly after school and went straight to his room for the afternoon. He

never had any friends over and appeared quite depressed. We got him into counseling and discovered that he was considering suicide. I felt much better keeping an eye on him during this fragile time. I would have worried sick about him if I was away from home all day.

Mary Kay consultant

The best way to work well with teenage children at home is to keep dialogue open, continue to have realistic expectations, and be prepared for good days and bad ones.

No matter what combination of work and parenting you choose, your family will experience frustration, guilt, anger, sadness, fatigue, and resentment. These experiences are natural and healthy, provided that you acknowledge them. There is no perfect setup that will eliminate all stress and difficulty. Raising a family and working is stressful, whether you work out of or in the home. You and your spouse must choose which set of challenges you wish to take on. Don't let anyone guilt or coerce you into their recommended option—like staying at home to raise your children or returning to the executive career you have worked hard to achieve. Find the right scenario for you, your spouse, and your children—at this time—and be willing to change it, as needed, throughout your family life.

DECIDING WHEN IT IS TIME TO MOVE THE OFFICE OUT OF THE HOME

Some entrepreneurs set up a home office when they start their business, and their business never leaves home. If the business prospers, the quality of their home office will improve—even to the extent of moving to a new home so that they can build a more spacious home office. The notion of eliminating a home office is out of the question. If relocating to a new house becomes necessary, a place for a suitable home office is a key criterion to the choice of a new house. They have discovered that their business, their personality, and their family needs are entirely conducive to a home office.

As an author, coach, and consultant, my home is where I work best. I conduct my coaching practice over the telephone, and since I schedule my clients throughout the day and evening, I can work easily around the schedule at home. I write in spurts, and I can maximize my productivity because there are always other business and household tasks to complete in between writing sessions. With my husband working outside of the house, having one of us home to care for the children's needs, to grocery shop and run to the bank, and to get dinner on the table has become essential to our family. Working at home is ideal for me and for our family.

Businesses typically move out of a home office for four reasons:

1. Zoning difficulties.
2. Business expansion.
3. Working at home doesn't work for either the entrepreneur or his or her family.
4. The business closes down.

Let's explore each of these scenarios.

Zoning

The town or city you live in determines whether it is legal for you to operate a business in your home, through zoning laws. Nine out of ten localities restrict using residences for offices or businesses in some way. According to the American Planning Association, these are the most common restrictions on home offices and home businesses (Edwards, *Working from Home*, page 217):

Restrictions limiting increases in vehicular traffic (46%)

Restrictions on use or size of outside signs (42%)

Restrictions on on-street parking (33%)

Limitations on employees (33%)

Limitations on floor space used (20%)

Restrictions on retail selling times on the premises (13%)

Prohibitions on outside storage of materials (11%)

Restrictions on inside storage of materials (8%)

Zoning ordinances, created on the local level, differ widely from town to town. Depending on your business of choice, they can severely restrict your ability to operate a legal home-based business. If you are conservative, law-abiding, and risk averse, you will check with your local city hall to find out what the restrictions are for your neighborhood *before* you set up the home office. This will be particularly essential if you are considering a business that will bring traffic, noise, or disturbance to your neighborhood. Complaining neighbors uncover most zoning violations.

If you take the route of selective denial or taking your chances by operating a home office that is not in total compliance with local zoning ordinances, you could get caught and wage an expensive battle to keep your business operating. Fighting a zoning ordinance can destroy your business *and* your relationship with your neighbors, so knowingly operating a home office in violation of zoning restrictions is risky. On the other hand, some home-based entrepreneurs have successfully defended their right to operate a business at home and have changed the zoning laws as a result. You may be able to band together in the fight with other similar home-based businesses in your neighborhood.

Business Expansion

For some entrepreneurs, the home office is a necessary first step to growing a business. The dream has always been to expand to a large facility with dozens of employees. For them, the move out of the house is cause for celebration, or at least a big leap of faith that their business is now ready to absorb the increased overhead. That doesn't mean that the move out is easy.

> My husband and teenage daughter forced me to move my business out of the house when our home started feeling as if we were living in my office. My business had taken over the dining room, the living room, half of our bedroom, and even the hallways. It finally got to be too much for my family to take.
> *Audio/video consultant*

This entrepreneur experienced the pull between striving for a successful, prosperous business, and wanting to work at home in a space too small to accommodate her growing business and a family. Some entrepreneurs intentionally limit their growth, or start charging higher fees, to work at home. The critical decision for some is whether to expand beyond a one- or two-person business, to a larger business requiring employees. Others use the profits from their business to improve their living space, build an addition, or finish the basement. Some entrepreneurs move to a larger home, rather than relocating their business.

You may feel claustrophobic after attempting to coexist in too small a space with a spouse, employees, clients, and children. Stepping all over each other in cramped quarters gets old. Without the opportunity for at least some privacy during the day or evening, work is less productive and conflict usually increases among family members.

Couples are imaginative with available space when the need dictates. One couple with two children turned a small, two-bedroom New York apartment into an office for their thriving service business. Every day they shared their one-thousand-square-foot apartment with three employees, two children, and a baby-sitter. Another couple created and delivered personal growth seminars in their home, turning their home over to a dozen people or more for a week each month when they gave the seminar. Both couples eventually profited enough to move their business out of the original home office, the first couple building a larger home in the suburbs to accommodate a more substantial office, and the second, a separate facility for delivering their courses.

If you are struggling with this dilemma, you may consider renting an outside office or professional suite on a part-time basis for selected work activities such as visiting with clients. Rent outside storage space instead of crowding your home with boxes and filing cabinets. House your staff in an outside office, but remain in your home office for most of your workday. Work in an outside office part of the day, but still work at home when it is preferable for you or your family.

I rent a professional suite that I share with three other women. Since none of us needs an office outside the house full-time, it's the perfect arrangement for us. I can still be home in the afternoon for my children.

Translator

It's Not Working to Work at Home

Working at home may not be conducive to business success and/or harmony in your marriage or family. Maybe you figured it out after just a few months, or after a year or two of valiant effort.

Stephen and I decided to move his office outside the home after six months, even though the additional overhead strained our budget. Stephen wasn't productive at home, and our relationship was suffering.

Sometimes the increased cost of overhead is necessary to improve business performance or to diminish tension in your relationship or family. Rather than seeing the move out of the home as failure, consider it feedback. You tried the home office approach, and it wasn't for you. Fine, try something else.

The Business Closes

A home-based business can be a lifetime career choice or a brief adventure. Your business may last a year or two or a decade or more. You may switch to a new business venture that requires working outside of the home. Many retired, laid off, or fired executives try their hand at self-employment and working from home after leaving behind their corporate routine. Contrast these two experiences:

When I stopped working as a controller I missed talking with people and having a secretary to type my letters and file my paperwork. I was lonely working as a self-employed accountant. After a year, I gave it up and secured a job as a controller again.

Controller

No more white shirts and ties, eating out in cheap restaurants, and sitting inside a building with no windows for ten hours a day. I would never go back to corporate jail, for any kind of money.

Consultant

Stephen elected to close down his business and return to corporate life when I quit my job to write this book full-time. With four children to support, one of us had to bring in some steady income. A home office continues to be an integral part of my work life and our marriage. You and your spouse may experience many variations on the home office lifestyle during your lifetime together, as your family and business needs change.

DISCOVERY EXERCISE FIVE: IS IT TIME TO MOVE THE OFFICE OUT OF THE HOUSE?
Completion time: 10 minutes.

The following quiz for the home-based entrepreneur will give you a sense of whether it's time to consider moving the office out of the home, for the sake of your business, your marriage, or your children.

Answer yes or no to the following questions.

1. Are you finding it difficult to focus on your work productively because household demands and repairs distract you?
2. Are your children complaining a great deal about the restrictions placed on them because of your home office? Are they rebelling frequently against your requests? Has it turned out to be impossible to create a productive work atmosphere because of your children's or spouse's presence in the home?
3. Are you and your spouse fighting more because of tension created by the home office? Do you argue over lack of space in the house, the blurring of personal and business conflict, boundaries around work and family time, or how you should manage the home office?
4. Is your home atmosphere interfering with the professional image you wish to project to your clients? Is it preventing or limiting new business development? Do you tend to network less often than you need to because your business is located at home?
5. Do you frequently feel torn between caring for your children and your spouse and caring for your business? Have you been unable

to do either one to your liking? Would it be easier for you to compartmentalize and separate those aspects of your life?

6. Have you been unhappy, lonely, anxious, or bored more often
   because of your dissatisfaction with working at home? Are bad
   habits, like overeating or sleeping too much taking over and jeopardizing your business and your health?

7. Is your presence at home unnecessary (for child care, elder care,
   or caring for a disabled spouse), so that you could consider other
   options that might work better for all concerned?

8. Do your gut sense and intuition tell you that it's time to move out?

If you answered *yes* to three to five of these questions, put some
serious energy into researching out-of-the-home office alternatives. If
you answered yes to six or more of these questions, start packing!

Expect to go through an adjustment period when the office
moves out of the home. Your spouse may be happy to reclaim his
or her house, sad to see you go, or a little of both. He or she may
feel more disconnected from you and your business once it's out
of the house. The routines of the family will change again.
Prepare children for the move and expect some adjustment difficulties. Remember, any change in the family system will disrupt
the routines you and they are accustomed to.

Memories of boxes on dining room tables, computers in the
kitchen, and baby's rooms converted to workstations bring a smile
and a feeling of disbelief—"how did we ever do it?" Most couples
are proud of what they have been able to pull off working at home
with limited resources. Most also acknowledge how much of a
struggle it was to keep their sanity and their relationship healthy
during this start-up period.

RECOMMENDED RESOURCES

Books

Country Careers: Successful Ways to Live and Work in the Country by Jerry Germer. John Wiley and Sons, 1993.

Homemade Money: How to Select, Start, Manage, Market, and Multiply the Profits of a Business at Home by Barbara Brabec. Better Way Books, 5th edition, 1994.

Making It On Your Own: Surviving and Thriving On the Ups and Downs of Being Your Own Boss by Paul and Sarah Edwards. Jeremy P. Tarcher/Perigee, 1991.

199 Great Home Businesses You Can Start (and Succeed in) for Under $1,000.00 by Tyler G. Hicks. Prima Publishing, 1993.

The Best Home Businesses for the '90s: The Inside Information You Need to Know to Select a Home-Based Business That's Right for You by Paul and Sarah Edwards. Jeremy P. Tarcher/Perigee, 1991.

The Complete Guide to Building and Outfitting an Office in Your Home by Jerry Germer. Better Way Publishing, 1994.

The Home Office and Small Business Answer Book: Solutions to the Most Frequently Asked Questions About Starting and Running Home Offices and Small Businesses by Janet Attard. Henry Holt and Company, 1993.

The Joy of Working from Home: Making a Life While Making a Living by Jeff Berner. Berrett Koehler, 1994.

Working from Home: Everything You Need to Know About Living and Working Under the Same Roof by Paul and Sarah Edwards. Putnam, 4th edition, 1994.

Working Solo: The Real Guide to Freedom and Financial Success with Your Own Business by Terri Lonier. Portico Press, 1994.

Working Solo Sourcebook: Essential Resources for Independent Entrepreneurs by Terri Lonier. Portico Press, 1995.

Newsletters, Magazines, and Newspapers

Home-Based Business News: Bimonthly Newspaper for the Home-Business Entrepreneur. John Knowlton, editor.

Subscription $15/year, 0424 SW Pendleton, Portland, OR 97201, 503-246-3452.

Home Office Computing. Focuses primarily on home-based computer entrepreneurs, but features articles relevant to all self-employed. Monthly magazine, P.O. Box 2511, Boulder, CO 80302, 1-800-288-7812.

Success Working from Home: Your In-House Consultant for Independent Professionals and Telecommuters. Jeff Berner Creative Services, bimonthly newsletter, subscription $36/year, P.O. Box 244, Dillon Beach, CA 94929 or fax at 707-878-2246.

Working Solo Newsletter: Quarterly Publication for the Self-Employed. Terri Lonier, subscription $24/year, sample issue is $4, Portico Press, Dept. Ws-Sb, P.O. Box 190, New Paltz, NY 12561-0190.

Associations and Conferences

American Association of Home-Based Businesses, P.O. Box 10023, Rockville, MD 20849, 1-800-447-9710. Nonprofit association provides a network of and for home-based businesses through local chapters around the country. Send a self-addressed stamped envelope for an informational brochure.

Home Business Institute (HBI), David Hanania, P.O. Box 301, White Plains, NY 10605-0301, 914-964-6600. Membership organization of more than 40,000 home-based businesses, provides a wide range of benefits, including newsletter, discounts, attendance at HBI conferences. Dues $49/year.

On-Line Services

America Online, 8619 Westwood Center Drive, Suite 200, Vienna, VA 22182, 1-800-827-6364. Microsoft Small Business Center.

CompuServe, Working from Home Forum, 5000 Arlington Center Boulevard, P.O. Box 20212, Columbus, OH 43220, 1-800-848-8199. On-Line Forum hosted by Paul and Sarah Edwards.

GEnie, interest-group bulletin boards, round tables and libraries, on-line conferences. 410 N. Washington Street, Rockville, MD 20850, 1-800-638-9636.

Part 2

Sustaining a Thriving Marriage

5

Communication Skills

Understanding Your Partner and Getting Your Point Across

I used to look forward to coming home to my wife, Susie. Now, I find myself making excuses to work late at the office because as soon as I come in the door she's complaining about one thing or another. When I tell her to hang in there, she just gets madder at me. I don't know what she wants from me.

Computer salesman

My wife and I share a home office. Lately, she's been driving me nuts. She talks to me all day long, even when I'm busy working. When I tell her to leave me alone, she does—she doesn't talk to me for the rest of the day. How can I get her to understand that I need privacy so that I can concentrate on my work? I wish she wouldn't take it so personally.

Environmental consultant

Are any of the following statements true for you?

I can have a great day at work, but when my husband comes home, he'll say something sarcastic to me that ruins my whole mood.

Sometimes I'm convinced that my wife and I are from different planets. We both experience the same event, but see it entirely differently.

I love my girlfriend, but I don't know how to make her feel better when she's upset. I wish I knew how to be a better friend for her.

When I tell my husband a complaint, I get a hostile defensive reaction. How can I make a simple request without causing a fight?

Sometimes talking about a problem with your partner only worsens the situation. How can you solve a problem verbally if you haven't learned how to communicate effectively? Repeating the same ineffective patterns, rather than making real breakthroughs in understanding, leads to greater conflict.

Without the right kind of communication between you and your spouse, the entrepreneurial journey will be rougher than it needs to be. Loving, empathic, and helpful communication will energize and support you. Unproductive negative communication will leave you lonely, angry, and overwhelmed. You may wonder about your sanity and the intimacy of your relationship after failing miserably to connect with your spouse. This chapter will show you simple changes you can make in the way you communicate to radically improve the results.

For example, Julia has repeatedly asked her husband, Wesley, to stop walking through the house with his dirty shoes on. He agrees but doesn't follow through. The more often she requests, the more he ignores her, until she nags him almost daily. He complains of being henpecked and she of being ignored. Julia and Wes wonder how they can negotiate more serious life issues together, if they can't even resolve a small disagreement like dirty shoes. A very good question.

When we communicate with our partners as we need them to communicate with us, we often feel frustrated and confused. Julia believes that asking her husband more often will get the desired response, because he will better understand how important a clean home is to her. She doesn't see that Wesley fears losing his independence. Wes needs to avoid taking orders from her, a need stronger than his desire to meet her standards for cleanliness. The more often she asks, the harder he resists. Using the information in this chapter, Julia and Wes can free themselves from their frozen positions, and both will more likely get what they need!

John Gray and Deborah Tannen, couples communication experts, have saved thousands of marriages by publishing their research on communication style differences between men and women. Couples on the verge of divorce report they forgave their partners when able to understand their behavior within the context of male/female dynamics.

The first section of this chapter, "Gender-Related Differences," focuses on solving communication problems, rooted in classic gender style differences.* You will learn how to manage four types of communication events experienced by all entrepreneurial couples, so that you can . . .

- comfort each other in times of distress.
- make requests that get results.
- offer constructive criticism that gets heard.
- connect more intimately, in ways that are meaningful to you.

The second section of this chapter, "Working with an Opposite," focuses on the challenge to working partners whose communication styles differ substantially. Though focused on working couples, anyone who lives or works with an "opposite," even within a corporate setting, can use this information. In section two, you will learn how to . . .

---

*If you are in a gay or lesbian partnership, or if classic gender-related research doesn't seem to apply to your partnership, substitute "right-brain" or "left-brain" for male and female or reverse roles if that seems more applicable.

- communicate effectively when one of you is right-brained and the other is left-brained.
- keep each other informed and make joint decisions.
- share work space when your work styles radically differ.
- plan a work project together.

GENDER-RELATED DIFFERENCES

Comforting Each Other in Times of Distress

One of the benefits of marriage or serious commitment to a significant other is living with a best friend—your sounding board, safe haven, and battery recharge. However, if your partner doesn't understand how you need to complain, solve problems, and be comforted, then your relationship can stress you more than relieve your pain. Too often we give our partners what *we* need in difficult times, rather than what *they* need. Though we mean well, our partners find no comfort in the results.

Life offers a daily series of problems to solve, from the mundane, such as what to wear to work, to the significant, such as how to increase sales. Although we dream of a life without problems, we get some daily satisfaction from solving our problems. When you live with a partner and children, your problems are not just your own. Your worries, complaints, and frustrations affect those dearest to you.

Georgia and Kurt are not responding effectively to the other's distress. When Georgia drags herself home after a horrendous day at work, she experiences the following unhelpful conversation with her husband:

I. Georgia: Somebody should shoot the idiot I work for. He treats me like a slave, and I can't take it anymore. The commute to work is driving me crazy. There are so many trucks on the Interstate. God, I'm so tired, I don't know how I'm going to make dinner tonight. Damn it! Andrew left his coat on the floor again. I'm sick and tired of cleaning up after everyone. No one ever helps me around here.

A. Georgia means: "I want empathy, support, a listening ear, and appreciation. I need to hear something like: 'Gee honey, it sounds as if you've had an awful day. You work so hard, you must be exhausted. Is there anything I can do to help?'"

B. Kurt hears: "She wants me to solve the problem for her."

Kurt responds:

II. Kurt: Don't you think you take things too personally at work? If it's so bad for you, why don't you just quit?

A. Kurt means: "I hate to see you this upset. It's OK with me if you quit your job, even if it would be hard on the family. I don't want you to have a nervous breakdown."

B. Georgia hears: "If you didn't take things so personally, there wouldn't be a problem. This is all your fault."

Georgia responds:

III. Georgia: You know I can't quit. We need the money. Don't accuse me of overreacting. I hate when you do that. If you could see the kind of abuse I put up with at work, you'd understand.

A. Georgia means: "I need validation and reassurance. I expect you to support me and say something like: 'You're right—no one should have to put up with that kind of crap. I'm sorry you feel you can't quit your job right now. It's really hard on you supporting the family while I get my business going. Let me give you a hug!'"

B. Kurt hears: "This is all your fault. If it wasn't for that stupid company of yours, I could quit my job and every thing would be fine."

Kurt responds:

IV. Kurt: I've had horrible bosses too. Sometimes you just have to toughen up and not let them get to you.

A. Kurt means: "I'm sorry that you can't quit your job and it's because my company isn't doing well enough yet. I know you are strong enough to handle a lousy boss. If you do what I've done in the past, when I've been in the same situation, maybe you'd feel better."

B. Georgia hears: "I've had a lousy boss too, and I had no problem dealing with him. You're just too much of a wimp."

What went wrong? Georgia wants to vent her misery and receive emotional support. Exasperated, she lets her husband know about four problems in the first thirty seconds. She doesn't really expect him to solve any of them. Complaining makes her feel better, even if some of the problems have no immediate solution. She exaggerates with expressions like "I can't take it anymore" because she is feeling overwhelmed and exhausted. She needs reassurance of her strength and to be assisted with something practical like cooking dinner that evening.

Kurt responds by giving her what he thinks she needs the most—a solution to her worst problem and reassurance that her problems aren't so bad. That's what he would want. He thinks her cry, "I can't take it anymore" signals an impending nervous breakdown, so he offers her permission to quit her job. He's trying to be helpful.

Georgia and Kurt can each improve their communication by making some small changes.

Georgia needs to:

- Reassure Kurt that she's really OK, even though it was an awful day.
- Tell Kurt clearly that she's looking for a listening ear, not a solution to her problems.
- Ask for help in the kitchen when she needs it.
- Complain to Kurt about a few things at a time.

Kurt needs to:

- Recognize Georgia's unspoken request for comfort and reassurance.
- Listen empathically and show concern.

- Remember that Georgia has always pulled out of it when she's hit a wall in the past.
- Remind himself that he is not responsible for fixing Georgia's problems.

A slight shift in Kurt's response will dramatically improve his ability to comfort Georgia when she is distressed. The following scene between Georgia and Kurt illustrates how a slight shift in Georgia's response to Kurt can also improve her ability to comfort him in distress.

Neck-deep in employee problems at his manufacturing plant, Kurt fired his vice president of operations for sexual harassment when several of the women in the plant threatened to sue. On a particularly harsh day, he gets home at 8:00 P.M. and just wants to bury himself in the newspaper, have a drink, and go to bed.

I.   Georgia: How was your day?

   A. Georgia means: "You are looking really upset and I'm worried about you. What happened today?"

   B. Kurt hears: "She's in one of those moods to talk, and I don't feel like it."

Kurt responds:

II. Kurt: Rough.

   A. Kurt means: "Please leave me alone to solve my problems by myself. I don't want to talk about it right now."

   B. Georgia hears: "It was so bad I will need some prodding to be able to open up to you."

Georgia responds:

III. Georgia: I can tell you're upset. If you tell me about it, maybe I can help. Burying yourself in the newspaper won't solve anything. Besides, just because you had a rotten day, you don't have to take it out on me.

A. Georgia means: "I hate to see you suffering and I want to make you feel better. It scares me and makes me angry when you pull away from me."

B. Kurt hears: "You have no right to be alone. Take care of making me feel better, along with whatever else is bothering you." He would rather hear something like, "I know you're having a rough time at the plant. If you want to talk about it, I'm here." Or, "I know you like to have your space when you're upset about work. Would you like to have dinner in an hour or so?"

IV. Kurt responds: Can't a guy get any peace and quiet?

What went wrong? While women usually feel better talking about what's bothering them, men often pull away to mull over the problem in silence. John Gray refers to the place they go as their "cave." Georgia is trying to help Kurt the way she would like him to respond to her, but her approach is not what he needs.

Men can often become distant and preoccupied when troubled, and therefore emotionally unavailable to their mates or family until they solve the problem. This behavior triggers fear and resentment in their female partners, who try to pull their husbands out of their caves, to make themselves feel better. Their efforts backfire, as the man retreats farther back into his cave and resents her intrusion.

Georgia needs to:

- Support Kurt's need for privacy.
- Let Kurt know she is available if he wants company, and then get on with her life so he doesn't have to worry about making her happy, along with all of his other problems.
- Refrain from punishing him or making a scene because he pulled away.
- Trust Kurt's ability to solve his own problems.

Kurt needs to:

- Reassure Georgia that he wants to be alone temporarily, but he'll be back.

- Appreciate her intrusiveness as a well-intended gesture to help.
- Reassure Georgia that his upset has nothing to do with her.
- Ask for the space that he needs, and thank her for giving it to him.

Both Georgia and Kurt have enormous power to help each other solve daily problems, if they can learn how to listen and communicate in the way that supports their partner's natural problem-solving process.

Making Requests that Are Heard and Responded To

When I was single, I did everything for myself. No one really needed or demanded anything of me, a huge difference from living with a spouse and family. Though I may fantasize about having no demands on my time other than what I choose to have, accommodating reasonable requests for assistance from my husband, children, and stepchildren is part of what it means to be a wife and mother. One of the benefits of marriage is that I also have people to ask for assistance. The key, I have learned, is to ask for help in ways that are not received as a demand.

Here are some simple techniques for getting the assistance you want or need. This section addresses the myriad of requests we make of each other to handle household and business details. For example:

Would you call the printer and ask what's holding up the sales literature?

Would you put the baby down for her nap?

Would you take these bills over to the post office?

Would you cook dinner tonight?

Men genuinely want to meet their partners' needs. They also need control over how they spend their time. Ironically, the easier you make it for a man to say no, the more willing he seems to be to say yes.

CLARIFICATION EXERCISE ONE: HOW I SOLVE PROBLEMS BEST
Completion time: 5 minutes.

How can your intimate partner best facilitate, and not frustrate, your problem-solving process? Complete the following questions, in the presence of your partner, and see for yourselves. Choose either *a* or *b* for the following statements:

la. When I have a problem on my mind, I tend to want to be alone to think about it.

b. When I have a problem on my mind, I generally want to talk about it.

2a. I don't even mention most problems to my spouse, unless my spouse presses me.

b. I tell all about the problems of my day, if my spouse is available to listen.

3a. I don't like to talk about a problem with my spouse unless I am asking for help to solve the problem directly.

b. I use my spouse as a sounding board when I want to think something out. I don't necessarily want my partner to solve the problem for me.

4a. I tend to focus on one problem at a time, so I don't get overwhelmed.

b. I usually think about several problems at the same time.

5a. I approach problem solving systematically, breaking problems down and analyzing them, and then looking for a rational solution.

b. I approach problem solving holistically, relying often on my intuition, as well as objective data, to reach a solution.

Discuss your differences and similarities and how they affect your daily communication with each other.

Men generally dislike when their partners:[†]	Try this instead:
Make a request that is really a demand, taking away his freedom to say no without being a "bad guy."	List household chores and star tasks where you need help. Discuss it at a time that works for him. Let him decide when to do something and leave him alone, unless you need something by a certain time.
Ask him to do something when he's in the middle of doing something else.	Don't interrupt him when he's concentrating, relaxing, and clearly doesn't want to be disturbed.
Ask him to do something by a certain time, without respecting his time frame for accomplishing it.	Don't bombard him with demands as soon as he comes in the door from work. When he's receptive, then start phrases with, "It would be great if. . . ," or "I'd love it if you would. . . ," or " I know you have a lot to do, but would you. . ."
Don't trust that he will take care of something he promised to do and repeatedly ask whether he's going to do it (nag).	Pick your best shots and postpone some requests for help, or skip them altogether, if it seems as though he is already feeling overwhelmed or not in a receptive mood.
Don't appreciate all he has already done with a thank you or acknowledgment, but rather bombard him with more requests.	Express more appreciation for what he has done, and complain less about what he hasn't.

---

†These general but mostly true statements come from my interviews with entrepreneurial couples and what I have learned living with my husband, Stephen.

[continued]

Men generally dislike when their partners:	Try this instead:
Act entitled to his positive response to your request, as if he owes it to you.	Ask "Will you . . ." rather than "Can you . . . ," since using the phrase "Can you" may suggest that you question his competence, rather than his willingness.
Pester him to do something he doesn't view as important or worth his time.	Accept his refusal of requests graciously, without a scene. Cut him some slack if he doesn't follow through exactly as promised.

Women genuinely want to meet their partners' needs. They also need to feel appreciated and to receive emotional and practical support at times. Generally, the more you give a woman, the more she will give back.

Women generally dislike it when their partners:	Try this instead:
Take them for granted and don't express appreciation.	Women love to feel cherished and appreciated. Express loving sentiments to her often, and she will be much more eager to fulfill your requests.
Act as if it's a big deal that he does one thing—like go to work every day—when she's doing twenty things a day.	Don't overload a woman with requests until she burns out. She may have trouble saying no until she has reached the point of exhaustion or resentment.
Don't offer to help with anything unless asked.	Do little romantic things for her like you used to when you were courting.

[continued]

Women generally dislike it when their partners:	**Try this instead:**
Assume that certain household and child-care jobs are "women's work."	Volunteer to help her with something without being asked.
Make a scene and act annoyed when she makes a simple request.	When she makes a request you can honor, smile and say "Sure, honey," instead of grumbling.
Ask for, or demand, sex without giving anything in return.	Give her plenty of physical affection.

Do you know what specific actions and expressions are the most effective for eliciting a positive response from your partner?

CLARIFICATION EXERCISE TWO: ELICITING POSITIVE RESPONSE TO REQUESTS

Complete the following sentences, and ask your partner to do the same.

1. I feel the most cooperative and respond the best to your requests when you _____ (positive actions). For example: give me a hug, thank me, give me sex.
2. I feel the most cooperative and respond the best to your requests when you refrain from _____ (actions). For example: nagging me, interrupting me when I am busy, lecturing.

Criticizing Your Partner and Asking for Change

We enter an intimate relationship hoping for unconditional love and acceptance. In our early romance, we focus on the positive aspects of our partner's character and ignore or are charmed by the idiosyncrasies that later become a source of irritation.

Delivering and receiving criticism in an intimate relationship can be our most painful communication challenge.

Sometimes you will speak critically to your partner directly and there will be no mistaking your message: *I'm sick and tired of you being late for dinner, and I want you to come home earlier.* Other times your critical message may be more indirect. Deborah Tannen stresses the importance of understanding the "metamessages of communication," that is, what we communicate through body language, tone of voice, how the words are spoken. These nonverbals often convey a deeper message than the words themselves. For example:

Request for change: Would you change the shirt you are wearing?

Metamessage the person hears: You are unattractive and it would embarrass me to be seen in public with you.

Interpretation: You don't love me the way that I am.

If the person delivering the request uses a disgusted or demanding tone, then the communication shifts from being about the shirt to being about love and approval.

Here's another example of a critical metamessage. Take the three letter word, *Why?* This innocuous word causes difficulty when it's used to convey indirect criticism. Most people react defensively when asked "Why . . . ?":

Question: Why did you mail this bill out late?

Metamessage: I don't approve of this bill going out late. I wouldn't have done that. You better have a good explanation.

Alternatives to asking "why," such as, "could you explain to me," or "how come," or "what do you think about. . . ," help soften the metamessage of interrogation and disapproval. It's also helpful to explain why you are asking the question. For example, "I am keeping track of our cash flow this month. I notice that you mailed the electric bill out late. Could you explain to me why, so that I can keep better control over our cash?"

One of men's greatest complaints about women is their tendency to become what John Gray refers to as a "Home Improvement Committee." To help their partners achieve their full potential, women often nurture their partners with a constant barrage of well-meaning suggestions and unsolicited advice. "Why don't you . . ." or "If you did this instead . . . ," or "Don't forget to. . . ." The overriding message to a man of constant requests for improvement is that she does not accept or love him as he is. By questioning his competence, he feels untrusted to take care of himself or his partner.

Helpful Hints for Managing Critical Communication

Weigh the pros and cons of criticism. Will the criticism help your partner? Is it a behavior that he or she is able to or likely to change? Do the possible benefits of speaking up outweigh the potential negative response from your partner? Keep quiet if a negative outcome is predictable.

Timing is everything. If possible, plan the time and place of your requests for change. Don't speak your mind whenever the impulse grabs you, if the moment is the worst time for your partner to hear your comments. Keep your primary goal in mind—to influence a change, not just vent a frustration.

Communicate critical feedback with "I" messages, and direct suggestions for a solution. Which complaint will likely result in positive change?

a. All you ever do is work. I don't even know why you bother coming home. Why don't you pay some attention to your family for a change?
b. When you work late into the evening, I feel lonely and ignored by you. I really miss spending time together. Can we schedule some time together this evening?

Sentence *a* will likely generate a defensive reaction and it doesn't tell the receiver how to solve the problem. Sentence *b* is more likely to create a loving and open response in the receiver by assuring him or her that a few hours of scheduled time that evening would be enough to satisfy the complaint.

Avoid late-night problem solving if possible. Women often have difficulty sleeping with an unresolved complaint between them and their partner, but men hate talking late at night when they are tired. They fear the discussion will go on endlessly and insufficient sleep will lead to an unproductive workday the next day. Postpone discussions of a critical nature until the right time for both of you. If you feel you must speak your peace before going to bed, get your partner's agreement for a time-limited, simple, and direct conversation.

Wait for your partner to ask for help. Your partner may ask for advice regarding how to change problematic behavior when you accept who he or she is right now. Create a feeling of safety for your partner, and he or she may come around. Your partner will change a problem behavior if self-motivated, not just in reaction to a complaint. Be patient.

Learn to let some things pass. Your relationship and the quality of your life together will disintegrate if you process every issue and confront every conflict. Talking about every complaint won't resolve every difference. Keep silent sometimes and bite your tongue.

Encourage and notice positive change. When children learn how to walk, we celebrate every clumsy attempt to move on wobbly legs. They soon practice the skill more often to get the applause. Adults need the same positive reinforcement of progress, no matter how small. If you demand a change of your partner and fail to acknowledge any improvement, then your partner will quickly develop a "why bother" attitude when you register your next complaint.

Connecting in Ways that Are Meaningful to Your Partner

The last time you went to the zoo you may have bought a twenty-five-cent bag of corn kernels to feed the giraffes. Would you get excited about a bag of corn kernels? Of course not, it's not your food of choice. To the giraffe, there's nothing better. Imagine that your partner is an animal from another kingdom. He or she may be nurtured, sustained, and excited by very different experiences than you are. The secret to meaningful connection is to know what to put in the paper bag that will get your partner salivating!

Expressing and Feeling Love

If you don't learn how your partner feels loved, you will automatically demonstrate love in the ways you want to receive love. Because your needs differ, neither of you will get what you are looking for. "If he really loved me, he would tell me more often." "If she really loved me, we would have sex more often." A sentence that begins with, "If my partner really loved me," expresses your need to be loved in a certain way.

You may have resented your partner because he didn't properly appreciate significant efforts of yours to express your love, only to discover that something else you did that took you no time at all was received with great enthusiasm. It is especially painful when efforts to be *loving* are actually interpreted as *unloving* behavior. For example:

> I couldn't wait to see my husband at the end of a workday. As soon as he pulled in the driveway, I had dinner waiting, and I was eager to talk to him about the day. My husband hurt my feelings when he told me he felt smothered. He preferred for me to delay dinner for an hour, so he could read the newspaper when he got home. How could he love me if he doesn't even look forward to seeing me?

> My wife is a great cook. Every night I come home to a gourmet meal. I should be grateful, but I've been trying to lose a few pounds, and it's impossible when she's feeding me all the time. I've tried to tell her that I would prefer simpler meals, but she doesn't really get it. She thinks she is loving me by serving me meals fit for a king—and his entire army!

> My husband is Mr. Fix-it. He spends all weekend working around the house. I appreciate being married to such a handyman, but I wish he would spend a little more time with me and less time with his tools and gadgets. If I got as much attention as his hammer, I'd be a lot happier!

Here are four secrets to expressing love to your partner in the most effective way.

1: Pay attention to what really works and what doesn't work, and give your partner more of what works for him or her.
2: Don't resent or judge your partner for being turned on and off by different experiences than you. No method of receiving nurturance is superior to another.
3: Express love as a daily habit. Don't wait for a good time or pour it on once a month. Find a way, every day, to let your partner know he or she is loved, appreciated, and cherished.
4: Timing is critical. Sometimes it's not what you do, but when you do it that counts. Connect with your mate on his or her schedule and you'll get better results.

You may be surprised when you discover how your spouse prefers to be loved. I feel most loved when my husband Stephen makes an effort to connect with me. Stephen often feels most loved when I give him space and independence. If you catch yourself thinking, "If my partner really loved me, he or she would know what I need," STOP and do this exercise instead. You have a much better chance of feeling satisfied by telling your partner exactly what you want than by demanding that your partner figure it out alone.

CLARIFICATION EXERCISE THREE: HOW I LIKE TO BE LOVED
Completion time: 10 minutes.

Number each of the following expressions of love according to the following scale. Then compare your responses with your partner.

1 = That behavior does nothing for me. In fact, it can turn me off.
2 = That behavior is neutral for me—it doesn't hurt, but it doesn't help.
3 = That behavior makes me feel somewhat loved and appreciated.
4 = Most of the time that behavior makes me feel really loved.
5 = That behavior always makes me feel sensational and much closer to you.

1. Written expressions of affection—notes, poems, cards.
2. Receiving a personalized gift, just because you were thinking of me.
3. Receiving a gift for my birthday or our anniversary.
4. Spending private intimate time with me.
5. Giving me a massage or a neck rub.
6. Sex.
7. Creating a special meal.
8. Calling me at work just to say "Hi" or to share something exciting.
9. Telling me that you love me.
10. Being affectionate in public.
11. Confiding in me your deepest feelings and secrets.
12. Telling me all the details of your day, after we've been apart.
13. Giving me space and privacy when I need it.
14. Listening to me attentively when I need to talk.
15. Keeping the household in working order.
16. Accepting me for who I am and letting me know.
17. Admiring me and telling me why you love and respect me.
18. Admiring me and telling others why you love and respect me.
19. Encouraging me when I am down.
20. Hugging, cuddling, and other physical expressions of affection.
21. Surprising me with a secret date or romantic rendezvous.
22. Offering to help me with household chores or the kids.
23. Keeping the house clean.
24. Complimenting me on my appearance.
25. Forgiving me when I've made a mistake.
26. Apologizing to me when you've hurt me.
27. Checking with me before you make plans that will affect me.
28. Talking about our future together, sharing your dreams.
29. Other: _____

WORKING WITH AN OPPOSITE

Working Together as Partners

Couples who work together usually have extraordinary communication challenges. They must learn how to manage different communication styles and to take advantage of complementary skills—or they can find themselves in divorce or bankruptcy court.

This section highlights the communication issues that predictably arise if you are a predominantly right-brained individual partnered in business with a primarily left-brained mate. The good news: Your business team is stronger and more complete. The bad news: You often need a translator or mediator to communicate.

As you read the following composite of a typical team profile, switch the *he* to *she* or the *she* to *he* to best describe your situation.

He is right-brained. He's the visionary, the idea man, the dreamer, the creative one. He's always in the middle of several projects at once, and he likes it that way. When we're at work, he wants to talk, talk, talk. He doesn't pay attention to details. He makes decisions intuitively, not always considering the facts. His highs are high, and his lows are low. He prefers to be spontaneous. Too much planning in his day will drive him nuts. He'll start a project, but if it goes on too long, he'll get bored or discouraged.

She is left-brained. She is the anchor that holds down the ship. She keeps the checkbook balanced and makes sure that business decisions are made with the facts in mind. She keeps the office in order and sets up routines and systems to organize the day. She brings logical, analytical thought to problem solving. She works best when able to focus on one project at a time. She makes sure that a long-term project gets finished. She encourages her husband over the long haul when he gets discouraged.

The Challenges of Working with an Opposite and How They Can Become Advantages

Making Decisions

The challenge: Right-brainers (RBs) who decide intuitively are frustrated by left-brainers (LBs) who focus on facts. LBs who decide rationally may fret when their RB partners make a spontaneous illogical decision.

The advantage: RBs learn to appreciate the "devil's advocate" position of their LB spouse. LBs come to admire their RB partner's creative ability to promote business growth.

Who Does What

The challenge: Working partners must share decision making and job responsibilities.

The advantage: Rather than arguing about "who does what better," RB and LB couples usually have very clear and distinct job descriptions, capitalizing on their individual strengths.

Sharing Work Space

The challenge: RBs and LBs usually disagree about what constitutes the perfect work environment. LBs want privacy, an organized office, and systems to rely on. RBs like someone to talk to, organized chaos, and clutter.

The advantage: If RBs and LBs can work in separate offices and meet throughout the day to converse, each can learn to respect the other's work space and style. Certain aspects of business development and operations lend themselves better to an LB or RB ideal setting.

Meetings

The challenge: RBs would prefer to keep meetings spontaneous, informal, and frequent. LBs like having at least one scheduled meeting a day, or week, with a planned agenda to keep on track.

The advantage: Sound business communication requires both forms of communication. If two RB's pair together, they may neglect planning details. If two LB's pair together, they could lose spontaneous inspiration.

The Seesaw

The challenge: The emotional experience of their partner frustrates or puzzles RBs and LBs. Why is LB making a mountain out of a molehill? Why is RB talking about closing the business down, just because it's been a slow month?

The advantage: RBs and LBs are rarely discouraged at the same time. What triggers one into despair or negativity bounces off of the other, and vice versa. When RBs and LBs move from judgment to compassion, they can lift each other up like partners on a seesaw.

Planning a Work Project Together

The challenge: RBs are impatient and resistant to LBs slow analytical thinking. They want to plan several projects at once and are often looking five years ahead. LBs prefer to carefully plan one project at a time. LBs may share a dream for five years ahead, but spend meetings talking about the practical details of how to make here and now work.

The advantage: An RB/LB team can handle long-range planning and current details, simultaneously. RBs don't sacrifice visioning and planning for the future for managing day-to-day operations. They encourage progress. LBs keep the company solvent and successful, building a foundation for future growth.

CONCLUSION

Most RB/LB entrepreneurial couples who thrive come to appreciate their differences. They offer these words of wisdom:

Trust each other, and respect each other's skills and experience.

Assume that your partner has positive intentions, even if the way he or she goes about getting something accomplished is foreign to you.

Concentrate on the positive results of working together, even if it makes the process more difficult at times.

Compromise is important, but let each of you get your own way some of the time.

Take the time to express appreciation to your partner for

the contribution his or her unique work style makes to the business.

Keep your sense of humor, and don't take your fights too seriously.

You both can be right.

Perfect communication between two human beings, no matter how much you love each other, is an unrealistic goal. In a thriving marriage, improving your communication with each other is a lifelong process. Perhaps at the deepest level, most daily communication with our intimate partner amounts to "Do you love me enough?" "Do you accept me completely the way that I am?" and "Do you trust me?"

RECOMMENDED RESOURCES

Books

He and She Talk: How to Communicate with the Opposite Sex by Laurie Schloff and Marcia Yudkin. Plume, 1993.

Men Are from Mars, Women Are from Venus: A Practical Guide for Improving Communication and Getting What You Want in Your Relationships by John Gray, Ph.D. HarperCollins, 1992.

Secrets About Men Every Woman Should Know by Barbara DeAngelis, Ph.D. Dell, 1990.

Talking from 9 To 5: How Women's and Men's Conversational Styles Affect Who Gets Heard, Who Gets Credit, and What Gets Done at Work by Deborah Tannen, Ph.D. William Morrow and Co., 1994.

That's Not What I Meant: How Conversational Style Makes or Breaks Relationships by Deborah Tannen, Ph.D. Ballantine, 1986.

What Really Works with Men: Solve 95% of Your Relationship Problems (and Cope with the Rest) by A. Justin Sterling. Warner, 1992.

When Opposites Attract: Right Brain/Left Brain Relationships and How to Make Them Work by Rebecca Cutter. Dutton, 1994.

Why Men Are the Way They Are: The Male-Female Dynamic by Warren Farrell, Ph.D. Berkley Books, 1986.

You Just Don't Understand: Women and Men in Conversation by Deborah Tannen, Ph.D. Ballantine, 1990.

Software

Me2: Easy to use software that can help you and your spouse understand the root of your frustrations with your work or each other. Explores your approach toward work and relationships. Available for MAC or IBM. For more information, call 800-TRUE-ME2.

Audiotape

The Magic of Differences, self-help tapes for couples and singles. Contact Judith Sherven, Ph.D., or Jim Sniechowski, Ph.D., at 12021 Wilshire Boulevard #692, Los Angeles, CA 90025, or call 310-829-3353.

6

Win/Win Conflict Resolution

Resolving Conflict at Work and at Home

In the beginning of our marriage, my wife and I couldn't decide how many pencils to order without questioning whether we should be married to each other. When I wanted to order office supplies in a smaller quantity than she, she accused me of being cheap. When she bought fresh flowers for the office staff, I complained she was being extravagant. We didn't trust each other, and every business decision became a forum for debating whether we should be married, instead of running a business.

Manufacturing business partners

I quit my job in my husband's store for four months, because I was sick of being unappreciated and taken for granted. Once when my husband was mad at me, he told me that no one would ever hire me. So I went and got another job in a week, just to prove him wrong. He apologized when he learned how difficult it was to manage the store without me. Now he's more conscious about expressing appreciation.

Wife of retail store owner

A *definition of conflict:* Webster's dictionary narrowly defines conflict as a fight or battle. The word *conflict* may lead you to think of a nasty fight with your spouse, or a mild disagreement over where to eat dinner. I've created this working definition of conflict: *An unresolved, or potentially unresolvable, disagreement between two people or parties that requires some resolution to ease tension, maintain goodwill, and strengthen the relationship.*

Why is there conflict between us, and what leads to it? Dr. Robert Schwebel, clinical psychologist and author, sees marital conflict rooted in power struggle:

> Most couples have no idea how to stay close when the going gets rough, and no awareness that it is possible to remain a team and to solve problems together. They lack a vision of cooperatively sharing power. We are thoroughly programmed to compete and to feel comfortable in power-based relationships—one person on top and the other on bottom. We tend to approach conflict as adversaries pitted against one another. We see the world as either I win and you lose, or you win and I lose. Or we hope to sidestep a power struggle by trying to avoid all conflict. In the long run, this eventually leads to even more trouble. (Schwebel, *Who's on Top, Who's on Bottom*, page 15)

Studies of thousands of couples reveal: "It is not how similar or different you are, it's how you handle differences when they arise that counts" (Notarius and Markman, *We Can Work It Out*, page 21). Interestingly enough, researchers Markman, Stanley, and Blumberg report that the way in which couples handle disagreement predicts with 93 percent accuracy whether the couple will remain married (Markman, Stanley, and Blumberg, *Fighting for Your Marriage*, page 5). When one of you wins an argument, and the other loses, you both lose to some extent. Mastering conflict resolution skills can protect your marriage as well as your business.

This chapter will coach you through some simple techniques for preventing and managing conflict, so that you reach win/win resolutions more often than not, avoiding or settling disputes in a way that allows both of you to feel satisfied.

Four Different Kinds of Conflict

In my coaching business and marriage, I have noticed that marital and business conflicts fall into four general categories:

1. *Taking responsibility*: Discord that you can mitigate alone by changing your own attitude or behavior.
2. *Preventable conflict*: Tension that is preventable with the help of clear agreements and understandings.
3. *Negotiated compromise:* Conflict that requires negotiation to resolve.
4. *Complex conflict*: Arguments that trigger deep emotional wounds, requiring outside help or refined communication skills to resolve.

LET IT BEGIN WITH ME: WHAT YOU CAN DO ALONE TO RESOLVE CONFLICT

Change Your Attitude, Not Your Spouse

We generally seek advice on conflict resolution for spousal transformation: how we can change our partners. We see ourselves as fair and reasonable and them as stubborn and irrational. Have you ever uttered, "If only my partner would . . ." We need a great deal of self-discipline and self-awareness to stop pointing fingers and start looking inward at how we contribute to the problem.

Rather than fretting over how we can change our partner's behavior, we might ponder how we can alter our attitude so that our partner's behavior no longer troubles us. A simple change in expression such as, "I would *prefer* if you . . . " rather than "I *need* you to . . ." can shift a destructive battle to a supportive discussion. The first step in resolving disagreement or tension is to examine how we can shift our own thinking or acting.

Resolving Conflict Through Acceptance and Positive Self-Talk

Sometimes the only resolution to a disagreement is for one of you to accept that the other will not or cannot alter a particular problematic behavior. Repeated confrontation proves only to be a waste of precious energy.

My husband, Stephen, works hard during the day. By early evening he's exhausted and often falls asleep by 9:00 P.M.—sometimes in the middle of a conversation. Early in our life together, I felt insulted or angry when he fell asleep during an important discussion or dozed off as we tried to watch a movie together. The only real way for me to resolve the tension this often caused was to accept that Stephen was not in conscious control of his fatigue and that he was doing the best he could.

To change my attitude about Stephen's sleep habits, I needed to change my internal monologue, without Stephen's involvement at all.

"Should" self-talk: Stephen shouldn't be so rude he falls asleep in the middle of an important conversation!

Positive self-talk: Stephen is usually a courteous listener. Too bad he's too tired to listen to me now. I'll wait until a better time for him.

"Always/Never" self-talk: Stephen always falls asleep when we're watching a movie together. I don't know why we even bother to rent a movie at all.

Positive self-talk: It's too bad Stephen fell asleep. I enjoy watching the movie more when we watch it together.

"Hopeless" self-talk: God, no matter how much sleep Stephen gets, he's always tired. What's he going to be like when he gets old? He'll probably sleep half the day!

Positive self-talk: Maybe there are some herbal remedies that would help Stephen stay awake longer. We should check out the health food store.

"Character assassination" self-talk: He's just like his father. He falls asleep in a chair halfway through the evening.

Positive self-talk: Poor guy has the same genes as his father. It's hard for him to stay awake at night (Notarius and Markman reveal these forms of destructive self-talk to be the most common instigators of relationship conflict. *We Can Work It Out*, page 148).

If you note those expressions that you say to yourself when your spouse irritates you, then your hostility might surprise you. No wonder a minor annoyance escalates to a major complaint. Your emotional and physical responses are natural manifestations of your internal thoughts.

SKILL-BUILDING EXERCISE ONE: ACCEPTANCE OF DIFFERENCES—CHANGING YOUR SELF-TALK

Use this exercise for any business associate or member of your family.

- What ongoing conflicts in your life will you best resolve by accepting another person's behavior, rather than trying to change it? (This exercise is not appropriate for physical, sexual, or verbal violence.)
- Select a current conflict that introduces negative energy into your home or business. Start with annoying behavior—"He leaves the toilet seat up"—not severely problematic behavior—"He drinks too much." For one week, practice accepting the behavior rather than trying to change it. When your urge to complain or advise arises, jot your inner dialogue down on a piece of paper instead of communicating aloud and directly to the person. Whenever possible, shift from destructive to positive self-talk.
- If you get positive results (more tolerance and less stress), then continue the exercise for another week with the same behavior or a new, more challenging one.

Most of us recognize the well known Serenity Prayer: "God grant me the serenity to accept the things that cannot change, courage to change the things I can, and the wisdom to know the difference." The prayer does not begin, "God grant my husband or wife the ability to change. . . ."

As a gift to my husband, I wrote the following Couple's Serenity Prayer.

SKILL-BUILDING EXERCISE TWO: COUPLE'S SERENITY PRAYER
(You can also use this exercise for business associates and other members of your family.)

God grant me the serenity to choose:
Acceptance over **A**nger
Believing in over **B**laming
Compassion over **C**riticism
Delight over **D**isdain
Encouraging over **E**nabling
Forgiveness over **F**ighting
Gratitude over **G**riping
Harmony over **H**ostility
Intimacy over **I**nsult
Joint problem solving over **J**udgment
Kindness over **K**illing
Listening over **L**eaving
Mutual interests over **M**y own
Negotiation over **N**agging
Openness over **O**bstinacy
Patience over **P**ickiness
Quality over **Q**uarreling
Resourcefulness over **R**igidity
Sacrifice over **S**elf-centeredness
Trusting over **T**error
Understanding over **U**nreasonableness
Validation over **V**enting
Wonder over **W**orry
e**X**citement over e**X**asperation
Yielding over **Y**elling
energi**Z**ing over polari**Z**ing
And the grace to apologize to my partner when I don't.

Starting with this week, choose **A**cceptance over **A**nger as your theme for communicating with your partner over the next week, then progress through the alphabet for the following twenty-five weeks. Substitute your own favorite words as you prefer.

When you catch yourself slipping into negative self-talk or engaging in a negative interaction with your spouse, repeat the relevant weekly affirmation silently to help you shift your mood.

Resolving Conflict by Acknowledging Projection

Sometimes changing your inner dialogue isn't enough. Understanding where the dialogue really originated is most important. Unwarranted criticism of your spouse can signal your judgment of yourself or another significant relationship from your past. Rather than pushing your spouse to change, you can identify and claim responsibility for the true source of tension. Sometimes other family members can help you see the projection you aren't aware of yourself.

> Whenever my husband worked late, I would give him the cold shoulder or whine and complain. I felt guilty for not being more supportive, but I couldn't help being enraged with him. One day my sister pointed out to me that my dad, also an entrepreneur, was absent all the time too when we were growing up. Then it all made sense. I wasn't just furious with my husband— I was also angry with my dad for not being around when I was a child.
>
> *Supportive spouse of an international businessman*

> When my wife decided to start her own business I thought it was going to be a little part-time thing that would bring in some extra cash and keep her busy. After a year she was suddenly running a big business. I started finding fault with everything about her and her company. Our marriage counselor pointed out to me that I was projecting onto my wife anger toward myself for not achieving my own goals. I got back to work on my

own career and started feeling better about myself—and my wife—again.

Supportive husband of clothing
manufacturer

If you acknowledge your own projected anger, then your partner will likely work *with* you instead of against you. An apology for any undeserved hostility and discussion of its roots puts blame where you can address it more effectively—*not* on your spouse! Often a marriage counselor must help you through deep-seated projection.

Eliminating Trigger Points

My husband, Stephen, knows how to anger me every time. When I make a request of him, all he has to do is roll his eyes and say "Yes, Dear," or "yeah, yeah, yeah," in a worn-out, annoyed tone of voice, implying that I am nagging him and he'd rather not hear it. When he does that, I immediately get defensive and angry at the implication that my request is unreasonable or that I'm a nuisance.

All of us have trigger points—or hot buttons—when a simple expression or behavior of our spouse hurts or enrages us in seconds. We all notice the power that we wield over our spouse in the same way, and we may even use our partner's hot spots to punish or control when we feel vulnerable.

The cost of exploiting your spouse's vulnerability is lost intimacy and trust in the relationship. Eliminate the charged expressions and behaviors that hurt or annoy your spouse, and ask that your spouse do the same for you. In his research with married couples, Dr. John Gottman discovered that you need at least five times as many positive as negative moments together to stabilize your marriage (Gottman, *Why Marriages Succeed or Fail*, page 29). The following exercise helps eliminate such negative expressions and erosive habits.

SKILL-BUILDING EXERCISE THREE: ELIMINATING NEGATIVE BEHAVIORS THAT TRIGGER YOUR SPOUSE

Completion time: 15 minutes.

The twenty expressions or behaviors below seem to have universal negative impact on communication. Here's how to use this exercise to help eliminate them.

1. Scan the list with your partner. Using a scale of 1 to 5, where 1=almost never and 5=frequently, first score *your perception* of how frequently you use these expressions or behaviors with your partner. Then score how often your partner uses these expressions or behaviors with you. Remember, you are rating *your perception* of the frequency, not taking an accurate count. If a particular behavior is a big problem for you, you may score its frequency higher than it actually occurs. Don't waste time arguing with your partner over frequency. For this exercise, perception is reality.
2. Using a scale of 1 to 5, where 1="no big deal" and 5="drives me crazy," rate how bothersome the behavior is for you.
3. Offer to eliminate or reduce for your partner any behaviors of yours that are a 3 or higher on his or her scale. Ask your partner to eliminate any of his or her behaviors that rank a 3 or higher for you.
4. Practice! You and your partner probably won't change these habits overnight. With due diligence, you can stop triggering your partner and decrease explosive conflict.

Expressions and behaviors:	**Frequency score**	**Bothersome score**

1. Rolling eyes and saying "Yes, Dear" in an annoyed tone of voice when your partner makes a request.
2. Yelling, using sarcasm, insults, or name-calling: "You selfish jerk!"
3. Interrupting, not listening, eyes wandering, cutting off conversation.
4. Mind reading, speaking for your partner, making assumptions about what your partner thinks or feels: "You're mad at me because . . ."
5. Offering excuses, explanations, and defensiveness in response to complaint: "I'm late because of traffic—it's not my fault."
6. Responding to criticism by changing the subject—"Well you do (fill in the blank), so my behavior isn't so bad."
7. Using "always/never," exaggerating, blowing trivial issues out of proportion.
8. Making vague general complaints instead of specifics: "You never help around here."
9. Using character assassination instead of speaking directly about the behavior: "You are a (fill in the blank), just like your father."
10. Threatening to exit the relationship, expressing hopelessness about the future.

Expressions and behaviors:	Frequency score	Bothersome score

11. Agreeing to a compromise or solution, but then not following through.
12. Asking questions instead of making statements—"Haven't we talked long enough?"
13. Apologizing insincerely or refusing to apologize.
14. Picking a fight at a bad time, when your partner is tired, distracted, depressed, overwhelmed, or angry—and *you* know it.
15. Running on and on, overwhelming your partner with long-winded complaints.
16. Digging up ancient history or a past issue that you didn't resolve.
17. Leaving the room, the house, the restaurant, hanging up the phone, or abruptly ending the conversation when it gets uncomfortable for you.
18. Complaining about and embarrassing your partner in front of other people.
19. Using the expressions, "You should," or "You have to."
20. Using the expression, "You make me feel (fill in the blank)."

Add to this list any particular expressions or behaviors that you or your spouse engages in that irritate or trigger hot buttons in the other.

Releasing Negative Feelings and Returning to a Loving Space: The Love Letter Technique

No one, except perhaps our parents, can distress us as deeply as our spouses. The price we pay for intimacy is vulnerability. Our partners can hurt us deeply because we intentionally let our guard down and invite them closer than anyone else to us. If you want an emotionally connected marriage, then your spouse will hurt you at times. Harville Hendrix believes that marriage is all about just that: the opportunity to heal old childhood wounds by working through the same wounding with our mates.

John Gray offers a technique, called "The Love Letter," for returning to a loving space after you and your spouse argue (for more detail see Gray, *Men Are from Mars, Women Are from Venus*, page 208).

The Love Letter exercise has three parts and you can do one, two, or all three by yourself.

1. Write a love letter to your mate expressing your feelings of anger, sadness, fear, regret, and love.
2. Write a response letter expressing what you want to hear from your partner (optional).
3. Share your love letter and response letter with your partner (optional).

Address the letter to your partner, starting with your negative feelings and ending with loving ones, which rekindle by writing the letter. I recommend the love letter technique as a method for releasing angry, resentful, or fearful feelings, so that you can resume your conversation later, when you are calmer and emotionally centered. I found the technique helpful when Stephen and I argued a few days before Mother's Day in 1995. Stephen and I were out for a morning walk before our workday began.

Azriela: So what did you have in mind for this weekend? (We often discuss logistics on our walk, but this time I'm also testing him to see if he has any plans for me for Mother's Day.)

Stephen: I'm going to spend a day and a half cleaning out the basement, and then I want to take Sarah to visit my Mom for a while for Mother's Day. What did you have in mind? (Stephen's use of the expression "I'm going to" sounds like he's made firm plans without consulting me.)

Azriela: I have two problems with what you just said. One, your decision to spend most of the weekend cleaning out the basement means that I take care of Sarah most of the weekend. You didn't check with me to see if that would work. (I feel taken for granted.) I'm also feeling disappointed that you didn't mention any plans to celebrate Mother's Day with me, only your mother. (I assume that Stephen has forgotten all about me. I feel hurt and rejected.)

Stephen rolls his eyes and groans. We walk separately around the track for a few laps and when we come back together I ask him to tell me what's wrong. He reluctantly tells me what's on his mind.

Stephen: We have very few weekends left until we move and I don't want to spend much time outside of getting things packed. (I have a problem now because you expect me to give you too much time and attention for Mother's Day. I want a card and a present to be enough to make you happy so that I can get some work done.)

Azriela: (Stephen's assumptions about what I want are inaccurate and I attempt to set him straight.) I don't have a problem with that—I'm not asking that you spend a lot of time with me. I just felt disappointed that you didn't mention anything about celebrating Mother's Day with me when I asked you about the weekend. (I felt as if I didn't matter when you made your weekend plans. I wanted some reassurance and some recognition.)

Stephen: We're just different about the way we treat holidays. You feel entitled to recognition, but when I have a birthday or it's Father's Day, I don't have any expectations. (Your expectations make me feel controlled and frustrated. You should be open to whatever I may do this weekend for Mother's Day. If it's enough to make you happy, great. If it's not, too bad.)

Azriela: (Now I defend myself against his negative judgment.) Just because I said I was feeling disappointed doesn't mean I feel entitled to a big deal on Mother's Day. A card and a gift, or even something as simple as a massage, would have been fine. Now I don't want anything at all, not if it's coming from such a negative place. (That's not true, I still want you to recognize and appreciate me, but I don't want to beg for it. I want you to give me your time or a gift because you love me, not from obligation.)

This fight continued for another twenty minutes, with no resolution and a great deal of distance between us. I went upstairs and cried. Stephen ate his breakfast and went off to work feeling angry and frustrated. I tried Dr. Gray's Love Letter technique during the day to calm myself while Stephen was at work.

Dear Stephen:

I am writing this letter to share my feelings with you.

Anger:

I don't like it when you make plans to work around the house and assume that I will take care of Sarah.

I feel frustrated that the fight escalated this morning and now we're so distant.

I am angry that you think I act entitled since I know you're really judgmental about that.

I feel annoyed that you didn't simply hear my feelings of disappointment and apologize.

I want you to give me a hug, apologize, and tell me that you love me.

Sadness:

I feel disappointed that you didn't mention celebrating Mother's Day with me this weekend.

I am sad that you went off to work feeling angry and we are distant from each other now.

I feel hurt that you think of giving me a gift as an obligation, rather than a desire.

I wanted to have a special Mother's Day celebration.

I want you and me to be back together again tonight.

Fear:

I feel worried that it will take us awhile to recover from this fight.

I am afraid that you think less of me because I want you to remember and acknowledge me.

I feel scared when we escalate so quickly into a fight.

I do not want you to give me anything out of duty or resentful obligation.

I need to know that you still love me.

I want you and me to make up.

Regret:

I feel embarrassed that I overreacted this morning. I should have trusted you.

I am sorry that I set you up from the beginning by asking you about the weekend, rather than just telling you that I hoped we would celebrate Mother's Day together.

I feel ashamed that I need so much reassurance and recognition.

I didn't want my telling you my feelings to turn into a fight.

I want you to forgive me.

Love:

I love you.

I want to trust you more.

I understand that you are doing the best you can with our busy schedule.

I forgive you for not mentioning Mother's Day and for accusing me of feeling entitled.

I appreciate all the ways you show me that you love me.

I thank you for being the kind of guy who makes me one of your highest priorities.

I know that we will come back together soon.

I love you,

Azriela

P.S. The response I would like to hear from you is a hug, a genuine apology for hurting me, acceptance of my need for you to recognize me, and your forgiveness, so that we can return to intimacy.

I left Stephen the letter on his pillow. When he read it before going to sleep, we hugged, and talked calmly about how we misunderstood one another that morning. The letter broke the ice, and we could apologize to each other.

Getting Angry at the Problem, Not Your Spouse

Couples who thrive through the rigors of entrepreneurial life don't stay angry with one another for long. Whether working together in the same business, or partnering to manage the demands of family and self-employment, you need to resolve conflicts quickly. It isn't just the marriage that is at stake, but the health of the business as well. One of the simplest and most powerful shifts you can make as a couple is to focus your anger and frustration on the problems at hand, rather than each other. A small change of words can divert you from a nasty fight.

> My husband was explaining to me why he would have difficulty collecting his expected fee from a client. I felt upset when I heard we probably wouldn't see the money we were expecting. Rather than reflexively blaming him ("Why can't you . . . "), I expressed in frustration: "God, I hate your business. First it's so difficult to get clients. Then when you finally get them, it's still hard to get paid." He just laughed and said, "I don't blame you for feeling that way." He didn't get defensive because I didn't attack him as the problem. I joined his side and empathized with how hard it was for him to collect the money he earned for his efforts.
>
> *Supportive spouse of struggling*
> *business consultant*

Under stressful circumstances, projecting our frustrations and anger on our spouse is easier but more destructive than directing the energy toward the problem itself. Watch for the pattern. If you find yourself growing hostile toward your spouse, ask yourself whether he or she deserves it. Would your anger energize you more productively if directed toward solving the problem or supporting your spouse in problem solving?

PREVENTING CONFLICT: STRATEGIES YOU CAN DO TOGETHER

While you can do plenty to prevent or mitigate conflict without even interacting with your spouse, sometimes involving your spouse is critical to tackling a joint problem.

Preventing Conflict by Joining the Same Team

John Gray postulates that most arguments escalate when a man invalidates a woman's feelings and when a woman responds to a man disapprovingly. A conflict escalates quickly from problem solving to counterattacking when you start blaming *each other* as the problem, rather than joining forces to address a mutual problem. When you both cooperate, rather than try to win the argument, you will likely find a mutually satisfying solution. Which one of the following statements is more likely to solve a problem?

Husband: You're always working and you're neglecting your family. Your job is more important to you than the kids or me.(Attack)

Wife: That's not true! You're just pissed off because I'm not here to wait on you hand and foot anymore. I'm not your maid! (Defense)

or

Husband: When you work so many hours the kids and I miss you.
        (I statement)
Wife: I miss you guys too. How can we find a way to spend
         more time together? (Joint problem solving)

These couples solved stubborn problems by creatively imple-
menting a joint solution, instead of continuing the blame/attack
syndrome:

> I tried helping my husband in his store on weeknights and
> weekends after my full-time job. It drove me nuts trying to
> straighten out his office and the paperwork. I tried to convince
> him that if he kept his office organized he'd be able to work
> fewer hours and be home more with the kids and me. He didn't
> see it that way. After six months, we knew we had to get me out
> of the store if we were going to stay married. We hired him a
> bookkeeper and payroll service to replace me. It was more
> expensive, but worth it!
>
> *Supportive spouse of store owner*

> My husband and I work the same MLM business in tandem,
> rather than as full partners. We each have our own separate
> downlines, even though we sell the same products. We had too
> much difficulty working together as partners. I am *always* on
> time for my appointments but my husband prefers to be spon-
> taneous and he's always running late. Now we take separate cars
> even if we're going to the same event. He gets there when he
> gets there and I don't worry about him being late anymore—
> except when we need to go to the airport together!
>
> *MLM distributor*

Preventing Conflict Through Clarifying Expectations

You enter your marriage and business with expectations of how people should treat you, based upon your upbringing, life experience, media exposure, and other people's opinions. Some expectations of your spouse are clear and unquestioned, like fidelity or physical safety, but some are not until you discover how the wants and needs of each of you clash. Sharing your expectations makes for effective problem solving, because you understand your starting point. These expectations couples had of each other, drawn from my interviews, could create conflict if not verbalized and agreed to.

Bedtime

When I married my husband, I expected us to go to bed together every night. My husband expected the freedom to go to sleep whenever he felt tired. Often that was a few hours before me. I felt abandoned and lonely when we slept separately, and my husband was resentful when he felt obliged to conform to my schedule for going to bed together.

> *Newlywed married to a real estate salesperson*

Time and Intimacy

My wife and I have different ideas about balance. For me, if I work for three months, seven days a week, sixteen hours a day, and then we take a break and go to Australia for a month— that's balance. Balance doesn't have to be an everyday thing, as it does for my wife.

> *Author*

Decision Making

When I was growing up, my dad made all the major decisions for the family. My husband was raised in the same kind of family. I warned him that if he wants a silent sheep, like his mother or mine, he's marrying the wrong lady. I have my opinions, and I expect him to consider them.

Female in early twenties

Financial Goals

My husband had a small established business when we married. I saw the business as an unpolished gem and planned to help him build the business to great success. I expected him to welcome my assistance. When he never implemented any of my ideas, I discovered we didn't have the same financial goals at all. Free time to play golf and tennis is more important to him than making money. I realized that if I wanted to make some money, I was better off starting my own business!

Female multilevel distributor

Privacy

I had been living alone for seven years when my male friend moved in with me. Every morning when I was getting ready for work, he would watch me get dressed and put on my makeup. When I requested that he give me more privacy, he took it personally. It turns out he had watched his ex-wife get dressed every morning for twenty-six years, and that's what he wanted with me.

Female in her fifties

CLARIFICATION EXERCISE FOUR: CLARIFY YOUR EXPECTATIONS OF YOUR PARTNER

Completion time: 30 minutes.

Record expectations of your partner which you have not yet verbalized. Your entries can be major expectations, like fidelity, or even small ones, like knocking on the bathroom door before entering, since the minor issues sometimes spark the biggest battles.

Write this sentence ten times, and complete it:

I expect that you will . . .

_____

_____

_____

_____

_____

_____

_____

_____

_____

_____

Examples: call if you are going to be late, spend Sunday with the family, stay monogamous when you are traveling, come home for dinner every night.

Write this sentence ten times, and complete it:

I expect that you will *not* . . .

_____

_____

_____

_____

_____

_____

_____

_____

_____

_____

Example: criticize me in front of our employees, read my journal, go out with the boys on Friday nights, talk to your friends about our sex life.

Initial and sign off on the expectations to which you each agree 100 percent. If your partner expects more than you can fulfill, use the skills that you've learned in this chapter to reach a mutually acceptable agreement.

Preventing Conflict Through Clarifying Roles and Responsibilities

Most people need clearly defined roles, responsibilities, and areas of authority to minimize conflict and manage demanding businesses and family life. Couples may designate roles according to several different criteria.

- We each do what we are best at, at home and at work.
- I earn the money and my girlfriend tends to all the details at home.
- We work different shifts so that we can share child rearing equally.

- I handle my business, and my spouse takes care of hers. We share all family decisions equally.
- I manage the people end of the business and my spouse supervises operations.
- I act as a sounding board for my life partner, offering advice or emotional support when I'm asked for it.

You should clearly delineate scopes of responsibility at home as well. List everything required weekly to keep your home neat and clean enough to meet *both* of your minimum standards—then divide the list in a fair and equal way.

> After years of fighting about how to divide household responsibilities fairly, we finally made enough money in our business to hire a full-time housekeeper and nanny. That's one of the best rewards we've received from working this hard to become successful.
>
> *President of multimillion-dollar company*

Job Descriptions

Corporations use job descriptions to clarify the company's expectations of employees. Job descriptions can get outdated quickly, encompass many unexpected tasks under "other duties as assigned," or prevent a willing employee from exceeding the basic requirements. Nonetheless, job descriptions provide good general outlines, so that both the supervisor and employee understand what the employer wants the employee to do, and how employees should interact with each other.

When we marry, or make a lifetime commitment, we implicitly agree to a loose job description called "husband" or "wife," or the equivalent thereof. If we work together as well, then we agree to "business partner or associate." The job description you imagine you have may differ from the one your partner expects of you. Significantly reduce both domestic and office tensions by forming a shared understanding of your roles and responsibilities at home and at work.

CLARIFICATION EXERCISE FIVE: DEFINE AREAS OF RESPONSIBILITIES THROUGH A JOB DESCRIPTION

Completion time: 30–60 minutes.

If you work or plan to work together, write a job title and description for each of you that clearly defines intended job responsibilities. Your title might be more traditional (head of operations) or innovative (office mover-and-shaker). You might divide responsibilities by functions, expertise, working shift, products/services, client needs, or site of activity, in or outside the office. If your business has identical or interchangeable roles for each of you, then write one job description and add details where relevant.

For example: "We both do therapy with clients, but Karen specializes in women with eating disorders and Gary in alcoholism. In those cases, we will refer clients specifically to one of us."

If you are in the process of deciding whether to partner in business with your spouse or life partner, create a help-wanted advertisement and a job description of the ideal business partner. It will help you decide objectively how your partner's skills and experience measure up to what you are looking for.

If you live together, create a job summary that clearly defines your separate duties at home.

You can detail your own job description as much or as little as you please, but plan to review and revise it at least once or twice a year. If appropriate, create a job description for your kids, nanny, or any other person who shares the requisite tasks for running a profitable business and an efficient household. You'll quickly discover that events like the birth of a child, a relocation, or a financial setback all affect your roles at home and office dramatically.

Imagine playing a baseball game without an umpire who has the authority to call the plays. When you assign responsibilities, you determine how and when to share decisions, and where to draw boundaries of authority. Setting decision-making guidelines with your spouse ahead of time prevents daily and long-term conflict.

In the beginning I would give a customer a refund and after the customer left the store my husband would complain I was giving away the store. We never argued in front of a customer, but you should have heard us in the back room! We finally got tired of fighting with each other. Twenty years ago we decided I take care of the customers and he takes care of the merchandise, and it's still that way. We stay out of each other's hair.

Co-owners of a retail store for twenty-five years

Set the stage for productive negotiation and problem solving by agreeing to the boundaries that will help guide your daily decisions.

CLARIFICATION EXERCISE SIX: DECISION-MAKING AUTHORITY
Completion time: 15 minutes.

With your spouse, review the following methods for designating authority over decision making in your marriage and business. Do your business rules differ from your marriage ones? Which of the following examples suit you the best for now?

- I am the decision maker, and my partner is the follower. My partner relies on me to lead the way and trusts my judgment entirely.
- We don't operate with any set rules. The one who feels stronger makes the call. We fight only when we both feel really strongly about a decision. It evens out over time.

- We make major decisions that affect the whole company (or family) jointly by consensus. Otherwise, we make individual decisions for our agreed-upon areas of responsibility.
- We make virtually all business and home decisions together, striving for consensus every time.
- I decide everything for my business, and my partner decides everything for his (hers). We make most of our home decisions jointly.
- Our decisions in the business are collaborative, but since my mate knows so much more about the business than I do, his (her) voice is still the louder.
- Our business differs from our marriage. In our marriage, we decide everything as equals. In business, I'm the employer and my spouse is an employee. I take full responsibility and make all final decisions for the business, though I do respect my partner's contribution to the process.
- In a tie or stalemate in a business decision, he's the tiebreaker. I'm the tiebreaker at home.
- Other:_____

_____

_____

Summarize with your partner your current perception of how you will make decisions at home and at work. The more detailed your statement, the less confusion later on, but a simple statement of general understanding will do. Review this statement periodically as your marriage and your business change.

CONFLICT RESOLVED THROUGH NEGOTIATION AGREEMENT

Later we will explore how to resolve conflict when one or both of you is too upset for a calm discussion. Now, we will focus on how to communicate effectively when you both are relatively calm and peaceful and need to resolve a difference of opinion. Reaching a satisfactory compromise in a productive way requires negotiation skills that accommodate both your needs—a win/win outcome.

You can tell if the discussion satisfies both of you. Even if you didn't get exactly what you requested initially, you both feel good about your exchange and closer to each other, with no negative residue or underlying resentment.

For many, the word *compromise* conjures up the unpleasant image of two people haggling for days and meeting somewhere between their needs, where neither person feels satisfied. The process can be so painful, the parties are simply relieved to be done. Sometimes compromise means that I get my way now and you'll get yours later—we trade off. That works occasionally, but not in the long run because one of you is unhappy half the time. Secretly you keep score, and your partnership starts feeling like a competition.

Focus on Interests, Not Positions

The most appealing version of compromise is discovering a brand-new solution, better than what each originally sought and more satisfying to both. To reach such innovation, try what Fisher and Ury suggest in their bestseller, *Getting to Yes: Negotiating Agreement Without Giving In*: focus on interests, not positions (Fisher and Ury, *Getting to Yes: Negotiating Agreement Without Giving In*, page 40).

Most of us bargain with our spouses over positions, defending and arguing our points of view against attack and insisting upon the validity of our position, not theirs. It's a win/lose proposition. Even if we "win" the argument, we lose something more meaningful and precious: an intimate and loving relationship. If our partner concedes by sacrifice and deprivation, the conflict often recurs in another more noxious form. A bittersweet victory indeed.

Ury and Fisher encourage both parties to focus on the mutual interests behind their respective conflicting positions. Often we convince ourselves that our position is the only way to address our underlying interest. Not true! Usually several alternatives can satisfy you if you fully recognize your deepest concerns. You may discover shared, compatible, even complementary interests behind seeming polarities.

This strategy works for Jerry and Frederick, gay partners who operate a midwestern floral shop together. Jerry is the accountant and operations manager. Frederick is the floral designer.

Jerry's position: We've got to watch the bottom line. That means we can't keep giving away extra flowers in each assortment just to make them look better.

Frederick's position: Our customers return to us because they know that we give them the best assortment possible. We shouldn't sacrifice quality and beauty just to save a few bucks.

Can you see how Jerry and Frederick could argue these positions endlessly, without resolution? What interest lies behind each position? Jerry's is profitable business, and Frederick's is happy customers and high-quality product.

Their positions seem different, but both want happy customers and high-quality merchandise so that they can have a profitable business. Jerry and Frederick can step to the same side of the problem and plan together how to achieve their shared goal. Perhaps they can raise prices, charge extra for special arrangements, cut operation costs to afford extra flowers in each arrangement, or seek a better price on wholesale flowers. They can consider several alternatives to meet *both* of their interests, instead of bickering over seemingly incompatible positions.

Considering Several Alternatives

We can quickly lock into narrow, one-option thinking. Have you ever presented an exciting idea to your spouse or colleague, and he or she doesn't see the genius in it? Rather than looking for other options or listening to reasons why the idea won't work, you defend your suggestion and insist that you are right and he or she is wrong. Your original idea twists into a demand, which your partner hears as "You jerk, anyone with intelligence would do this my way!" Naturally your partner defends him- or herself and loses sight of shared interests.

The following ineffective dialogue between Stephen and me intensified into an argument. I rewrote the dialogue as it might have been had we paid attention to shared interests.

Version One: Ignoring Shared Interests

Azriela: Let's go away for the weekend to a romantic bed and breakfast in Maine. We could really use the break from working and taking care of the kids.

Stephen: I don't think that will work for me. I've got too much to do around here. The idea of driving five hours up and back in one weekend doesn't thrill me.

Azriela: You've always got too much to do, and besides, five hours is no big deal. You like to drive in the mountains. (I'm smarter about what you need than you are.)

Stephen: My idea of relaxation isn't spending ten hours driving in a car. I'd rather relax here with you at home. (Defending his position but still open to some intimate time.)

Azriela: Sure, that's what you say, but I know how it will be. You'll get distracted by all the things on your to-do list, and we won't spend any time relaxing together at all. (Still maintaining that my original suggestion is a good one by making him wrong for his concerns.)

Stephen: That's not true! Last weekend we stayed here and we spent a whole evening together. (Feeling exasperated—"Will I ever be able to satisfy this woman?")

Azriela: Going out for dinner is hardly the same thing as going away for an entire weekend. I want to get away for an entire weekend with you. (I see no other acceptable options other than the one I originally presented. If we don't go to Maine, I'll be unhappy.)

This dialogue spins further away from satisfying my initial goal of spending romantic time away with Stephen. I actually create the opposite effect of my intention, argument instead of intimacy. Had I changed my response to Stephen's initial resistance, the dialogue might have been as follows:

Version Two: Recognizing Shared Interests

Azriela: Let's go away for the weekend to a romantic bed and breakfast in Maine. We could really use the break from working and taking care of the kids.

Stephen: I don't think that will work for me. I've got too much to do around here. The idea of driving five hours up and back in one weekend doesn't thrill me.

Azriela: I can understand why you'd feel that way after commuting such a long distance to work each day. I know you're concerned about getting the house packed for our move. Can you think of any other way we could spend some romantic getaway time that would work for you? I really miss you. (Focusing on my underlying interest—intimate time with my husband—rather than insisting on my original position.)

Stephen: I'd like to spend time together, but I'd rather relax here with you at home. That way we wouldn't have to spend half the weekend in the car. How about if we plan on all day Sunday together? (Open to romantic time together, but not an entire weekend.)

Azriela: Maybe we can drive just an hour or two away and spend Sunday at the beach. I'd really like to get away, even if it's just for a day. (Restating my interest but showing openness to another alternative.)

Stephen: If we spend Sunday together, is it OK with you if I work down in the basement on Saturday night, instead of going out for our regular Saturday night date? I'm really concerned about getting the basement packed up in time for our move. (Negotiating so that he also cares for his interest in getting his work done.)

Azriela: Sure, I'll plan on getting some writing done too. That sounds like a good compromise. We'll have some time away together and be able to finish some work too.

With version two, we both satisfy our interests. Even though Stephen turned down my original idea, our final solution still meets my primary need. Going to Maine wasn't my actual need, just a means to the real need for intimate time with my husband. Keeping the primary desire in mind is key to negotiating beyond positions to the underlying interests.

DISCOVERY EXERCISE SEVEN: FINDING YOUR COMPATIBLE INTERESTS

Completion time: 30 minutes.

This exercise can be done with your spouse, or any family member or coworker.

Select a current scenario of incompatibilities, from any place in your work or family life. Write down your individual positions on a piece of paper. Separately, write down the immediate interest behind your stance. Then dig deeper for an interest behind the first. Keep digging until you find the core need or desire driving your overt request. Compare notes with your spouse or whoever you are joining with to do the exercise. Where are you compatible? Identify and write down a joint solution that meets both of your underlying interests when you find one. Repeat this exercise whenever you must negotiate a solution to seemingly incompatible positions.

COMPLEX CONFLICTS: WHEN BUSINESS AND PERSONAL CONFLICTS MERGE

If only all conflict were simple enough to handle with straightforward negotiation and agreement upon compromise. Throughout your entrepreneurial journey, you will struggle to resolve complex issues in your relationship that require greater communication skill and technique, and sheer endurance. Such is the work of all married or long-term committed partnerships.

According to family firm consultant and therapist Jane Hilburt-Davis, "Complex conflicts are those in which emotional issues obstruct the resolution of critical business decisions." In complex conflict, family issues tangle with business ones nonproductively and communication grows adversarial. Here are three examples of complex conflict, one from my own marriage.

Fred and Joanne, a young couple who run an East Coast consulting agency together, held different opinions of how the new company brochure should appear. Fred preferred a slick, bold look, whereas Joanne wanted an elegant and classy presentation. They met twice with their graphic designer, fought with each other both times, and accomplished nothing. The graphic designer wisely refused to return a third time.

The brochure became the centerpiece of a much deeper unresolved problem: Joanne was furious at Fred for often making major business decisions unilaterally without consulting her. At home, Fred domineered and controlled and expected Joanne and their kids to respond promptly to him. Since Joanne lacked courage to complain about his ill-treatment of her and the family, she argued over the brochure. In effect, she picked a minor fight to avoid a much larger more risky one. But neither brochure nor family benefits from her displaced self-assertion.

Daisy and Mario both own their own businesses, a successful interior design firm and a psychotherapy practice, respectively. But before Mario began his practice, their twenty-year marriage almost ended.

> Looking back now, I realize the affair had nothing to do with my feelings for that woman, or my wife for that matter. The truth is, I hated my job and I didn't have the courage to quit. I created some excitement in my life by starting an affair, rather than making the career move I needed to. In counseling I faced the truth about how much I needed to make a career change. Thank God my wife stood by me while I worked all this out.
>
> *Psychotherapist*

I was seven months pregnant, and Stephen and I were on our way to "baby" class. The car trip itself plus the class time gave us some time alone to enjoy each other's company and to focus on the upcoming baby. But I turned instead to my financial concerns about his business and asked when he expected to receive $2,000 from a client I knew he had billed several months ago. Worried about our finances, I needed Stephen to reassure me that money was coming. Stephen explained that, despite his efforts, the company wasn't paying, and he wouldn't waste any more time on it. How could Stephen write this money off so easily? I was scared of running out of money and I fired back.

On the surface, I criticized his handling of an accounts receivable problem. At a deeper level, I was attacking our relationship and Stephen as a man. Stephen wasn't caring for me financially the way I had hoped for as a married woman, and I resented his business's drain on our savings account and relationship. My venomous words and angry tone of voice hurt Stephen deeply, because he felt as if he was failing me as a husband. I had reached my limit of being a "supportive spouse" to a business I no longer supported. It took a long while for us to recover from that argument.

Amidst tears later that night, I conceived of the idea for this book and shifted my focus from trying to fix Stephen's business to healing myself and our relationship.

If destructive futile conflict erodes your relationship, and begins to wear *you* down, then seek counsel from an objective third party, trained in conflict resolution, marriage counseling, or entrepreneurial coaching. Most of the couples in my research sought outside assistance at the toughest times. If you have accounting troubles in your business, you find a trustworthy accountant to advise you. When unraveling a tricky legal matter related to your business requires a competent lawyer, you find one. Hire the right professional, if necessary, to guide you through your interpersonal disputes as well.

The Speaker–Listener Technique

Drs. Markman, Stanley, and Blumberg, seasoned researchers and couples therapists, recommend the "Speaker–Listener" technique (Markman, Stanley, and Blumberg, *Fighting for Your Marriage*, page 71) to help couples communicate more effectively on hot issues. The technique involves structured conversation, paraphrasing, and giving one partner the floor to speak uninterruptedly until that person feels heard. These three therapists suggest assigning an object to represent the floor, like a paperweight or stuffed animal, to designate the speaker visually at any time. Using this technique helps liberate couples from the following patterns that normally destroy, rather than create, intimacy.

Escalation. The act of paraphrasing everything, though tedious at times, slows the dialogue, reduces the reactive tendency toward escalation, and with enough practice, spares you both a nasty fight.

Invalidation. By not listening to our partners or instantly attacking their point of view, we invalidate them and spark a combative dialogue, rather than a calm conversation in which both partners feel heard. Paraphrasing promotes the latter.

Withdrawal and pursuit. When one partner withdraws from conflict, the other usually pursues the conflict even harder. The Speaker–Listener technique affords the withdrawn person safety, since the discourse is less likely to escalate. When the withdrawer sticks around, the chasing partner gets a chance to voice the issues and feel heard, thus diminishing the need to pursue.

Filters. Internal and external filters—the way that we hear and interpret what is being said to us—interfere with straightforward communication with our partners. The Speaker–Listener technique gives each partner the opportunity to say, "That's not quite what I mean." You can then clarify and modify the message until your partner understands.

Let's look at how the Speaker–Listener technique could have been helpful to Armand and Kirsten, an entrepreneurial couple who manage an office supply business. When Kirsten was fired from her job, she joined Armand in his established business as a new business partner. This dialogue takes place:

Kirsten: I'm sick of doing all the copying and filing around here. What do you think I am, your secretary?
Armand: Don't be ridiculous. I didn't tell you to do it; you just started filing one day so I let you.
Kirsten: Someone has to file around here. If I didn't do it, it would never get done. You do all the fun work and you leave the scut work to me. I thought we were going to be business partners. I feel more like your unpaid servant.
Armand: That's your problem. Ever since you lost your job,

you've been really touchy. Your feelings about our business are all in your imagination.

What did Armand and Kirsten accomplish in this conversation? Both partners angered and alienated each other, and Kirsten got no satisfaction. Let's revisit the same dialogue using the Speaker–Listener technique. Kirsten has the floor:

Kirsten: I'm sick of doing all the copying and filing around here. What do you think I am, your secretary?

Armand: You're tired of doing secretarial work. You want me to do it instead.

Kirsten: No, that's not true. I don't want you to do all of it. I just want you to share some of the responsibilities with me. It seems as if all I do all day is copy and file and you get to do the fun work.

Armand: You want me to help you with some of the copying and filing?

Kirsten: That's right. Ever since I started doing it, it seems like I do all of it.

Armand asks for the floor.

Armand: I appreciate the copying and filing that you do to make our business work. It's true that I don't do much of it. The truth is, I can't stand doing the paperwork part of our business. I'd rather hire someone than do it myself.

Kirsten: You don't want to help me since you hate paperwork.

Armand: It's not true that I don't want to help you. I feel bad that you're so unhappy. I think we should consider hiring someone part-time to help you rather than expecting me to help. I probably won't follow through on my promise to help and that will just make you madder.

Kirsten: You're suggesting we hire someone to help me since you don't want to do the work, and you agree that I need help.

Kirsten asks for the floor.

Kirsten: The problem is not really that I need help, but that I feel unappreciated for the work I do. You never thank me and the clients never thank me. You have all the glamorous work and I have the behind-the-scenes work that everyone takes for granted.

Armand: You feel unappreciated and you would like to work more with the clients.

Kirsten: I think it would help a lot if you thanked me occasionally for doing the work that I do. Maybe if I didn't feel taken for granted, I wouldn't mind it so much. You know I'm still a little raw from being fired. I need some extra reassurance that I'm useful to the business.

Armand: You would like me to thank you more often so you feel appreciated. You also mentioned earlier that you want to work more with the clients.

Kirsten: That's right. I know that sales and marketing is your forte, but I wish I could have a bit more interaction with the clients. I want to go on sales calls with you, rather than being stuck at the office all day while you're out on the road.

Armand: You'd like to go out on the road with me.

Kirsten: Not all the time, just once in a while to help me get to know the clients and to get out of the office.

At this point Armand and Kirsten can stop the structured dialogue and move into joint problem solving. Using the Speaker–Listener technique, Armand heard Kirsten's complaint without invalidating her or defending himself. Kirsten clarified the underlying reasons for her feelings so that they could find a mutually pleasing solution. Without a full discussion, they may have prematurely agreed to hire additional help, which didn't solve her real issue about being underappreciated and wanting more client interaction.

The most common objection to using methods like Speaker–Listener is, "It's too contrived." Most couples overcome that objection when they get results and can talk about a hot issue without a blow-up. Structuring your dialogue gives you the power to discuss an otherwise volatile topic with uncharacteristic serenity.

SKILL-BUILDING EXERCISE EIGHT: USING THE SPEAKER–LISTENER TECHNIQUE TO RESOLVE A COMPLEX CONFLICT

Completion time: 30–60 minutes.

Try the Speaker–Listener technique to reach a compromise on a highly charged issue—business, personal, or a combination—that you and your spouse have been unable to resolve satisfactorily. You might practice the technique on comparatively minor problems before you tackle your most difficult issues. Don't give up if your first attempts don't go perfectly, or you don't get ideal results. Like learning any new language, you need time and practice to become fluent. You may find your best results from using the technique in the presence of a trained counselor.

Slow It Down and Take the Time You Need

Most couples try to solve their problems before they have a full, clear discussion of the issues. It's no wonder that the solutions don't stick, or that the problem escalates instead of dissipates. If you combine a fast-paced overloaded day with an aversion to conflict, you often get quick-fix decisions that aren't really solutions in the long run. There is no shortcut; communicating well takes time and concentration.

When you corner your partner at a bad time—right before an important client meeting or while helping a child with homework—to attend to a problem for immediate resolution, you take a hostage rather than find a listener. You achieve your primary goal better if you wait for a time when both of you are intellectually and emotionally present and attentive.

You may be telling yourself now: "Wait a minute! We don't have the time to negotiate everything at length. We grab moments when we can." Couples skilled in negotiation and problem solving find that planned business or couple meetings, even if they are short, are more effective for solving some problems than ill-timed conversations on the fly.

Couple Meetings

Partners who handle conflict well speak highly of regular couple meetings, which marriage counselors unanimously endorse. These meetings—scheduled times for the couple to concentrate on speaking with each other without interruption or distraction—need not be long because you can get a lot accomplished when you are focused. Some couples meet at the start or end of every day. Others prefer meeting once a week, biweekly, or monthly.

> My husband and I tried having regular business meetings in the morning to start off the day but it didn't work. Charlie is a night owl, and he can stay up all night working. I do my best work from six to eleven in the morning but Charlie is usually too tired then to have a productive meeting. We compromised and now we talk over business or personal concerns at lunch twice a week. If something comes up on a day we're not having lunch together, we save it until our lunch meeting unless it's urgent.
>
> *Newsletter publishers*

> My partner and I meet at a local café one evening every two weeks. We've created a list together of our values and goals as individuals, a couple, and for our businesses. The first hour and half of the meeting we go over each goal and value and talk about how we're each doing, measured against that list. We encourage and congratulate each other, as well as give feedback and acknowledge where we've fallen short. Then we set goals for the next two weeks. We've been meeting like this for five years. I think it's the most important thing we do for our relationship.
>
> *Lawyer and corporate consultant*

The Power of an Apology

Never underestimate the power of a sincere apology. Why is offering an apology to our partners during or after a conflict so difficult? Like the word *compromise, apology* carries a lot of negative baggage. When we compete habitually with one another for the superior position, apologizing feels like surrender or admission that our partners are right and that we are wrong.

Properly timed, an apology can prevent a disagreement from becoming a volatile argument. An apology is a sincere expression of regret that your partner feels hurt, angry, sad, or otherwise upset by your actions *even if you don't agree with his or her point of view.*

If you say "I'm sorry" insincerely just because your partner wants to hear it, or your "I'm sorry" is followed immediately by a defense of your actions, the effect is negligible. On the other hand, demanding an apology from your spouse will get you little except defiance. If your spouse thinks he or she deserves an apology, hear this demand as a clue that he or she is feeling invalidated and needs acknowledgment of his or her point of view.

Childhood Wounds

Complex conflicts trigger emotional outbursts when they reopen childhood wounds. Sharon Kleinberg and Patricia Zorn, both New York psychotherapists trained by Dr. Harville Hendrix in Imago Relationship Theory, find that Hendrix's teachings help their clients who are entrepreneurial couples.

Imago Relationship Theory asserts that how individuals experience childhood partially determines their choice of partners in adulthood and how they will behave with their partners. When a controversial issue arises, conflict becomes calamitous because couples tune out, interrupt, criticize, give unwanted advice, or attempt to fix the problem. When a fight reopens childhood wounds, couples react defensively to each other. Criticism becomes the adult equivalent of the screaming child. Couples must look behind the criticism for the underlying childhood frustration, hurt, fear, or other emotion.

When Kim criticized my work, she talked down to me just like my father used to. It upset me so much I would cry. She accused me of being overreactive and too sensitive, but as soon as she yelled at me in that condescending tone, I would just lose it.

Business owner who had difficulty receiving criticism from her business and life partner

Understanding childhood wounds helped Ed and Julia, co-owners of a multimillion-dollar manufacturing company. Before counseling, they had this typical hurtful argument.

Ed: I'm sick and tired of having a business partner who isn't pulling her weight. The clients are very demanding and you don't offer any help.

Julia: That's ridiculous! I'm in the office plenty, but you never take my suggestions anyway. You're sick and tired of me not pulling my weight? I'm always the one who takes care of the house and kids—besides working at least forty hours a week.

Ed: I'm never home because I have to work all the time to make up for the fact that you sit on your butt all day and talk to your friends. If I had a real working partner maybe I could come home more often. Someone has to keep this business afloat!

Julia: Just because I'm not a social hermit like you doesn't mean I don't pull my fair share.

This fight led Ed and Julia to seek counseling, where they talked about their early childhood experiences. Ed came from a family of six kids; as the oldest, he was often left in charge of his siblings without much support from his parents. His perception that Julia also left him responsible for the business without adequately supporting him instigated his childhood rage. In contrast, Julia's family communicated, "Children are better seen than heard." Her overworked and inattentive parents largely ignored Julia's opinions, feelings, and needs. Her perception that Ed ignored her contribution to the business sparked her childhood hurt and frustration.

A replay of the former dialogue, redrafted with an understanding of childhood wounds, illustrates a more effective dialoguing process.

Ed: I'm sick and tired of having a business partner who isn't pulling her weight. The clients are so demanding and you're never there to help.

Julia: You think I'm not doing enough.

Ed: I know you're very busy with the kids and the house and the office. It's just that I'm exhausted. Some days I just want to walk away from the whole damn thing. It feels just like when I was growing up as the oldest kid, responsible for taking care of my brothers and sisters.

Julia: I bet you would give anything for some time off. May I speak?

          I'm feeling really frustrated. You say you are overwhelmed and that I don't help you enough, but you don't listen to my opinions and you make your own decisions anyway, no matter what I say.

Ed: You think I don't take your advice when you give it.

Julia: You make decisions on your own and then get mad at me for not helping you. You say you want a business partner, but you also want total control. It really pushes my buttons because my parents were always making decisions without involving me, just like you do.

Ed: I've spent time with your parents so I know what you mean about them. May I speak?

          I didn't mean to exclude you. I'm used to doing everything myself, and I thought you wanted it that way too. Why don't we start having regular business meetings first thing in the morning, before the clients start calling. Maybe you can take over some of the problems that have been weighing me down. I would really appreciate your help.

Julia: That sounds good to me. I'd like you to involve me more. Let's try eight tomorrow morning. And one more thing. Can we get a baby-sitter this weekend so we can go out for a date? I miss having fun together.

Ed: Sure, that sounds good.

DISCOVERY EXERCISE NINE: RECOGNIZING CHILDHOOD WOUNDS

Completion time: 30–60 minutes.

While you should seriously consider seeking professional help for resolving deep emotional pain from childhood, you and your partner can still consider how your most troubling conflicts may be rooted in childhood trauma. Set aside a period of uninterrupted time to share your insights with each other. Use a structured dialogue technique if it helps you to communicate with each other. You may find your hostility diminish afterward and be able to empathize more tenderly. With increased awareness, you will be less apt to blame your partner for not giving you what you needed, but never got, as a child.

CONCLUSION

Relationship techniques or counseling will never eliminate conflict entirely between a husband and wife or two intimate partners. You may benefit from individual therapy to take the charge out of your vulnerable "hot buttons." Couples counseling and workshops can instruct you on shifting from destructive to constructive communication, and reading some of the books in the Recommended Resources section of this chapter can improve your awareness and introduce you to new communication skills. Every action to prevent, reduce, or resolve conflict between you will enrich your relationship and strengthen your business partnership as well. You may eventually welcome the opportunity to work through some of your differences. Focus on the process and be satisfied with small accomplishments along the way. *Progress,* not perfection, is a worthy goal.

RECOMMENDED RESOURCES

Books

Conscious Loving: The Journey to Co-Commitment: A Way to Be Fully Together Without Giving Up Yourself by Gay and Kathlyn Hendricks, Ph.D. Bantam, 1992.

Couple Skills: Making Your Relationship Work by Matthew McKay, Ph.D., Patrick Fanning, Kim Paleg, Ph.D. New Harbinger Publications, Inc., 1994.

Fighting for Your Marriage: Positive Steps for Preventing Divorce and Preserving a Lasting Love by Howard Markman, Ph.D., Scott Stanley, Ph.D., Susan L. Blumberg, Ph.D. Jossey-Bass, 1994.

Getting Past No: Negotiating Your Way from Confrontation to Cooperation by William Ury. Bantam, 1993.

Getting the Love You Want: A Guide for Couples by Harville Hendrix, Ph.D. HarperPerennial, 1988.

Getting Together: Building Relationships as We Negotiate by Roger Fisher and Scott Brown. Penguin, 1989.

Getting to Yes—Negotiating Agreement Without Giving In, by Roger Fisher and William Ury., 2nd ed. Penguin, 1991.

In Love and In Business: How Entrepreneurial Couples Are Changing the Rules of Business and Marriage by Sharon Nelton. John Wiley and Sons, 1986 (out of print).

Intimate Partners: Patterns in Love and Marriage by Maggie Scarf. Ballantine, 1987.

Men Are from Mars, Women Are from Venus: A Practical Guide for Improving Communication and Getting What You Want in Your Relationship by John Gray, Ph.D. HarperCollins, 1992.

Now That I'm Married, Why Isn't Everything Perfect? The Eight Essential Traits of Couples Who Thrive by Susan Page. Little, Brown and Company, 1994.

The Dance of Anger: A Woman's Guide to Changing the Patterns of Intimate Relationships by Harriet Lerner, Ph.D. Harper and Row, 1985.

The Seven Basic Quarrels of Marriage: Recognize, Defuse, Negotiate, and Resolve Your Conflicts by William Betcher, M.D., and Robie Macauley. Villard Books, 1990.

The Tao of Negotiation: How You Can Prevent, Resolve, and Transcend Conflict in Work and Everyday Life by Joel Edelman and Mary Beth Crain. HarperBusiness, 1993.

We Can Work It Out: Making Sense of Marital Conflict by Clifford Notarius, Ph.D., Howard Markman, Ph.D. G.P. Putnam's Sons, 1993.

Who's on Top, Who's on Bottom: How Couples Can Learn to Share Power by Robert Schwebel, Ph.D. Newmarket Press, 1994.

Why Marriages Succeed or Fail by John Gottman, Ph.D. Simon & Schuster, 1994.

Video- and Audiotapes

Fighting for *Your Marriage* by S. M. Stanley, H. J. Markman, and S. L. Blumberg (1994). Video- or audio-tape series teaches couples a skills-based approach for staying married and happy. Denver, PREP Educational Videos, Inc. Call 1-800-366-0166.

Franklin Reality Model Kit. Improve family relationships and control addictive or destructive behaviors. Videotape, audiocassette, workbook, and hardcover book *Gaining Control*. Call Franklin Quest, 1-800-983-1776 or fax 1-800-242-1492.

John Gray, Ph.D. Large collection of audio- and video-tapes available by calling 1-800-821-3033.

The Magic of Differences. Self-help tapes for couples and singles. Contact Judith Sherven, Ph.D., or Jim Sniechowski, Ph.D., at 12021 Wilshire Boulevard, #692, Los Angeles, CA 90025, or call 310-829-3353.

The Hendricks Institute sells ten different audio- and videotapes on a rage of topics including "The Heart Of Conscious Loving," "Creating Conscious Relationships," and "Creating Abundant Wealth." Call 719-632-0772.

Workshops, Seminars, and Consultation

Joel Edelman, J.D., M.A., mediation and conflict consultant, offers seminars, workshops, and consultation to couples and organizations for preventing and resolving disputes. Write: 169 Pier Avenue, Santa Monica, CA 90405, call 310-392-4830, or fax 310-392-6331.

Fighting for Your Marriage workshops given around the country. Call 303-750-8798 (Denver) or write: Fighting for Your Marriage, c/o PREP, Inc., 1780 S. Bellaire Street, Suite 621, Denver, CO 80222.

John Gray, Ph.D., offers relationship seminars in major cities around the country. Write: 20 Sunnyside Avenue, Suite A-130, Mill Valley, CA 94941, or call 1-800-821-3033.

Harville Hendrix, Ph.D., The Institute for Relationship Therapy, offers couples workshops, therapy, and professional training in Imago Relationship Therapy. Write: The Institute for Relationship Therapy, 1255 Fifth Avenue, Suite C2, New York, NY 10029, or call 1-800-553-9025.

Kathlyn and Gay Henricks offer seminars for couples and individuals nationally on conscious relationship training and body-centered transformation. Write: The Henricks Institute, 409 East Bijou, Colorado Springs, CO 80903, or call 719-632-0772.

Jane Hilburt-Davis, cofounder of Key Resources, offers seminars, workshops, and private consultation for family businesses, copreneurs, and closely held businesses. Lexington, MA, 617-861-0586.

Sharon Kleinberg, CSW, and Patricia Zorn, MSN, Relationship Resources. Certified Imago Relationship therapists and business relationship facilitators. Offer seminars, consulting, and workshops nationally for couples, small groups, and small businesses. Also offer couples therapy in the New York City area. Call 212-864-0331.

Richard Levin, Ph.D., Work/Life Enterprises, offers couples counseling, workshops, and seminars on couples communication, conflict resolution, and change management. Write: 1330 Beacon Street, Brookline, MA 02146, or call 617-566-1995.

Drs. Markman and Notarius maintain counseling practices in Washington, D.C., and Denver and Boulder, respectively. They also offer seminars and workshops to couples and professionals. Call 303-750-3506.

Marriage Encounter offers inexpensive weekend retreats for couples all over the world. For information write: Worldwide Marriage Encounter, 1908 East Highland Avenue, Suite A, San Bernardino, CA 92404, or National Marriage Encounter, 4704 Jamerson Place, Orlando, FL 32807-1024. Include an SASE.

Olivia Mellan, psychotherapist with practice devoted to assisting individuals and couples with money issues, conflict resolution, and business therapy. Olivia Mellan and Associates, 2607 Connecticut Avenue N.W., Washington, D.C. 20008-1522, 202-483-2660.

Dr. Robert Schwebel provides individual and couples counseling, as well as lectures and workshops for couples on sharing power and problem solving. Write: 431 South Brighton Lane, Tucson, AZ 85711, or call 520-748-2122.

Dr. Douglas and MaryElizabeth Welpton offer individual and couple therapy and weekend workshops based on Harville Hendrix's and Pia Melody's work. Write: 116 Old Orchard Road, Chestnut Hill, MA 02167, or call 1-800-525-1979 or 617-232-6378.

7

Keeping the Romance Alive

Creative Ways to Protect and Nurture the Intimacy of Your Relationship

After working together for a number of years, we filed for divorce. We endured the heartbreak of not only losing our marriage, but also the businesses we had worked so hard to create. We were always working and never took any personal or relationship time away from the business. Instead of being lovers, we became only business partners.

Divorced entrepreneurial couple

After thirty-five years of marriage I have deepened my love for the lady I married. Before we began working together, she was a trophy wife, a beautiful woman who took care of my kids and stood at my arm when we went to business functions. I never discussed my business with her because I didn't know she had anything to contribute. When my wife came to work with me in

my business, I discovered a brilliant, creative woman and I fell
in love with her in a whole new way.

Professional speaker and consultant

When you hear the word *romance*, what comes to mind?
Images of giving or receiving candy, flowers, and expensive gifts?
Whatever the image, the allure of romance is universal. Romantic
love is the seductress that brought you together and compelled
you, for better or worse, to spend the rest of your lives together.
Romance naturally fades with time and the pressures of daily life.
When you are struggling to manage both business and family
affairs, sustaining romance in your marriage may fall low on your
list of priorities. This chapter will help you find ways to express
love amidst the stress of entrepreneurial life and child rearing.

You'll learn how to cultivate romance in both attitude and
action and how to overcome the most common obstacles to preserving a loving, romantic relationship.

WHAT IS A ROMANTIC MARRIAGE?

Romance may include buying gifts, sending flowers, and leaving
love notes for each other, all traditional modes of romantic
expression. But it is far more than that. "Keeping the romance
alive" means maintaining a relationship with each other in such a
way that you both feel loved, appreciated, cherished, and admired
daily. Your love for each other will change and mature over time.
Your heart may not palpitate the way it used to when your spouse
walks into the room, yet your love for each other can deepen into
an even more satisfying feeling over the years.

Paying bills, raising children, maintaining a household,
responding to medical crises, and, of course, starting a business,
zaps your energy and thwarts intimate connection. Sustaining the
expression of love in your marriage is one of the most essential
skills you can develop to protect and enrich your marriage.
Without romantic rituals, every day passes like all the others.
Without expressions of love, spouses and soul mates become
merely roommates and business associates.

The Ten Characteristics of a Romantic Marriage

How romantic is your marriage in terms of the following checklist of qualities normally found in a romantic, passionate, thriving marriage?

1. You express reverence and respect for the other's abilities, and accept each other for who you are.
2. You often focus your attention on how to please your spouse and regularly go the extra distance to help your spouse feel cherished and loved.
3. You delight in the companionship of your mate. You can experience togetherness side by side, even when doing different activities at the same time.
4. You have developed joint hobbies or pursuits such as raising kids, grandchildren, travel, business, antiques, religion, music and the arts, or sports.
5. You carry in your heart a constant gratitude and appreciation for your spouse and express these feelings often.
6. You usually look for the good in your mate and focus on the positive in your relationship and life together.
7. You have fun, laugh together, and savor spontaneous, creative romantic activities from time to time.
8. Your relationship fulfills you on many levels: recreational, sexual, intellectual, emotional, and spiritual. You regularly share activities in each of these spheres of life.
9. You have learned over time how to accept each other's weaknesses and to release resentment.
10. You have learned how to forgive each other and give each other grace.

DEVELOPING A ROMANTIC MARRIAGE

What if you spent only one half hour a week taking care of your customers, developing your marketing plan, or collecting your receivables? Your business would die of neglect. The same goes for marriage. The first step toward a romantic marriage is to make keeping the romance alive in your marriage a priority in your life.

Yet, as several experts report, most couples spend fewer than thirty minutes a week sharing intimate feelings or private time. No wonder the divorce rate now exceeds 50 percent.

Give Your Relationship Regular Attention

"Romance is the environment in which love flourishes," according to Greg Godek, author and romance expert. Romance is the garden where our relationship can bloom with great beauty, or wither from inattention. My husband, Stephen, nourishes our lawn and garden with only the highest quality organic fertilizers, soil rich from composting, and regular attention to weeding. If Stephen only spent thirty minutes a week on the garden, or waited until June and put his hands in the soil for forty hours, the garden wouldn't flourish. Stephen makes time to mow and weed during an extraordinarily busy week because he prioritizes the health and beauty of our land above many other items on his to-do list. Just as gardening results are in direct proportion to the effort you put in, the same is true for marriage.

Treat Your Spouse Like Your Best Client

If you work hard to acquire a client who becomes your biggest income producer, you provide the best service and consideration possible. Imagine if after a few years you decide that you now need to pay more attention to your newer clients, so you stop giving that client your best service. Your prize client will become dissatisfied and take the business elsewhere.

Your mate is your most important life client. Satisfying this person with high-quality attention should be a major investment of your time and energy. For many couples, a marriage license becomes permission to relegate their relationship to the lowest priority on the never-ending list of things to do. If you are a married entrepreneur, or if you married an entrepreneur, you cannot wait for time to romance your intimate partner. If your business depends on getting clients, you create the time to get clients—or you go out of business very soon. If you don't make romance a priority, then you may find your marriage going bankrupt as well.

Keep Business in Perspective

Entrepreneurial life can absorb all of your physical and mental energy. Entrepreneurs who value their marriages and family life learn how to leave their business worries at the office and return in the morning with a fresh mind and heart. Transition rituals can help you make the transition from work to home, so that you can be fully present for your spouse and kids when you are at home. Take a half hour to read the paper before joining the family, work out at the local club, or take a bath before making dinner and putting the kids to bed. Ease into the transition, and then be as fully present as possible.

How much of your personal time in the evenings will you devote to discussing work, working on the business, taking care of kids, or sharing intimate time with your spouse? Every couple needs different amounts of daily intimate contact. Some guard their evening time together carefully and leave work entirely at the office. Others live, eat, and breathe the business day and night, by choice. Although some outsiders label this behavior as unhealthy, these couples remain happy, excited, and connected to one another passionately. For them, cocreating the business is as good as sex: working toward a common goal is as romantic an activity as they can imagine. If you have workaholic tendencies and your spouse is complaining, you may need to curtail your commitment to work in exchange for attending to your spouse's intimacy needs.

> As long as my needs are getting met, I enjoy helping my husband with his business. When he isn't there for me emotionally, I resent him and his business. My husband has learned to take care of me, so that I am more supportive about his regular absence from our home.
>
> *Spouse of physician*

Communicating What You Need

What makes you feel loved, respected, and connected to your lover? "If I have to ask for it, it doesn't count" is a defeating attitude that guarantees unmet needs. Don't expect your spouse to be a mind reader—give him or her specific guidance on how to make you happy. Ask for what you need to feel loved by your partner. You may want your spouse home at 6:00 P.M. for dinner every night, but your expectation may be entirely unrealistic given your mate's business. You can at least ask when to expect your spouse home, and if you want your spouse to be home for dinner more often, say it.

DISCOVERY EXERCISE ONE: WHAT MAKES ME FEEL LOVED
Completion time: 30 minutes.

Write this sentence on a piece of paper. Then draw twenty blanks underneath it: "I feel loved, cherished, and appreciated when you _____." Fill in the blanks and share your list with your spouse.

For example, I would tell Stephen:

I feel loved when you offer to take the babies for a few hours so that I can get some work done or have some private time.
I feel loved when you spontaneously give me a hug—just because you feel like it.
I feel loved when you look at me admiringly and tell me I look beautiful.
I feel loved when you leave me a love note before you go to work.
I feel loved when you make us a special dinner.

Commit to do something loving for your spouse every day, weekly, or monthly. Post the list on the wall by your bed, in the bathroom, on the refrigerator, or on your desk at work. Carry it around in your wallet, refer to it often, and add to it whenever an idea comes to mind. Create and share new lists every six months.

Schedule Intimacy

"It's not romantic to schedule sex." "My whole life is planned for me; I don't want to have to plan intimacy with my spouse too." "We keep saying we're going to spend some time together, but the day just disappears before you know it." Do you recognize any of these common complaints of entrepreneurial couples? Couples thriving in the midst of entrepreneurial demands often schedule intimacy as a priority. Dates—even sex—with your spouse get put on the agenda, with baby-sitters hired on retainer to ensure a regular date night. Couples become creative and insist upon new ways to spend time together. Scheduling intimate time doesn't preclude spontaneous closeness when time allows, but it ensures a baseline of connection to hedge against a hectic business schedule.

SKILL-BUILDING EXERCISE TWO: SCHEDULING INTIMACY
Completion time: 30 minutes.

Create a system with your spouse to schedule intimacy. Refer to the previous exercise, "What Makes Me Feel Loved," for ideas. Your scheduled activities may include:

sex
private dates
celebrating special days
daily connection
vacations

Buy a special calendar just for planning your relationship activities, or put the ideas directly into your daily agenda. Plan your calendar for the following month and repeat this exercise monthly.

ROMANCE KILLERS—THE EMOTIONAL WEEDS OF THE ENTREPRENEURIAL ROMANCE GARDEN

Even planting heirloom seeds purchased from the best source won't guarantee an abundant flower and vegetable garden without rich fertilization and careful pruning. Entrepreneurial life has its own weeds and slugs that overrun the garden of romantic love first planted during courtship. The next section of this chapter looks at the negativity, "the weeds" that you need to eradicate so that your relationship can flourish. We will examine five common business-related causes for boredom or distance in your marriage, followed by concrete ways to rise above these challenges.

During a difficult time in our marriage, I complained to my husband, Stephen, about the perceptible lack of intimacy and romance between us. Stephen, in a decidedly unromantic mood for several weeks, used the following metaphor to explain his feelings:

> Picture a delicate bud vase holding a single red rose. The rose represents romance and intimacy; the vase our marriage. Now imagine dropping a pebble in the vase. The pebble represents disapproval, resentment, demands, or my beating myself up. That first pebble in the vase may displace some water, but the rose can still live. But pebble upon pebble in the vase eventually displaces all the water so that the rose withers and dies. With so much negativity between us lately, too many pebbles crowd the rose for me to feel romantic.

The next section explores how to protect your marriage garden from being overrun by the following weeds:

1. anger and resentment
2. depression and melancholy
3. fatigue and feeling overwhelmed
4. disappointment or disenchantment
5. boredom
6. lack of personal space
7. worries about money

Anger and Resentment

Driving home from my job as a critical care nurse, I was exhausted by the demands of a fifty-hour workweek, terminally ill patients, and demanding families. I wanted to work part-time but I couldn't as long as my husband's business wasn't earning any money. I was furious when I drove up the driveway and saw him polishing his car. "Why isn't he in his office making business calls and getting some clients?" I ranted to myself.

Critical care nurse

The Pebbles

"I'm exhausted and it's all his fault."

"He doesn't deserve to have fun while I'm working so hard."

"He isn't doing what it takes to make the business work. He's incompetent."

"Damn it, I deserve to be taken care of. This isn't what I bargained for when we got married."

Shifting Attitude

When anger clouds the picture, romance is the farthest idea from your mind. Rather than wanting to give to your spouse in a generous and loving way, you want to punish and withdraw from your spouse in anger and resentment. If you express your hostility ineffectively, then your partner may retaliate. If you swallow your feelings and numb yourself out, then you choke the positive, passionate feelings as well, so that your loving connection frays anyway.

"Not communicating the truth in your relationship is sure to kill the passion. Passion comes from feeling intensely. When you suppress the truth, you are destroying your ability to feel. And when you stop feeling, you stop loving," instructs Dr. Barbara DeAngelis, author and relationship expert (DeAngelis, *How to Make Love All the Time*, page 67).

Tell the truth to yourself and to your partner in a loving way. Dr. DeAngelis states that the key to telling the complete truth is to peel back and examine all your feelings about the issue, not just the outermost layer. For example, when you react with anger as your primary defense, you may also discover hurt, fear, and regret beneath the rage. If you communicate only the angry message, you sound unloving and your partner may react defensively. If you learn to express the range of emotions, then you uncover loving feelings behind the angrier hurt ones, and your partner will be better able to hear you. Locating deeper feelings isn't easy because the intensity of the first layer blocks our feelings. Like all skills and positive habits, slowing down the process and looking for hidden emotion takes practice and determination.

Consider the wife who finds her entrepreneurial husband polishing his car. She feels rage instantly upon seeing him caring for his car instead of working. But she also feels hurt: "He doesn't love me enough to protect me and make sure I don't have to work this hard when I'm exhausted." She feels fear: "If he doesn't make any money, then I'm going to have to keep working this killer schedule. I don't know how I will manage that." She feels remorse: "I wish I could be more compassionate and forgiving about his difficulties getting clients." Beneath all of these emotions she feels love: "I love my husband and I want to feel reconnected to him again instead of feeling angry."

With intention you can learn to pause in the middle of anger and tell yourself the whole truth about your feelings. In a calm voice, perhaps after a cool-down time, use "I" statements to communicate your feelings and needs to your spouse. Try the Love Letter technique (chapter 6) for a structured way to write all your feelings when speaking is too difficult. With this new awareness, the critical care nurse returning home from work might be able to communicate the following to her husband:

"I am exhausted and overwhelmed today and I'm feeling angry that you aren't contributing more income to the family. It's hard for me to continue to be supportive of you starting your own business when I'm so scared of running out of money at the end of this month. I love you, and I want you to be happy. What can you say that would reassure me?"

If the timing wasn't right to tell the truth to her husband as she pulls in the driveway, then she could request a couple's meeting, wait until she has calmed down and he is in a receptive mode, or at least tell herself the whole truth. By doing so, she opens the door for intimacy.

Depression and Melancholy

When my husband declared bankruptcy and closed his business, he moped around the house for six months in a deep
depression. He didn't shower, hardly ate, didn't want to be near
the kids or me, and wouldn't socialize with any of our friends.
Our sex life was nonexistent. I didn't mind losing the business
or our money as much as I mourned losing my husband.

Spouse of former clothing store owner

The Pebbles

"I lost everything we worked so hard to save. I'm a loser."

"I'm so ashamed of myself. I can barely face my wife or kids."

"I'm sure my wife doesn't even want to make love with me
anymore."

"My wife and kids would be better off without me."

Romance as Unconditional Love

One entrepreneur referred to the state of mind of the gentleman above as "mental knots." When our spouses are depressed,
we hurt too, and want to "unknot" the twisted thinking behind
their depression so that they can forgive themselves and again
enjoy life as our partner. We move from compassion to impa-
tience, through fear to anger as we wait for time to heal our partner's wounds—and our own. Most entrepreneurs are resilient, but
even six months of depression and disconnection can feel like an
eternity. When your mate suffers and your life together loses virtually all expression of love and romance, then you have the
opportunity to continue creating what Dr. Harville Hendrix calls a
"conscious relationship."

One of the hardest things about a conscious relationship is that
we have to give up the fantasy that the right partner will come
along and magically make everything okay—or that if our part-

ner would change what is wrong with them, everything would be fine. At times we need to put the focus on learning to love instead of being loved. Real love is not an emotion; it is a decision to act unconditionally in the interest of your partner. (Hendrix, *The Couples Companion: Meditations and Exercises for Getting the Love You Want*, page 13)

When our partner is depressed, unattractive, and unavailable, we learn about real love. For a time, the relationship is neither balanced nor fair. We give more than we get, suffer from a lack of intimacy, and fear that our partner will never be loving toward him- or herself or us again. During this time, romance rises above flowers and cute little gifts. If your partner is depressed, then express your ongoing and unconditional love for your spouse often, even if your spouse does not reciprocate. Newlywed couples habitually keep score, measuring their output against their spouse's. Mature loving couples assess fairness over time, knowing that at any moment in marriage, one spouse may be more available to give than the other.

The most romantic gesture that you can make for your depressed spouse is to *be there* unconditionally, with compassion, acceptance, and a whole lot of patience. Be persistent in your efforts to reassure and love. Eventually your spouse's wounds are likely to heal. Find unique ways to express your love daily, even if your spouse has difficulty receiving it, or doesn't know how to thank you. Eventually the interminable winter blossoms into spring, and your lover will warm to your gestures and receive again. Partnership is as much about cycles as it is about constant growth.

I was a bear to live with when my restaurant went under. My wife kept on taking care of the kids, making dinner, offering to make love, and reassuring me that she still loved me. I don't know how she put up with me. One day she arranged for the kids to spend the weekend at their grandmother's. She booked us for a three-day weekend at the cabin we honeymooned in. At first I didn't want to go, but she insisted. Getting away really helped. I have never forgotten how my wife was there for me during my lowest point.

Bankrupt restaurant owner

Fatigue and Feeling Overwhelmed

My husband got the ax and decided to go out on his own as a consultant just when my home business was getting started and wasn't bringing in much money yet. We both tried to work out of our home offices during the day with two toddlers running around. It was nuts! At 8:00 P.M. we'd finally get the kids to bed, and then we'd head back to the office until midnight. Sex, intimacy, personal time with my husband? You've got to be kidding. All either of us wanted to do when we had some free time was sleep!

Business consultant and Shaklee distributor

The Pebbles

"We're going to lose the house if we don't make some money quick."

"The kids have got to come first."

"I can survive without sex."

"Who's got time for romance? I'd rather sleep."

Staying Anchored

When you combine entrepreneurship, children, and financial worries, you may easily feel overwhelmed and exhausted. Creative romantic ideas usually take a back burner. When you've little time and energy to invent new romantic rituals, then identify the anchors in your marriage that sustain your commitment and connection. Keep some of them in your daily life. Every day you find a way to eat, bathe, and get dressed. You decide to prioritize the essentials, even when you have too much to do in too little time. Put on your priority list the anchoring rituals you share with your spouse.

Anchoring rituals may be as simple as:

We say "I love you" every day.

We hug before we leave the house.

We take a walk together on weekends.

We talk over breakfast about the day.

We go to church together on Sundays.

We talk at least once a day on the telephone.

When you find yourself saying, "All the romance is gone in our marriage," remember to count those daily rituals taken for granted. Look for and acknowledge the simple daily routines and habits you have developed together that demonstrate your ongoing love and connection with each other.

DISCOVERY EXERCISE THREE: ANCHORING RITUALS
Completion time: 20 minutes.

Complete the following sentence with your mate ten times:

Amidst these crazy times, it's important that, as a minimum, we do the following with and for each other, every day or week:

_____

_____

_____

_____

_____

_____

_____

_____

_____

_____

We commit to each other that no matter how busy we get, we will make the time for those activities that center us and sustain our marriage during difficult times.

Sign your names at the end of the sentence.

Anchoring Rituals Stephen and I Have Created Together

Stephen and I struggle to keep romance alive creatively during harried times. With four children to support and two busy careers, our courtship passion has been hard to sustain. We have excelled however in keeping anchoring rituals an everyday part of our marriage. Here are some of those that compose our life.

Couple's journal. Since we began dating, we have kept a couple's journal, with written entries by both of us, to record special events, offer loving and encouraging thoughts, and communicate difficult feelings. When one of us makes an entry, we leave it on the other's pillow to read. On special anniversaries, we sometimes review the entire journal together and reminisce. We also include memorabilia like the personal ad that united us, our wedding photo, and our children's birth announcements and newborn pictures.

Wedding vows. We wrote and memorized our own wedding vows and repeated them aloud to each other *every day* for the first year and a half of our marriage. With two babies, two stepsons, and scarcer time, we now repeat them weekly. We say them when we are feeling loving or angry toward each other, reaffirming our solid commitment. As our marriage grows and matures, the words take on even more meaning. We even calligraphied our wedding vows and hung them at our bedside.

Couple's mission statement. Shortly after we married, we created a joint mission statement to express and affirm our goals, dreams, and aspirations for our life together. We recite our mission statement aloud to each other when we recite our wedding vows.

Dry erase board. Hanging by our bedroom door is a dry erase board we use occasionally to leave each other private love notes, notes of encouragement, support, and apology.

Walking together. As our schedule and the weather allows, we walk around the neighborhood together with the babies in their carriage. We appreciate this brief time to catch up with each other.

Sabbath. We observe the Jewish Sabbath from Friday sundown to Saturday sundown as a special time set aside for focusing on family, intimacy, and relaxation, a time apart from the rigors of the workweek.

Saturday night date. Now that the babies are here, we don't go out on Saturday nights too often, but we try to maintain the spirit of Saturday night date night by spending time together at home. Occasionally, we treat ourselves to a baby-sitter.

I love you. Stephen and I end virtually every phone call with "I love you." Before one of us leaves the house in the morning we exchange a hug and an "I love you."

Daily calls. We talk at least once during the day by telephone to touch base, share information, and maintain our connection throughout the day.

Disappointment or Disenchantment

When I first married my wife, I thought I had found the perfect woman. She was beautiful, she wanted to stay home and raise my kids, she was intelligent enough to converse with my clients, and she was a great cook. But after the second baby came, she wasn't the same woman anymore. She gained forty pounds with her second pregnancy and never took it off. She didn't want to stay home with the kids full-time anymore. She got involved in this MLM business that took her away practically every night of the week to one meeting or another. Instead of coming home to dinner on the table, I usually cooked the meal and put the kids to bed by myself. When she came home from her meetings she wanted to tell me all about it, but I didn't really want to hear it. I wanted my old wife back.

Husband of MLM distributor

The Pebbles

"If I wanted to marry a business woman I could have done so."

"My wife belongs back home with the kids."

"I'm sick of handling the kids every night while she's out having fun at her damn meetings."

"Why doesn't she lose weight? She's gotten so fat and unattractive."

Romantic Illusions Versus Mature Love

When our romantic illusions fade and we realize that our partner lacks certain personal qualities we wish they had, it's called "disenchantment." Dr. Larry Bugen, author and couples expert, notes:

> Disenchantment is a painful but necessary process that all relationships must pass through in order to enter maturity. It arises in progressive cycles of increasing frustration, disappointment, anger, resentment, apathy, and withdrawal. (Bugen, *Love and Renewal, A Couple's Guide to Commitment*, page 6)

Going into business together, or dealing with the strains of self-employment accelerates the disenchantment phase of your marriage. Working in close quarters, you will see aspects of your spouse's character that may irritate you. The frustrations associated with a demanding business speed the transition from light-hearted courtship and romance to unpleasant realities that will test your marriage.

Larry Bugen's book, *Love and Renewal*, describes how you can transform romantic love into a more rewarding and deeper love by learning how to do the following (Bugen, *Love and Renewal, A Couple's Guide to Commitment*, page 24).

Transform intense passion into genuine intimacy and warm loving affection.

Replace your loss of judgment and blindness to your spouse's flaws with generosity of judgment, an acceptance of flaws, and the tenderness and tolerance that promotes a safe, loving environment for both to heal.

Temper your desire for exclusive time alone with your spouse with an affirmation of your life's complexity, and an ability to enjoy quality moments instead of hours and days of extended romance.

Move beyond the self-centeredness of early romantic love—when you focused on being loved the way you want to be loved, toward a dedication to the fulfillment of the relationship's demands and needs.

Prize your commitment to a lifetime journey, more than personal qualities frozen in time or idealisms of each other.

Entrepreneurial couples with a strong commitment to a life-long partnership convert the hardships of business ownership into bedrock for building a greater, more dependable relationship. Mature and lasting love replaces the idealized infatuation of your courtship.

Boredom

I remember how excited my husband and I were many years ago when we opened our first store. As newlyweds, every day was different and exhilarating. Even though we have plenty of money now and our first store has turned into twenty stores, I miss the struggling years in a way—they were more fun.

Franchise owner

The Pebbles

"My marriage has become dull and boring. Life isn't any fun anymore."

"I miss the earlier years when our marriage was more exciting."

"Working together as business partners has killed our sex life."

"I don't know if we have what it takes to turn each other on anymore."

Fighting Inertia

Even though a long-term, stable marriage lets you relax and be yourself around your spouse, putting no effort into being attractive, sexy, or interesting to your spouse will result in a dull, distant marriage. My mom, married to my dad for thirty-eight years, still dresses up nicely every day for my dad, even though they retired a few years ago. She takes pride in her appearance, and Dad appreciates her beauty and self-respect. Even if your marriage is like a perennial garden that needs little daily care, you should still attend regularly to it or the flowers will eventually die.

Boredom is best eradicated with mutual commitment and energy to shake up the status quo. Buy one of the romance books recommended at the end of the chapter and try some of their creative, spontaneous, and easy to implement ideas. Enroll your spouse on the mission or start making a few changes yourself. Your spouse will eventually respond. Romance is contagious.

Lack of Personal Space

> I get up at six o'clock in the morning, help get my kids ready for school, and then leave for the office. I work in a cubicle all day, surrounded by hundreds of other employees. When I get home at night, my family is waiting with dinner. After helping the kids with their homework and cleaning up the kitchen, it's time for bed. The only moment I've been alone all day was in my car. I have no opportunity to unwind and recharge my batteries so that I can be available for, or even interested in, intimacy with my wife.
>
> *Corporate accountant*

The Pebbles

"I want to get away from everyone and be by myself."

"I wish I could have a drink and read the newspaper without interruption."

"Sometimes I wish I was single and coming home to an empty house."

"Every day it's the same old routine. I'm trapped in all my obligations."

Finding Personal Space

A lifestyle that deprives you of personal space will limit your desire for romance with your spouse. Without minimum privacy, you may seek solitude rather than togetherness, common behavior of men and women who work in a job all day, then return home to a family. Burned out by interacting with people all day, you quite naturally crave at least an hour alone, and may sacrifice intimate relationship time to make it available to yourself.

Successful entrepreneurial couples create strategies to provide both partners with replenishing private time. Sometimes one partner must sacrifice—baby-sitting the kids, postponing dinner, forfeiting conversation or sex, or even spending weekends apart occasionally—to make private time available for the other partner.

If you do not find ways to get your necessary space, then you both may unconsciously create it for yourselves in destructive ways, by distancing emotionally, starting an argument, turning on the TV, sleeping, or other habits that annoy your spouse. Sacrifice intimate time with your spouse in the short-term, and you will probably receive greater passion and intimacy over the long term.

Worries About Money

We were barely scraping by on my teaching salary while my husband started his own high-tech company when quite unexpectedly I got pregnant. In those days, they didn't let a pregnant woman teach in the classroom beyond her fifth month, so this was really bad timing. Looking back, I don't know how we made it, except I know this. The most expensive date we had all year was going to the drive-in movies for $2.00!

Retired schoolteacher

The Pebbles

"We don't have enough money to even think of doing anything romantic."

"If my husband wasn't chasing this foolish dream of his, we'd have the money to have some fun together."

"Laura is so lucky. Her husband takes her out to a nice restaurant every week."

"I have no idea what to give my wife for her birthday since we're so short on cash."

Romantic Gifts that Don't Cost Money

One of the misnomers about romance is that it has to cost a lot of money. Some of the most romantic experiences shared by couples require no money and only a little time. In fact, many report deeper satisfaction with a personal and creative gift, than with an ostentatious one. The first step toward weeding the garden of money worries that are keeping you from being romantic is to seek out creative noncash gestures for keeping the romance alive. The Resources section of this chapter offers books with hundreds of suggestions. Here are twelve ideas from my marriage.

Love notes. Leave each other love notes in unexpected places—on the dashboard, on the computer desktop, on the bathroom mirror written in soap, on your pillow, in the car, or in a briefcase.

Doing chores. As a surprise, do one of your spouse's chores for him or her. Fill up your spouse's gas tank without him or her even asking. Lighten the daily load just a bit.

The gift of time. Designate a period of time on the weekend when your spouse can consider him- or herself completely free of child-care and household responsibility, to spend the time as he or she chooses.

Flowers. Place a single flower from the garden on your spouse's dashboard, pillow, or in the bathroom, just to let your spouse know you were thinking of him or her.

Prepare a meal. Create and serve a delicious dish that took some time and effort to prepare. You don't need to go out to a restaurant for a fine-dining experience.

Massage. Give your spouse a neck, back, foot, or hand massage for twenty minutes.

Napkin notes. Make your spouse lunch for work and include a special poem or love note written on a napkin as an extra unexpected surprise.

Phone call. Call your spouse at an unexpected time just to say "I love you and appreciate you." Depending on your mood and your spouse's, the phone call could even be erotic.

Compliment. Take a moment to compliment how your spouse dresses, cooks, takes care of the children or the house, or brings home a paycheck.

Kiss and a hug. A no-cost and practically no-time way of saying "I love you." Give your spouse a sign of affection at an unexpected moment with some heartfelt enthusiasm!

Sex. This may be one of the most direct ways to your spouse's heart, and it won't cost you a dime.

Listen. Give your spouse the gift of your undivided attention and support when he or she needs it most.

KEEPING THE ROMANCE ALIVE WHEN YOU ARE RAISING KIDS

> It's hard to think about being romantic with my wife when I've got three kids crawling all over me, a house to keep up, and a demanding business.
>
> *Restaurant owner*

Setting Boundaries

As a mother of two teenage stepsons and two infants fifteen months apart, I know the difficulties of maintaining romance in a marriage while raising kids and growing a business. When the kids and your careers are so demanding, it takes due diligence to keep the romance alive in your marriage. I am the romance police-woman in my relationship, reaching out to my husband, Stephen, to rekindle intimacy when we drift too far apart.

The secret to sustaining a vital couple connection is the ability to set and maintain boundaries, refusing to give yourselves entirely to the incessant demands of business or children. The best gift you can offer to your children is a solid intimate relationship that energizes and supports you.

With children around, you learn to grab intimacy when you can, in the middle of the night or at dawn if necessary. You no longer hope to spend entire weekends together in romantic privacy. Children get sick, need your attention, and take much of your time. You become grateful for an occasional night out, rather than a weekly date. You are happy for sex twice a month, instead of twice a week.

If your children are old enough, put that Do Not Disturb sign on your bedroom door, and teach your children to respect your privacy. If your children are young, then put them on a regular bedtime schedule so that you get some adult time together in the evenings. When you spend most of your time as "Mom and Dad," feeling or acting like lovers takes effort. If you tell yourselves that the romance will end once the children come, then it probably will. If you commit to keeping romance alive, despite family pressures, then you can sustain a satisfactory level of intimacy. But you will have to work hard to achieve it.

Give your spouse the gift of freedom from child care for a while so that he or she can recharge and be more emotionally and sexually available to you. Take turns allowing one of you to sleep late on the weekend or hire a teenager to entertain the kids during a weekend afternoon so you have the time to clean the bedroom or take an extra long shower. If your spouse usually gets up in the middle of the night to take care of the baby, offer to take over for a night.

The key is balance: have reasonable expectations of each other—yes, children do change things substantially—but don't give up entirely on keeping romance alive. As long as you keep the embers burning, the hot flames of passion are still within your reach when the time and mood are right. Let the fire grow cold between you, and when the children are raised and out of the house, the fire will be much harder to start again.

COMMUNICATING ABOUT SEX

How often have you heard: "He wants sex and she wants romance." A more accurate statement is: "If you ask a man what his number one favorite romantic and intimate activity is, he'll tell you it's sex. If you ask a woman what her favorite romantic and intimate activity is, she'll tell you it's talking and cuddling with her mate." Does that mean that a woman doesn't want sex or a man doesn't want romance? Absolutely not. Most men and women want and appreciate both expressions of love and intimacy, but they prioritize specific activities differently. Couples who thrive learn how to meet the sexual and romantic needs of both individuals, so that there is a natural flow of goodwill between them. He's enjoying plenty of good sex so he naturally expresses love and romance to her in a way that encourages her to want to make love to him (or vice versa).

Never mind what a "normal" sex life is for a married couple. Throw out the stereotypes and discover what really turns on your mate. Perhaps great sex monthly satisfies you, or maybe you need sex every other day to feel connected, or ten minutes of cuddling to get warmed up. Can you enjoy quick sex when the opportunity arises, or do you need more time? Do you prefer to make love in the morning or the evening? Do you need a certain amount of emotional closeness in your relationship to be in the mood or a certain amount of sleep?

Authors of sex and relationship books often speak about how hard communicating about sexual needs is for couples. Shyness, modesty, and fear of rejection often keep us silent, and we hope that our spouse figures out what works for us. To maximize your time together and strengthen your relationship, you both must get specific about your sexual preferences. The Resources section of this chapter lists excellent books on communicating about your sex and intimacy needs, and enhancing sexual creativity with your partner.

AN IMPORTANT MALE/FEMALE DIFFERENCE

Keeping Score

John Gray revealed that men and women can easily fall into a vicious cycle of dissatisfaction with how the other acts romantically. A significant difference in the way each gender values a gift provides some perspective (Gray, *Men Are from Mars, Women Are from Venus*, page 177). For a woman, no matter how big or small a gift is, it scores one point; each gift has equal value. A spontaneous hug and an "I love you" are equal in romance value to an expensive dinner at a romantic restaurant. In contrast, men measure gifts by their perception of how much it costs or how much effort went into creating it. A man thinks that he earns one point for a small gift and thirty points for big one, so he focuses on giving one or two big gifts which "last" in value. The problem is, a woman usually prefers ongoing steady gifts, no matter how small.

In a relationship, women need many expressions of love to feel loved. Dr. Gray equates women to a gas tank that needs repeated filling. When a woman doesn't appropriately recognize a man for his big romantic gifts, he stops giving. "Why should I bother?" he asks himself. When he starts giving less, her resentment grows and the vicious cycle begins. Women must learn how to give men adequate appreciation for their romantic gifts, and men must learn how to prime the pump more regularly.

KEEPING THE ROMANCE ALIVE WHEN YOU WORK TOGETHER

Sustaining an active intimate sex life with your business partner is tricky business. Can you allow your spouse to be your lover as well as your business partner? There is often a period of adjustment.

> I love working with my wife, but for a while it ruined our sex life. I wasn't sure it was worth the trade. In bed, instead of mak-

ing love, we discussed our clients or the mailing we had to get out. We'd go out for a date and argue over how a business matter should be handled. We had to learn how to be business partners at the office and lovers at home.

Psychotherapist

Romance arises from feelings of goodwill and love, and the desire to give a gift to your lover. But when tension exists between you at the office and you carry it home with you, you may shut off any romantic energy between you.

My husband and I had a passionate, romantic relationship before we became business partners, but we became so frustrated working with each other, we stopped making love and romance went down the tubes. After six months my husband got a new business partner and I went back to my old profession as a nurse. It took about six more months, but eventually we started making love again. We would never work together again!

Nurse married to an advertising executive

The first step to maintaining the romance of your relationship if you work together is to recognize that it can be a challenge. Communicate early with each other about the issue. Bring the romance of your relationship into the office if that helps keep you intimately connected. Leave your mate a steamy love note in his or her in-box, or seduce your husband at lunch if you share a home office. Give your spouse a hug, or even flowers, when you land a great deal. Use your imagination without crossing professional boundaries. Check out what is appropriate so you don't offend your spouse by trying to make love while he or she is in work mode.

Each couple needs a different degree of separation from work to maintain a desirable level of sexual and romantic intimacy. Set boundaries together around your personal relationship to protect its sexual and romantic nature. Business ground rules can include agreeing not to discuss work in the bedroom, before breakfast, in the home, or during date time.

On the bright side, working together may improve your romantic and sexual life considerably. More flexible time to make love, the chance to share a dream, a renewed respect and admiration for each other, and spending more time together, can fan or rekindle the flames of passion.

> The first time I saw my wife give a presentation to our board of directors, I was stunned by her beauty and power. It was a real turn on for me to see her in the role of executive VP of operations, not just Susie, my wife. I appreciated her in a whole new way, and it increased my desire for her.
>
> *President of multimillion-dollar sales organization*

CLARIFICATION EXERCISE FOUR: MAINTAINING ROMANCE WHEN YOU WORK TOGETHER

Completion time: 20 minutes.

Write the following on a piece of paper:

"It is important that we maintain a healthy romantic and sexual relationship while working together as business partners. To that end, I would like you to _____, and I would like you to refrain from _____."

List at least five ideas in each blank, and share your requests with your spouse. Update these lists quarterly.

CONCLUSION

Most choose the entrepreneurial path to overcome banality and complacency. Entrepreneurs want to go for it, to have it all: passion, accomplishment, prosperity. fame, and meaningful contribution in both work and marriage. Keeping romance alive is hard work and great fun too, the difference between a boring, vulnerable marriage or a stupendous, dependable one. You can have a marriage without romance, but why?

Entrepreneurial couples experience the joy of achieving a shared dream, the creativity, spontaneity and rewards of struggling together to forge a thriving business and a rewarding marriage. I haven't met an entrepreneur yet who didn't also acknowledge that when his or her marriage is vibrant, strong, and loving, the business performs better, and life in general is more fun and rewarding. There is great synergy between romantic fulfillment at home and entrepreneurial achievement. Romance is good for marriage and business.

Review the Resources section at the end of this chapter and the creative ideas throughout. Make immediate moves toward keeping the romance alive in your marriage. Select a new and different way to express your love for your spouse and implement it—now! A woman in her sixties who works full-time with her husband laughed when I told her I was including this chapter in my book. She said, "Tell them, sometimes you just have to bring out the old black negligee!"

RECOMMENDED RESOURCES

Books

Courtship After Marriage: Romance Can Last a Lifetime by Zig Ziglar. Ballantine, 1990.

How to Make Love All the Time by Barbara DeAngelis, Ph.D. Rawson Associates, 1987.

How to Stay Lovers While Raising Your Children by Anne Mayer. St. Martin's Press, 1990.

Love and Renewal, A Couple's Guide to Commitment, How to Get Past Disenchantment, The Impasse Between Romance and Lasting Love by Larry Bugen, Ph.D. New Harbinger Publications, 1990.

Men Are from Mars, Women Are from Venus by John Gray, Ph.D. HarperCollins, 1992.

1001 More Ways to Be Romantic by Gregory J.P. Godek. Casablanca Press, 1993.

1001 Ways to Be Romantic by Gregory J.P. Godek. Casablanca

Press, 1991 (to order any of Greg Godek's books, call
1-800-444-2524, ext. 65).

Romance 101: Lessons in Love by Gregory J.P. Godek. Casablanca
Press, 1993.

*The Book of Love, Laughter and Romance: Wonderful Suggestions
and Delightful Ideas for Couples Who Want to Stay Close,
Have Fun, and Keep the Enchantment Alive* by Barbara and
Michael Jonas. Games Partnership Ltd., 1994.

*The Couple's Comfort Book: A Creative Guide for Renewing
Passion, Pleasure and Commitment* by Jennifer Louden.
Harper San Francisco, 1994.

*The Couples Companion: Meditations and Exercises for Getting
the Love You Want* by Harville Hendrix, Ph.D., and Helen
Hunt, M.A. Pocket Books, 1994.

*The Lovers Bedside Companion: Romantic Inspiration and
Meditations* by Gregory J.P. Godek. Casablanca Press, 1994.

*The Portable Romantic: An Indispensable Pocket Guide to
Creating Loving Relationships* by Gregory J.P. Godek.
Casablanca Press, 1994.

Newsletters and Magazines

The LoveLetter newsletter. Presents romantic ideas,
strategies, and tips from Greg Godek, author of *1001
Ways to Be Romantic*. First year's subscription is free
($25 value). Write to LoveLetter, Box 226, Weymouth,
MA 02188.

Marriage magazine. "Celebrating the Potential of
Marriage"—spin-off from the well-respected Marriage
Encounter organization; $15/year. Write to *Marriage*, 955
Lake Drive, St. Paul, MN 55120, or call 612-454-6434.

Romantic Traveling newsletter. Quarterly newsletter with
specific recommendations and reviews of romantic desti-
nations; $15/year. Write: Winterbourne Press, 236 West
Portal, Suite 237, San Francisco, CA 94127, or call
415-731-8239.

Seminars, Workshops, and Games

Club Mom. Creates get-away weekends in Newport, Rhode Island, for frazzled mothers. Massages, manicures, and meals included. Write to Jean Paulantonio, P.O. Box 1485, Newport, RI 02840.

Marriage Encounter. An international organization that focuses on the spiritual as well as practical needs of couples dedicated to their long-term, monogamous relationships. Call 1-800-795-5683.

The PAIRS Foundation (Practical Application of Intimate Relationship Skills). PAIRS is a 120-hour course for couples that provides a guided series of lectures and experiences. Write: 3705 South George Mason Drive, Suite C-8, Falls Church, VA 22041, or call 703-998-5550 or 1-800-842-7470.

Purchase a romantic board game and have an unusual Saturday night date: "An Enchanted Evening," or "Getting to Know You . . . Better," or "SEXsational." Over half a million sold. Call 1-800-776-7662; $25 plus $4 shipping and handling, or look for the games in gift and lingerie stores.

8

This Isn't What
I Bargained For

Coping with Hard Times
and Coming Out Stronger

It was bad enough when my husband, Bill, lost his job. Then he invested all our savings in a small business that went bankrupt two years later. I don't know what was worse, losing all our money or losing Bill for two years while he was working ninety hours a week trying to make the business successful. Sometimes the only thing that kept me from walking out the door was the commitment I made to him on our wedding day.

Supportive spouse of bankrupt entrepreneur

The incessant demands of entrepreneurship and the ever present risk of business failure can jeopardize or strengthen your marriage. If you battle together against difficult circumstances, rather than fight each other, then you improve your chances of surviving as a couple. When you are constantly overworked, deprived of sleep, or worried about finances, then you might find yourself really struggling to stay happily married or even in relationship.

Before my husband and I bought a waterbed, we considered how "wave-free" the mattress should be. We could choose one extreme, where one person's movement sets the other side rolling dramatically, or complete wave reduction, where one sleeper scarcely knows the other is there. We chose complete wave reduction. In entrepreneurial life, some partners can cope with waves, but others completely lose their peace of mind. If every action your partner takes in his or her business—or in your business together—ruins your serenity, it's like sleeping on a waterbed with no wave control. This chapter doesn't guarantee complete wave reduction, but its eight strategies can help you to maintain some stability in your relationship while riding out the waves.

DIFFERENT PERCEPTIONS OF STRESS

I'm not the brave, athletic sort. When a friend pressured me into white-water rafting, I responded to turbulent waters as if we were going to die. I was in crisis until that dreadful trip ended and my feet were ashore! To my thrill-seeking friend, the river lacked enough white-water action to stimulate her, so she experienced virtually no stress.

If you approach entrepreneurship as I did white-water rafting, where the slightest turbulence threatens your feeling of safety, the entrepreneurial journey will terrify and exhaust you. A smooth, calm entrepreneurial journey is an unrealistic desire.

Most of us can distinguish between a daily frustration, like traffic, and a devastating tragedy, like a fatal car crash. However, your idea of crisis may be your partner's notion of disappointment. When financial difficulties prevented one entrepreneur from paying for his daughter's college education, he considered suicide for a short time, as he confronted his feelings of failure as a father. Since his wife didn't measure her success as a mother by her ability to provide for their family, she coped better with their financial circumstances than her husband did.

What unsettles one of you may actually excite the other at any given time. Financial uncertainty of a husband's self-employment gave his wife many sleepless nights and anxiety attacks. The challenge excited him. In fact, he enjoyed the adrenaline rush of the game—until they faced bankruptcy and losing the company. Then *he* crashed. His wife, on the other hand, calmed down, faced the worst, and accepted that business failure wasn't so bad after all. This husband and wife, on the journey together, each experienced personal crisis at different times.

CLARIFICATION EXERCISE ONE: DEFINING THE LEVEL OF CRISIS
Completion time: 15 minutes.

Consider the following questions and share your responses with your partner. How do you differ? Where do you agree? Refrain from judging your partner's response as wrong if it differs from yours. Answers to these questions will help you understand how you and your partner differ in response to stressful events in your life together.

The top five daily frustrations of my (our) business:

_____

The top five daily frustrations of my (our) personal and family life:

_____

The current business problem I find the most distressful:

_____

The current relationship/family problem I find the most distressful:

_____

I am feeling devastated by (if applicable):

_____

I would be devastated by:

_____

COMMON STRESS RESPONSES TO ENTREPRENEURIAL LIFE

Throughout your life, uninvited circumstances may precipitate crisis in your relationship, family, business, health, or other aspects of your life. One couple I interviewed lost everything they owned in a house fire a week after they opened their new business. Another couple lost their business in a California earthquake, and they were totally uninsured. A third couple lost an adult son in a car accident, while they negotiated a deal to sell their business. A fourth couple dealt with the wife's breast cancer and their subsequent inability to find affordable health insurance. All of these couples were resilient enough to survive, and even thrive, in the midst of crisis. You'll learn some of their secrets in this chapter.

Entrepreneurial couples who have met with business failure or struggled with the hardships of building a business frequently report the following:

- depression, anxiety, loss of self-esteem
- guilt, inability to forgive oneself or partner
- anger or rage at self or partner
- loss of sex drive, exhaustion
- health problems
- addictive behaviors—overeating, smoking, drinking, gambling
- financial difficulties
- emotionally unavailable for relationship or children
- disintegration of intimate relationship

If any items on this list are too familiar, then your relationship or personal well-being may be severely impaired. Seek professional help immediately—a trained marriage counselor, business or personal coach, financial consultant, or clergy.

EIGHT STRATEGIES FOR MEETING CHALLENGE SUCCESSFULLY AS A COUPLE

Strategy One: The Importance of Flexibility

To survive hard times, you must shift gears to meet changing conditions. Dr. Al Siebert, an expert on the survivor personality, found that life's best survivors are highly adaptable, with a wide range of responses to any given situation. Not fixed on one emotional state or personality characteristic, a survivor can seemingly contradict him- or herself at any one time, selfish and unselfish, cooperative and rebellious, whatever the situation requires. A survivor may appear paradoxical and unpredictable, but that flexibility protects the survivor in crisis.

Thriving couples avoid fixed ideas of what must be. Flexibility is evident daily and in the big picture as well. In the first two years of my marriage to Stephen, custody arrangements for Stephen's boys changed four times. If I had fixed ideas as a stepparent of how his sons' living arrangements *had* to be, we would have suffered more as a couple.

Flourishing entrepreneurial couples make decisions based on the outcome for everyone in the family—not just the entrepreneur's need. Each member of the family may sacrifice momentarily to support the entrepreneur and to reap long-term rewards for the family. When the entrepreneur ignores family needs, trouble is on the horizon.

> My wife refused to accept that her business was a failure. Seven years, and she still hadn't turned a profit. Working two jobs, one hundred hours a week, just to support our family, wiped me out. I begged her to get a part-time job, but she refused. She was so self-centered, I got fed up, and we finally separated.
>
> *Divorced entrepreneur*

> I pleaded with my husband to cut back on his working hours so that we could have a life again. He was never home and our relationship was fading away. All he could think about was work, making money, and feeding his ego. I was so lonely, I had an affair that destroyed our marriage.
>
> *Divorced from an entrepreneur*

The "family plan," not just the business plan, drives successful entrepreneurial couples. They willingly make personal sacrifices, like the following, in response to family circumstances.

Twenty years ago my husband quit a lucrative and enjoyable job to relocate with me to another state, where my company offered me an exciting career opportunity. He took a lot of flack for his decision. Back then men didn't make career sacrifices for their wives. He's always been as committed to my success as to his own.

Health care consultant

When my daughter was born, I wanted to quit my job and stay home with her full-time. My job was pulling in $70,000 a year for our family, so that was no easy decision. My husband took a second job, we moved to a smaller house, and we quit our membership to the golf club. It wasn't easy, but my husband was totally behind my decision.

Former marketing executive

Daily flexibility is as important as a willingness to make major life changes. If you must have dinner at six every night, and a predictable cash flow every month, don't marry or become a business owner. Successful entrepreneurial couples are like a pair of willow trees—strong at the roots, but bending with the weather.

Strategy Two: Find Outside Support

Your intimate partner may be your best friend and confidant, but make sure he or she isn't your *only* one. A healthy relationship requires two kinds of outside assistance: objective advice and emotional support.

Jim and Suzanne, partners in a troubled business, lost money at a frightening rate and fought constantly about how to remedy the situation. Each blamed the other for the company's decline. Their marriage, like their business, was almost bankrupt. They credit their marriage's being saved by their joint decision to call upon an outside third party, a seasoned businessman who could advise them on restructuring their company. Since the consultant had no bias or loyalty to either Jim or Suzanne, the couple could hear constructive criticism from him more easily than from each other.

Whether you work with your spouse or use your partner as an unpaid business adviser, you will still need occasional objective and neutral input, as from a board of directors, a consultant or business partner, or business coach. You may invite or even encourage your partner's opinions, but not as your only source.

Kathi Elster, founder of New York City–based Business Strategy seminars for entrepreneurs, urges entrepreneurs to form or join an entrepreneurial support group for emotional backing and practical advice. She notes that many entrepreneurs who come to her support groups have burned out their intimate partners and endangered their relationships.

Frustrated with aspects of entrepreneurial life, supportive spouses will have difficulty demonstrating support if they lack a place to vent their frustrations other than on their partner. A friend, neighbor, coworker, therapist, coach, business association, or clergy may fill that role.

> I joined a businesswoman's association that meets once a month at a local restaurant. I've met some terrific women whom I confide in when I'm having a hard time. After going to so many business meetings where I focus on putting my best foot forward to attract business, I appreciate the opportunity to be honest from time to time.
> *Mary Kay distributor*

> As a man, I found it very difficult to talk about the emotional problems I was having in my business. I didn't want other men to think I was a wimp. One day, over lunch, I mentioned to a business colleague that I was having a hell of a time prospecting new clients. He admitted he was having the same trouble, and we talked openly about it. We agreed to check in with each other once a week. Having a "buddy" to bounce things off was critical to building my business.
> *Salesman*

My business coach is as essential to my business success as my investors. Once a week my coach listens to my problems and helps me find solutions. He helps me think creatively and keep my spirits up when I get discouraged. It's great to have a cheerleader other than my wife.

Stockbroker

Isolation and emotional hardship can lead the business owner either to bottle everything up or to shower his or her intimate partner with troubles. Neither response leads to a healthy relationship. Channeling some of the need to complain, brainstorm, or get reassurance will protect your significant other from burnout. Connecting to a spiritual source, a group of like-minded people, or even just one good friend or a journal, can save your marriage during challenging times.

Strategy Three: It's All How You Think About It

You can convert even the worst disasters into good fortune, with the right perspective and enough time. How you cope with unexpected and unwelcomed turns of events directly affects how you explain the meaning of the events to yourself. Are you basically an optimist or a pessimist? Dr. Martin Seligman, author of the bestseller *Learned Optimism*, distinguishes between optimists and pessimists (Seligman, *Learned Optimism*, page 44).

Pessimists dwell on the worst possibilities, blame themselves for the problem, expect bad events to persist forever, and let problems in one area spill over to all aspects of their life. Depressed pessimists can stay depressed for a long time.

A pessimist might respond to business failure: "It's all my fault, we're never going to recover from this, and it's going to ruin every aspect of our life."

A disaster to a pessimist is a mere setback to an optimist who sees bad events as temporary and surmountable. Optimists, ever-resilient, rarely get down for long and can contain worries about one issue of their life without spreading them to all aspects of their life. An optimist blames circumstances and other people, not just him- or herself, for failure.

An optimist might say: "The business failed because of my limitations, the economy, and circumstances beyond my control.

We'll bounce back from this. I'm not going to let a business disappointment ruin our life."

The main difference between an optimist and a pessimist is the amount of hope brought to a difficult situation. Thriving entrepreneurial couples maintain an optimistic long-term outlook, always converting lemons to lemonade and reframing life events to see the positive.

No one wants adversity. If you can avoid hard times, all the better. But reframing your circumstances in a more optimistic light is a skill that you can learn to manage whatever adversity comes your way. You can train your mind to shift from negative to positive thinking. (After all, worry is simply imagining over and over again the worst happening. Praying for the positive repeatedly is much more productive.) Strategies to shift your mindset include replacing negative self-talk with positive, disputing catastrophic thinking, and distracting yourself when negative thoughts overwhelm or consume you.

Pessimistic thought: "I'm a real jerk. We're going to lose everything. My wife will probably leave me, and my kids are going to have no respect for me."

Reframed positive thought: "It's too bad that the business didn't make it. It's a good thing that my wife is sticking by me. I guess the kids are going to get a lesson on what the business world is really like."

Catastrophic thinking: "Running a company together is much harder than I expected. We'll probably be divorced in a year."

Reframed positive thought: "Everyone says we'll be a stronger business team because we don't always think alike. I hope that we can learn how to accept our differences."

SKILL-BUILDING EXERCISE TWO: REFRAMING UNWELCOME CIRCUMSTANCES

Completion time: 30 minutes.

Take a few moments with your partner to review your life together. Select three unwelcomed events since you met, and answer the following questions about each.

1. What good has come of that difficult circumstance?
2. What lessons can you now apply to the future?
3. What strengths have you developed individually and as a couple as a result?
4. What are you thankful for?

   Sample event: Miriam was hospitalized for depression and anxiety after she lost her job.

1: Kevin's business performance improved when Miriam's hospitalization forced him to be the sole provider for their family for a year. Miriam opened up emotionally to Kevin after her hospitalization, and they are closer now as a result.
2: We've learned that we can survive tough times together, and that we're going to make it no matter what.
3: Miriam has learned how to stop some of her negative thinking, and how to lean on Kevin for support when she needs it. Kevin has learned how to focus on his business productively, even when his personal life is in upheaval.
4: We're thankful that our relationship has survived and that we're still able to live in the house we love. We're lucky to still be living a middle-class lifestyle.

When You Are Upbeat and Your Partner Is Not

When you can view circumstances brightly, but your partner remains entrenched in toxic thinking, try some of the following approaches:

- Listen without reacting to any negative statements. Give your partner a chance to vent without arguing about his or her right to that point of view.
- Listen for a few moments, and then change the subject. Don't participate in your partner's ruminations beyond what is productive.
- Don't dismiss everything your partner says. You may discover an element of realism worth your attention and immediate acknowledgment.
- Set limits. When you can't handle hearing negative talk, ask your partner to respect your request and explain carefully why you need to keep your positive frame of mind.
- Ask your partner how you can help ease his or her mind or remedy the situation. A simple action like a hug, or a nonaction such as not leaving the room when your partner starts to cry, can make a huge difference.
- Be patient and kindhearted. See the world through your partner's eyes and feel compassion for his or her suffering. Accept his or her negativity as what's true for your partner and hope that in time he or she will come around.
- Reward your partner with affection and positive reinforcement when you spot any signs of optimism.

Strategy Four: Take Action and Celebrate Your Progress

When you are overwhelmed and discouraged, you are particularly prone to paralyzing depression and inertia. A downward spiral takes you further from a solution and toward a more monumental problem.

If one is depressed, the other may take the lead. Suggest that the two of you picnic in the park, clean out the garage, or go for a bicycle ride. Action can break a depressive cycle. Respecting your partner's mood and need for solitude, you can coax him or her gently into a change of scenery.

> My wife and I had a business in our basement. Sales weren't coming in, and I was having panic attacks throughout the day. One beautiful spring day my wife demanded that we get out of the house and go to the local park. I protested taking time off from the business during the day, but by getting out of that dark basement I was able to relax and gain a more optimistic perspective. Now, whenever I start to have a panic attack, I go for a walk and it helps me calm down.
> *Toymaker*

When I was in labor with my first daughter, my midwife coached me to get through one contraction at a time, viewing each contraction as an accomplishment in itself. She assured me that after a finite number of contractions, my daughter would be born. By focusing on the moment and experiencing the progress of labor, I kept my fear and frustration to a manageable level.

Couples in any kind of crisis need analogous concentration on the moment. Break your largest challenges into manageable steps and celebrate the small victories along the way. Recognize your partner's progress toward personal and business goals and don't wait until the big moment at the end. When your partner overcomes even one obstacle, express your excitement in a tangible way.

When I set the goal of getting a contract for this book from HarperCollins, I was standing in front of a formidable mountain. My husband and I celebrated each victory along the way—finishing the necessary book proposal, the sample chapter, acquiring an agent, etc. When I felt disheartened or pessimistic from time to time, I would sink into those feelings for a few hours or a day, but then I got back to work, focusing on my next manageable goal. When I finally landed the contract, that accomplishment was the culmination of six months of smaller completed goals.

DISCOVERY EXERCISE THREE: SMALL ACTIONS I/WE CAN TAKE TO RESTORE HOPE AND BALANCE

Take a moment to write down—alone or with your partner—ten simple daily actions you can take when you are depressed or overwhelmed that have a history of making you feel better. For example: taking a walk, cooking a meal, buying flowers, petting the cat. Keep it simple. Think of activities you can do by yourself or with your partner.

_____

_____

_____

_____

_____

_____

_____

_____

_____

_____

Strategy Five: Shift from Dwelling on the Past to Focusing on the Future

Studying the past to learn something, rather than dwelling on it regretfully, is a productive use of energy. Couples who thrive during hard times shift their mental and emotional attention to building a new future. The entrepreneurial phoenix rises from the ashes of failure and flies toward the couple's new vision.

We originally had big dreams for a nationwide franchise, at least twenty stores, when my husband and I were childless and driven by ambition. Then I got pregnant unexpectedly with twins. Due to complications, I spent four months of my pregnancy in bed. Our franchise plans went on hold. Once the twins were born, devoting the same level of energy to our business was impossible. We refocused on making our one store the best it could be and raising our family. We aren't as wealthy now as we had hoped we could be, but our decision was the right one for us, and we're happy.

Gift store owner

My wife and I moved our family to a new state and bought a small business where we hoped to retire. Six months later, my wife was diagnosed with multiple sclerosis. There we were, in the middle of nowhere, far from decent medical care. We sold the business, moved back to a metropolitan area where she could receive the finest care, and took in a foster child, whom we have since adopted. Our daughter would never have become part of our family had the diagnosis not forced us to move. God had different plans for us than we had for ourselves.

Midwest entrepreneur

CLARIFICATION EXERCISE FOUR: CREATING A NEW VISION
Completion time: 30–60 minutes.

Consider your short-term and long-term goals, as an individual and as a couple. Write down, or articulate to each other, a new vision of your future in the next six months, year, and five years. Get the children involved and encourage some family brainstorming, where all ideas, no matter how fantastic, are put on the table.

Goals	6 mo	1 yr	5 yrs
Financial			
Career			

[continued]

Goals	6 mo	1 yr	5 yrs
Business direction			
Relationship			
Children			
Social			
Community			
Spiritual			
Health			
Education			

Revise these goals when new circumstances have entered the picture.

Strategy Six: Solidify Commitment to Your Relationship

People and events will test your commitment to your significant other repeatedly over your lifetime together. In crisis, you may reevaluate your relationship, question your belonging together, even fall out of love temporarily when hard times bring out the worst in your partner. No, you never bargained for such unpleasant times, but it's what you've got for the time being. Will you walk away when it isn't fun anymore, or will you remain committed to your partner?

Some breakups, precipitated by business crisis, are inevitable. You discover that you have completely incompatible life goals, or you or your partner becomes an uncontrolled alcoholic, adulterer, or workaholic who is never home. Your relationship's dissolution may be a necessary, though painful, part of your journey.

Dr. Scott Stanley, a national expert on commitment, distinguishes between two kinds of commitment between couples: constraint commitment and dedication commitment (Stanley, *Fighting for Your Marriage*, page 165).

Constraint commitment rests on obligation or the perceived negative consequences of breaking up. If you run a business with your spouse, then you may stay married because dividing the business is too much of a hassle. Your children's well-being may concern you, or you may question your ability to support yourself on your own. These thoughts constrain you to stay in relationship.

During hard times, you may rely on constraint commitment to pull you through. A deeper form of commitment is that of dedication. You have dedication commitment when you devote yourself to your partner's well-being, growing old together, and developing a healthy, nourishing, and mature relationship. Your marriage/partnership is one of your highest priorities.

When you commit strongly to each other, you sustain your long-term vision toward being in a relationship with your mate. When you experience periods of relationship dissatisfaction, you don't leave; over the long haul, life with your partner is truly satisfying.

When you feel the least in love with your partner you may need to express your lifelong commitment even more. Say to your mate something as simple as "We're going to stay together through these difficult times, no matter what," or "I'm having trouble expressing affection to you right now, but I still love you." Pull out your marriage vows and reread them to each other. Give your spouse a card that conveys your commitment. Pray for the ability to live up to your commitment that you struggle to keep.

In difficult times, a man in financial trouble needs frequent reassurance that his wife won't leave him for a more potent provider. A woman, when she's not at her best, needs to feel loved, cherished, and reassured that she won't be abandoned. When you are in a crisis or struggle to stay connected, reaffirm your ongoing love and commitment frequently.

DISCOVERY EXERCISE FIVE: REMINDERS OF YOUR STRENGTH
Completion time: 30 minutes.

This difficult time in your relationship is probably not the first. Yet, you are still together. Rejuvenate your commitment and optimism by reminding yourself of your history as a couple, and your success in overcoming previous obstacles. What previous obstacles have you overcome and with what unwelcome circumstances have you managed to cope? How has your relationship grown and thrived as a result of challenge?

What five challenges have you met as a couple?

_____

_____

_____

_____

_____

What strengths have you developed individually and as a couple as a result?_____

How has your previous experience together prepared you for your current challenge?_____

Strategy Seven: Accept and Appreciate Differences in Coping Styles

When Carol faces crisis, she tends to grin and bear it, keep her feelings to herself, and act as if everything is fine. Paul deals with his intense anger by immersing himself in distracting activity. Suzanna prays a lot and seeks out a good friend to talk to. Jeffrey analyzes all the different components of the problem and searches for a logical solution. Each has a unique coping style, one no better than another.

From a distance, we can forgive total strangers for their response to crisis. But what about our own partners? When we fear, despair, or fume we may demand that our partners respond the same way that we do. If they don't, we criticize them. "He's in denial." "When will he deal with his real feelings?" "She's so damn hysterical all the time." "Why can't she control herself?"

When we hurt, we want our partners to validate and comfort us, not reject or judge us incompetent. The greatest gift you can give your partner is what *he or she* needs, *not what you need*. As you each move through stages of denial, anger, depression, and acceptance, you advance at different paces and use different coping strategies. One partner may prefer solitude, another companionship. One partner may need to talk about the problem repeatedly, the other only a little. One partner may rush to solution, while the other weighs the possibilities for a long while.

Regardless, expending all your energy to convert or coerce your partner into your way of healing loses a valuable opportunity to support your partner. You likely alienate, rather than comfort, them. Reach out your hand, stretch yourself, and be there for your partner as he or she needs you to be.

Supporting your partner's emotional process is not incompatible with helping them reframe their perceptions when their view of reality has become distorted. Describe to your partner your more hopeful vision and show them a more optimistic way of looking at the same situation without invalidating their feelings.

Preston: We're going down the tubes and we're going to lose the house. What a disaster!

Kim: You're right, the business may be closing. That doesn't mean we'll lose the house. We have enough in savings until we find jobs, and in the meantime, my parents will help. We'll be OK.

Cheryl: All of our employees hate me. I'm a lousy boss. I should never have agreed to supervise operations.

Phil: Sure, some employees are angry with you because of our new work rules. But being the boss is tough sometimes. I still think you're doing a great job.

George: That damn insurance company is trying to screw us again. Why is everyone out to get us these days? Why do I even bother trying to be a nice guy?

Fred: The employees in data entry wrote a thank-you letter about how much they appreciate not being laid off after the fire. They really appreciate you. Here, let me show you that letter—it might cheer you up.

CLARIFICATION EXERCISE SIX: DEFINE YOUR COPING STYLE

Completion time: 15 minutes.

You may assume that your partner knows exactly what you want or need when you are in distress. Explain these needs clearly so that your partner can better support you as you desire. Complete the following sentences with your partner.

When I am tired, or overwhelmed, I need you to

_____.

When I am angry at circumstances or other people, I need

_____.

When I am depressed, I need you to

_____.

When you _____, I usually feel so much better.

Strategy Eight: Forgive Your Partner and Yourself

What if you struggle because your partner made a serious error in judgment or did something entirely wrong in your estimation? Now you must live with the consequences. Can you forgive your partner? What if you yourself screwed up? Can you forgive yourself and move on?

Forgiveness is a process. It begins with a willingness and a desire to forgive, even if you can't do so right away. To forgive does not mean to condone the hurtful experience. To forgive is to let go of prolonged guilt, regret, or resentment that poisons your ability to move beyond unfortunate circumstances.

A business or personal crisis can capsize some of your cherished beliefs. If you always believed that your husband would provide for you, how will you respond when your husband's business fails? Couples who work through these disillusions emerge with a more impenetrable love and a stronger relationship, but disillusionment can be the most painful experience of your marriage. Get outside help if you need it or even think you do.

If you forgive your partner, communicate your forgiveness directly and often. Put it in writing. Partners may need to hear it, or read it, several times and experience you behaving as if it's true, before they trust you. Remember: If your spouse cannot forgive him- or herself, it will be difficult for him or her to believe in your forgiveness. As you both get on with your lives, and positive directions emerge, your partner may only then be able to see his or her actions in a brighter light.

My husband Stephen's start-up business didn't achieve what we had hoped for, battering Stephen's ego as well as our bank account. He went through periods of depression and guilt, and I experienced anger and disappointment as well. Our business struggles led to the idea for this book and ultimately a new career for me as an author, business coach, and public speaker. As new positives emerged, and as Stephen secured other successful employment, we recast the entire trial affirmatively.

If your partner is angry at you, don't underestimate your power through a simple and direct "I'm sorry." Refrain from either of two extremes—denying your responsibility or exaggerating the magnitude of your sins. An error in judgment is not a failure in life or a sin. Above all, be patient with yourself and your partner. This too shall pass, though perhaps not as quickly as you would like.

KEEP PERSPECTIVE AND REMEMBER YOUR PRIORITIES

When business challenges throw us off center, we may take actions inconsistent with our deepest values or concerns. Although many entrepreneurs describe a stable, satisfying marriage with healthy and happy children as a higher priority than having business success, many admit being locked into daily business routines that preclude time with their family. Long hours, emotional absenteeism, and money pressures all contribute to temporary amnesia. Some entrepreneurs lose perspective and forget their deepest priorities until a family, health, or business crisis forces them to reorient themselves.

> We learned a big lesson seven years ago. My father died, and we had to bury him within twenty-four hours because he was Jewish. My husband and I were working on three tight deadlines, but we wanted to go to the funeral. One client threatened to sue us if we didn't stick with our original commitment. We were so scared of being sued and losing everything in the business, we didn't go to the funeral. Now we regret our decision.
>
> *Husband and wife business partners*

> On the worst days, what helps most is knowing that the alternative is working for someone else in a job. When I think about that, I make a conscious choice again to keep struggling in my own business.
>
> *New England entrepreneur*

Some entrepreneurs rise to the top, acquire material wealth, and then lose all of their assets in a subsequent humiliating business failure. After rebounding, they never look at business success or prosperity in quite in the same way. Those who kept their sense of humor and connection as a team coped best.

> In 1990 the bank that financed me ran into big trouble and demanded payment for my loan, due in full immediately. I knew I hit bottom when I traded in my Porsche for a 1974 Pinto.
>
> *Business consultant*

CONCLUSION: BROKEN BONES OR
SHATTERED GLASS

Brian G. once described his previous marriage as a crystal pitcher that shattered into thousands of pieces when his wife had an affair. No amount of effort or love could glue those pieces back again. Some crises hit so deep, you have no way to recover and you lose the relationship forever.

Stephen and I prefer the broken bone analogy for any crises we've weathered. A broken bone heals stronger at the break and so can your relationship with optimism and reflection.

Dr. Mihaly Csikszentmihalyi counsels, "Adversity, unfortunately, is a fact of life. It will always be present in one form or the other. The question is, are you going to let it destroy the quality of your life, or are you going to find ways of making it a springboard for some new adventure or growth? One way or another, you have to cope with it. You might as well find a way that will make life richer" (Wholey, *When the Worst that Can Happen Already Has*, page 151).

Flexibility is essential for any entrepreneurial journey. The Japanese observe how, during a heavy snowfall, the resilient bamboo bends but the unyielding oak breaks. I hope that you learn what you need to learn quickly together, and in such a way that strengthens your relationship and brings your life eventual lasting joy. May you and your partner celebrate your successes, learn from your mistakes, and thrive as a couple on your entrepreneurial adventure. May you come to view all aspects of your life together through this Hebrew phrase: *Gam zu letovah*, meaning, "This, too, is for the best." God bless you, your partner, and your family on your journey.

RECOMMENDED RESOURCES

Books

Big Ideas for Small Service Businesses: How to Successfully Advertise, Publicize, and Maximize Your Business or Professional Practice by Marilyn and Tom Ross. Communication Creativity, 1994.

Fighting for Your Marriage: Positive Steps for Preventing Divorce and Preserving a Lasting Love by Howard Markham, Ph.D., Scott Stanley, Ph.D., Susan L. Blumberg, Ph.D. Jossey-Bass, 1994.

Getting the Business to Come to You: Everything You Need to Know to Do Your Own Advertising, Public Relations, Direct Mail, and Sales Promotion, and Attract All the Business You Can Handle by Paul and Sarah Edwards and Laura Clampitt Douglas. Jeremy P. Tarcher/Perigee, 1991.

Growing a Business by Paul Hawken. Simon and Schuster, 1987.

Guerrilla Marketing Excellence: The Fifty Golden Rules for Small-Business Success by Jay Conrad Levinson. Houghton Mifflin, 1993.

Learned Optimism: How to Change Your Mind and Your Life by Martin Seligman, Ph.D. Pocket Books, 1990.

Making It on Your Own: Surviving and Thriving on the Ups and Downs of Being Your Own Boss by Paul and Sarah Edwards. Jeremy P. Tarcher/Perigee, 1991.

Making It through the Night: How Couples Can Survive a Crisis Together by Pat Quigley and Marilyn Shroyer, Ph.D. Conari Press, 1992.

Marketing Your Services: A Step-by-Step Guide for Small Businesses and Professionals by Anthony Putman. John Wiley and Sons, 1990.

Mastering the Winds of Change: Peak Performers Reveal How to Stay on Top in Times of Turmoil by Erik Olesen. HarperBusiness, 1993.

The Power of Optimism by Alan Loy McGinnis. HarperCollins, 1990.

The Survivor Personality by Al Siebert, Ph.D. Practical
   Psychology Press, 1994.
*When the Worst that Can Happen Already Has: Conquering Life's
   Most Difficult Times* by Dennis Wholey. Hyperion, 1992.

Support

Business Strategy Seminars. Strategy and support programs
for entrepreneurs. Write: Kathi Elster, President,
120 East 34th Street, #15L, New York, NY 10016, or
call 212-481-7075.

Let's Talk Business Network. Assembles diverse entrepre-
neurial resources for small business owners. Write: Larry
Kesslin, partner, LTBN, 20 Exchange Place, 16th Floor,
New York, NY 10005, or call 212-742-1553.

How to Contact
the Author

Azriela Jaffe is the founder of The Critical Link, a coaching and consulting firm helping entrepreneurs and their intimate partners to achieve personal and business success. Azriela welcomes reader response to *Honey, I Want to Start My Own Business.* For more information about her private telephone coaching services and public speaking availability, send a self-addressed, stamped envelope to P.O. Box 209, Bausman, PA 17504, or e-mail azjaffe@aol.com.

Index

emotional balance with left-
brained person, 183–4
job responsibilities of, 183
meetings, style of, 183
planning methods, 184
profile of, 182
sharing work space with right-
brained person, 183
Lesbian partnerships, communication in, 165n
Love:
communicating what you
need, 237–8
expressing and feeling, 179–81
see also Romance and sex life
*Love and Renewal, A Couple's
Guide to Commitment*
(Bugen), 249–50
Love Letter technique, 198–202,
242
Love notes, 253

Male supportive spouse role,
61–2
Manufacturing business, pros
and cons of, 13
Markman, Dr. Howard, 188, 219
Marriage and entrepreneurship,
models of combining,
20–65
dual entrepreneurship, *see*
Dual entrepreneurship
full partnership, *see* Full partnership
spousal support, *see*
Supportive spouse
Marriage counselors, 62, 102,
266
Massage, 254
Mature love versus romantic illusions, 249–50

Meal preparation as romantic
gift, 254
Media, risk personality, influence
on your, 74
Medical insurance for full partners, 25–6
Meetings:
couple, 224
style for, 183
Mellan, Olivia, 71
*Men Are from Mars, Women Are
from Venus* (Gray), 59,
198, 257
Money discussions, time and
place for, 103–7
ground rules, 105–7
Money Harmony (Mellan), 71
Money management guidelines,
95–100
checking accounts, joint or
separate, 95–6
exercise, 98–100
financial decisions for the
business, 96–8, 99–100
resolving disagreements, 98
Money philosophy, 76–7
Money styles, taking a positive
view of differences in,
100–3
Money worries as romance killer,
252–4
Mood swings:
balancing each other's, 35–6,
183–4
of dual entrepreneurs, 47
in full partnerships, balancing,
35–6
supportive spouse dealing
with entrepreneur's,
60–1
Mortgages, 25–6